NEW YORK REVIEW BOOKS
CLASSICS

PART OF OUR TIME

MURRAY KEMPTON (1917–1997) was a columnist for *Newsday*, as well as a regular contributor to *The New York Review of Books*. His books include *Rebellions, Perversities, and Main Events* and *The Briar Patch*, as well as *Part of Our Time*. He won the Pulitzer Prize in 1985.

DAVID REMNICK is the Pulitzer Prize–winning author of *Lenin's Tomb, Resurrection*, and *King of the World*. He is the editor of *The New Yorker*.

D1248674

Mark -

Sitting at this desk in our
Library, trying to pinpoint what
a fellow like you, with the
leisure to read at length, plus
the conviction that doing so
would be to one's benefit, would
enjoy reading.

Settled on a literate book filled
with literary people, at times of
strain and renovation of their
belief/es and loyalties.

I found the book a means of
understanding the world inhabited
by our Fathers.

Would be interested to learn of
your own reactions.   JOHN

FOUR SEASONS
Hotels and Resorts

PART OF OUR TIME

SOME RUINS AND MONUMENTS
OF THE THIRTIES

MURRAY KEMPTON

Introduction by
DAVID REMNICK

NEW YORK REVIEW BOOKS

New York

This is a New York Review Book
Published by The New York Review of Books
1755 Broadway, New York, NY 10019

Library of Congress Cataloging-in-Publication Data
Kempton, Murray, 1917–
  Part of our time : some ruins and monuments of the thirties / Murray Kempton ;
introduction by David Remnick.
    p. cm. — (New York Review Books classics)
  Originally published: Simon & Schuster, 1955.
  ISBN 1-59017-087-3 (pbk. : alk. paper)
  1. Subversive activities—United States—History—20th century. 2. Radicals—
United States—Biography. 3. Communists—United States—Biography.
4. Labor unions—United States—History—20th century. 5. United States—
History—1933–1945. 6. United States—History—1919–1933. 7. Nineteen
thirties. I. Title. II. Series.
  E743.5.K4 2004
  973.917'092'2—dc22

                              2004003004

ISBN 1-59017-087-3

Printed in the United States of America on acid-free paper.
10 9 8 7 6 5 4 3 2 1

March 2004
www.nyrb.com

Introduction

BY THE TIME he died on May 5, 1997, Murray Kempton had written more than eleven thousand newspaper columns, mainly for the *New York Post* and *Newsday*, as well as hundreds of freelance essays on everything from his experience as a hapless mugging victim (for *Playboy*) to an abbot-close reading of the Newark federal prosecutor's collected wiretaps of Simon Rizzo DeCavalcante (for *The New York Review of Books*). He was the one reporter in New York capable of covering a housing court trial on an August Tuesday in the Bronx through the dramatic prism of Aeschylus. Reliably, but without pretension or evident strain, he could summon a passage in Henry Adams's *Mont-Saint-Michel and Chartres* as a way of explaining the wayward faith of John Gotti, late of Leavenworth maximum security. Kempton did not think much of secret sources, but over the years his subjects and acquaintances ranged from William F. Buckley, Jr., to Carmine (the Snake) Persico; he was equally at home at the Morgan Library and the Ravenite Social Club. He got around. His targets were the men of arrogance, the ones who believed in nothing and risked less; he went to his grave disdaining Bill Clinton. His sympathy, which far outstripped his disdain, went to the weak, the mistreated, the lost, and the fallen. One of Murray's conceits was that, despite his own politics, it often seemed his affection and pity for Richard Nixon only increased as Nixon fell deeper into the abyss. When Mario Cuomo once asked Sydney Schanberg at *Newsday* how he could get Murray Kempton to love him, Schanberg replied, "Try getting indicted, Governor."

Both as a man and as a reporter (Murray hated the grasping professionalism of "journalist"), Kempton was admired more widely and more deeply than anyone else in the trade. Younger reporters (and they were all younger after a while) loved him. He was, in so many ways, our ideal: a man of erudition and experience, of wit and character, of unbelievable energy and even greater generosity. His judgments only seemed surprising; as you came to know Kempton's codes of forgiveness, chivalry, and grace, you could begin to anticipate him and understand why he would shed tears for a soul such as Jean Harris—though fewer tears, perhaps, after he learned that she'd fired her gun a second and third time at the diet doctor who'd broken her heart.

Kempton was not unaware of the reverence directed toward him, nor was he unaware that he had become in some quarters a kind of New York character, an urban legend: the city's last gentleman, the besuited reporter bicycling off to a Bellvue press conference while smoking a pipe and listening to the Diabelli Variations on his portable CD player. He enjoyed the admiration but was more than a little embarrassed by all the fuss. I never knew quite how embarrassed he really was until he was gone. The funerals and memorial services of reporters and even editors are, almost invariably, occasions for storytelling, myth-making, and self-celebration. The last great gesture of Murray's character was the funeral he designed for himself: On a fine spring morning, hundreds came to a grand Episcopal church on the West Side expecting to hear the name Kempton uttered many times in affection, but Murray made sure we heard, again and again, the name of God. There was no storytelling at all, no charming speeches; rather we heard the elevated language of prayer, of Murray's favorite hymns, we heard the music he loved, and, finally, the sound of a bell tolling off his years. I can hear that bell now. Afterwards, Murray's daughter and sons, their families, his friends, his colleagues—even the mayor of the City of New York—came down the steps and into the sunlight; we'd been made a little better once more, by the craft and spirit of Murray Kempton. Once more he had proven himself an artist. As I say, the man knew how to write, even when he was quoting.

But while his friends and acolytes will tell Murray stories and quote his columns and remember him for many years to come, there is no getting around the fact that as the author of books Kempton was, in his lifetime, treated disgracefully. Only the publication in 1994 of *Rebellions, Perversities, and Main Events*—an omnibus collection of columns and essays—made a rotten situation a little less so. When Murray died his other books—*Part of Our Time*, *The Briar Patch*, and *America Comes of Middle Age*—had been out of print for years. For a reader of nonfiction, of journalism at its best and most ambitious, this was rather like being unable to find copies of *Homage to Catalonia* or *Patriotic Gore*, *The American Scene* or *The Fire Next Time*. It was intolerable.

What you hold in your hands was the most sorely missed of all of Kempton's books, his masterpiece. Kempton published *Part of Our Time: Some Ruins and Monuments of the Thirties* in 1955, when he was thirty-eight. His hair was still red. His sentences were a good deal simpler than the more baroque ones that would come to be his later (and inimitable) voice. He was, in years, still young, and yet *Part of Our Time* is a book of almost autumnal reflection on the radicals of his childhood and youth.

In form, *Part of Our Time* is a series of profiles or, as Kempton put it, "a series of novellas which happen to be about real persons": Alger Hiss and Whittaker Chambers, the Hollywood Ten, Elizabeth Bentley, Paul Robeson, Joe Curran, the Reuther brothers. Kempton takes on both the familiar and forgotten figures of the era and tries not merely to account for what they did, but to think about why. It is only secondarily important to him, for instance, that Alger Hiss was guilty as charged; what matters most is what led this sorry man to his sins and, not least, how much the sins —and others like them—mattered at all. He surveys the literary figures of the era and tries to determine for himself the difference between the complicated commitments of the first-rate and the zealotry of the second-rate, the differences of mind and political passions between the authors of *To the Finland Station* and *Marching! Marching!*

But, more, *Part of Our Time* is a book about idealism, myth, engagement, commitment, foolishness, pride, delusion, and, finally (and above all else) forgiveness. *Part of Our Time* is the book of a profoundly experienced man, one who came out of the world of shabby gentility in Baltimore (the world, Kempton tells us, of Alger Hiss); one whose reaction to national collapse was a short stint first with the Young Communist League and then with the Socialist Party. After finishing Johns Hopkins, Kempton fought in the Pacific with the Fifth Air Force and then came home to be a newspaperman at the *New York Post*. I am just about the same age now that Kempton was when he wrote *Part of Our Time* and when I reread that book I find in it a maturity, a sympathy and patience with the gods and the fools of his time, that is beyond me or any of my similarly coddled peers. It seems that Kempton had lived so much by the time he began writing *Part of Our Time* that he was beyond the cynicism and the unforgiving impulses of the young. Writing on a subject that is almost always given to accusation or defense, Kempton adopts both a prose and a moral stance that speaks less of his understanding of Lenin and Marx than of Matthew and Mark.

"The thirties were a part of my life like any other," Kempton writes in his author's note, "I am aware that there are things in it for which I must apologize; I am also aware that in the whole of my life, there will be many things for which I must apologize, under what have to be compulsions stronger than a Congressional subpoena."

It is worth noting that no one was more delighted by the tragicomical end to Soviet communism than Kempton. And yet it is also worth noting the courage it took him, in 1955, in the America of Joseph McCarthy, to write with sympathy about those radicals of the thirties who believed in the myths of their decade. After living four years in Moscow and witnessing the downfall of Soviet communism, I came home at the end of 1991 to read article after article of triumphalism, of vitriol dumped in retrospect on the heads of men and women who, fifty and sixty years before, had made the mistake of showing sympathy to the foreign radical left. For so many of those writers I was reading then, figures such as Robeson, Walter Reuther, and Clifford Odets were but mere punching bags set in a row for a good time. *Part of Our Time* goes a long way toward recreating not merely the privations of the thirties, the economic and political conditions that led imperfect men toward foolish and violent ideologies, but also a moral landscape that was "blighted more than anything else by the absence of pity and mercy." Because Murray Kempton had more pity and mercy within him than any writer of his time, he is the best writer to read on his time, of which he was so much a part.

—DAVID REMNICK, 1998

PART OF OUR TIME

A Prelude

EACH of us lives with a sword over his head.

There are those who can ignore its shadow and those who cannot. Those who cannot are not necessarily better than those who can. But they are the creators of the special myth of their time, because any myth is the creation of the very few who cannot bear reality.

This is a book about the myth of the nineteen thirties.

Most of all it was a social myth. No man was an island. He could not escape history. If Madrid fell, he fell with it. In his own time, he would know the night of defeat or the morning of final victory. The instruments of his salvation were his to command.

The language of the myth was abstract and collective. Its key words were symbols like "labor," "people," "youth," and "history." It was a language of exhortation, and it was graceless by choice, written on a drumhead, to be read to an impatient army. Those who wrote it assumed that, in years to come, their words would be read by people who would judge them only as the words of the winning side or the losing one They would be tested by victory or defeat, and not by the judgment of neutrals. The heart of the myth of the thirties was that there were no neutrals.

Yet the reality, as we know it now, is that most people are neutral. Only the very few give their lives to the myth of any decade; and, in America, only a limited few lived by the myth of the thirties. They were the committed and the dedicated, and they are the subjects of these studies.

Time has altered them and their circumstance beyond recognition, and yet I wonder now whether their place in our lives is not more important today than it was when the myth was fresh in their vision. For they are with us still, not as the prophets they thought they were, but as the scapegoats of an aggressive new myth which has shoved their own aside. The bearers of the myth of every decade seem to carry in their hands the ax and the spade to execute and inter the myth of the previous one.

As an instance, the bearers of the myth of the thirties did all they could to destroy the myth of the twenties. The myth of the twenties had involved the search for individual expression, whether in beauty, laughter, or defiance of convention; all this was judged by the myth of the thirties as selfish and footling and egocentric. It did not seem proper at the time to say that the twenties were not quite so simple, and that their values were mixed, some good and some bad. It is a perilous thing for any generation to misjudge its immediate past. The prisoners of the myth of the thirties threw away most, I think, when they applied their brooms with such impartiality to that which was paste and that which was diamond in the myth of the twenties. There are signs that a myth is developing in our time; and its panel of judges has brought all the thirties to the prisoner's bar. These studies are not offered as material for the defense; they are only an essay toward a selective understanding of this myth which judged once and has now come itself to so terrible a judgment. The only thing current in them is the sense that the past we lived through is a part of ourselves, and that no part of ourselves is without its portion of guilt and its portion of glory, and that any summary judgment of our past is a peril to our present.

My subjects, as I have already said, are a very few people whose lives were changed because they were committed to the social myth of the thirties. No one of us, of course, can know just what his commitment will exact from him. The social revolutionary of the thirties thought that he was prepared to die by violence. He thought that he was prepared for an America destroyed by war and fascism. His imagination covered, in fact, almost every disaster except the one which has now overtaken him.

For he could not have known that, within twenty years, he would live in an America made glorious according to every dream of the economic materialist. Its wealth, its resources, its almost universally exalted living standards would not have seemed to him possible except in the triumph of his own revolutionary program.

And yet this America had fixed him with a harsh and chilling eye. To the extent that it remembered him at all, this America sought from him no enlightenment except as to whether he was or ever had been a member of the Communist Party or any of that cluster of organizations which the Department of Justice has found to be under its control. He could communicate only defiance or penitence.

If he were still a Communist, he could refuse to answer and be left with whatever comfort there might be in the knowledge that no triumph was possible for him except as the quisling of a Soviet Army of Occupation. If he had been a Trotskyite or some other kind of revolutionary, he could generally expect to be left alone, assuming he was uninterested in a place in government. For him, the price of commitment was to be alone and unattended.

The Trotskyite's own god had at least defined for him the enormity of his present disaster. Shortly before he was murdered, Leon Trotsky had cast out some three hundred, roughly half, of his American followers. He was, said Trotsky, consigning them to the dustbin of history.

The dustbin of history was, to the revolutionary of the thirties, what Hell was to the Maine farmer. To fall out of history, to lose your grip upon its express train, to be buried in its graveyard—

the conflicting metaphors descriptive of that immolation recurred again and again. But who could have believed that it could happen to so many so young?

For all of them are so long gone; the parades for Spain, the concerts for the anti-fascists where everyone sang about the Peat Bog soldiers, the dinners for the sharecroppers, the college girls throwing away their silk stockings to defeat Japanese aggression, the lectures on the crimes of Trotsky, and the counter-lectures on the crimes of Stalin.

The author of *The Coming Struggle for Power* peacefully joined and peacefully left a British cabinet. The first chairman of the American League against War and Fascism has become J. B. Matthews, laboriously assembling the names of all those treasonable enough to have followed his call, a Pied Piper entombing his children. A thousand different pamphlets, written at night, approved by the committee, wheedled past the printer on the barely believed, barely meant promise of payment, all buried now and of interest to no one except the Federal Bureau of Investigation and the odd new entrepreneurs to whom the letterhead of a dead subversive organization is at once a weapon and a commodity.

They were a very few people, but they made a great noise, although not so great a one as the noise being made over them now. And yet, few though they were, each was in some way different from any other, and the consequences of their involvement with the social myth of the thirties were different for each of them. Julius Rosenberg accepted the myth and became a traitor. Walter Reuther accepted the myth and became a highly useful citizen.

Any experience deeply felt makes some men better and some men worse. When it has ended, they share nothing but the recollection of a commitment in which each was tested and each to some degree found wanting. They were not alike when they began, and they were not alike when they finished. T. S. Eliot says in one of his Quartets that time is no healer, because the patient is no longer here. The consequences of the journey change the voyager so much more than the embarking or the arrival.

It is already very hard to remember that, only a generation ago, there were a number of Americans, of significant character and talent, who believed that our society was not merely doomed but undeserving of survival, and to whom every one of its institutions seemed not just unworthy of preservation but crying out to be exterminated.

And it is also hard to re-create that storm which passed over America in 1929, which conditioned the real history of the thirties, and which provided what the subjects of this inquiry at least thought was the impulse of their social myth. The year 1931 was not a time when the American businessman held his head high. All the ancient values he represented seemed to wither around him. The early thirties tried bankers and found them guilty as steadily as the fifties were to try Communists. The image of the American dream was flawed and cracked; its critics had never sounded more persuasive. It is especially hard to remember how persuasive they were, because so many of them have ceased to persuade themselves. Fred J. Schlink, who wrote the most widely circulated attack on industry's treatment of the consumer, is a Republican now. John T. Flynn, author of *Graft in Business,* lifts his voice over the radio now against all that he helped inspire. But these men were reformers and not revolutionaries; the force of their criticism then and the changing of their passions now reflect a public temper. The great body of Americans did not believe that their system was mortally ill. Its decline was far more surprising to them than its subsequent recovery.

But there were a few who sought some revolutionary shelter from the storm; and they are the subjects of these studies. They believed in Marx and, with a few exceptions, in Lenin. Marx had said that history, by its own iron and necessary laws, progresses toward the breaking of nations and the destruction of the rich and the mighty. The triumph of the wage earner, the most abject victim of society's injustice, was to Marx a matter of historic inevitability.

And Lenin taught that the destruction of the mighty and the elevation of the humble would not be an easy or peaceful process. Even the West was ruled by men who wrapped repression in the sham of a democratic government; the owners of capital also owned the press, the Congress, the army, and every instrument of the state.

"The liberation of the oppressed class," said Lenin, "is impossible, not only without a violent revolution but without the destruction of the apparatus of state power."

And Lenin spoke with the authority of success. Only in the Soviet Union was the revolution triumphant. The Soviets survived and America declined; and therefore was it possible to believe that, as Lenin had achieved the revolution, Stalin was building the new Jerusalem.

Germany was drifting to the Nazis. The British Labor government had expired, and recriminations still echoed around its deathbed. The radicals of Europe had lived for years by the dream of a sure and peaceful progress toward the broad, sunny uplands of social democracy. Now they were stragglers broken in the valley; nowhere did there appear any hope for these gentle apostles of the peaceful and the legal.

The Socialists of Vienna had built themselves an oasis of pensions and co-operatives and workers' houses in the social desert about them. In 1934, the Chancellor of Austria, as if to underscore Lenin, turned his guns on all they had put together. The workers of Vienna chose to stand and die, half-armed and half-fed, in their Karl Marx Hof and their Matteoti Hof, the first named for the symbol of socialism's prophecy in the nineteenth century and the second for a symbol of its martyrdom in the twentieth.

The survivors were heroes of sorts. But, for American revolutionaries, their true epitaph was the bitter legend that they had rallied their forces to seize Vienna's City Hall, only to be halted in full sweep by a "Keep off the Grass" sign in a public park and dispersed by the *polizei.*

After their defeat, the leaders of the Viennese Socialists sought refuge abroad. Most of those who went to the Soviet Union were eventually shot as political unreliables; some of those who went to the United States found at first only the freedom to sleep in doorways. They, of course, understood the difference; the American revolutionaries understood only that the Viennese were out of fashion wherever power lived. And they were at one with the historic American progressives, whose earnest faith in peaceful, slow reform seemed now as lost in the storm as poor Herbert Hoover.

Sitting in America with ten million unemployed and looking out at the world, it was possible to read Lenin and believe he was right. Not many people read Lenin, but more did read John Strachey or Louis Fischer or even Richard Halliburton and learned about a magic land where man had eliminated unemployment and was conquering poverty.

For diversion, among a great many other things, they could listen to a song called "Brother, Can You Spare a Dime?" They had no reason to know that the depression's theme would become prosperity's forbidden melody and that its lyricist, Jay Gorney, would be brought before the House Un-American Activities Committee twenty-three years later as a Communist.

Carl Sandburg inserted "I built a railroad/now it's run" into a poem which can be found in the *Oxford Book of American Verse;* the speech and aspirations of the common man had become the stuff of poetry or at least of fashionable verse.

Archibald MacLeish, after a decade of experimentation with

the French *symbolistes* ("A poem should not mean but be"), began writing affirmations of the American earth and of those true
comrades "who have fought the police in the parks of the same
cities."

John Dos Passos, an anarchist then and a Republican now, was
writing the collective novel. It seemed as though man could never
be alone again, even in the craft of fiction.

Some of the poets had caught a mood; but the primary actors
in these studies were not poets. For the poets admitted of doubt,
as MacLeish said:

> Preferring life with the sons to death with the fathers
> We also doubt on the record whether the sons
> Will be shouting around with the same huzzas—
> Besides, Tovarish, how to embrace an army?
> How to take to one's chamber a million souls?
> How to conceive in the name of a column of marchers?
> Is it just to demand of us also to bear arms?

But there was a poet named Shaemus O'Sheel who wrote some
lines that were about persons like the objects of these studies and
were warmly esteemed by many of them: "He that a dream has
possessed knoweth no more of doubting."

O'Sheel abandoned any faith in the Soviets in the late thirties
and was encountered many years later moving like an uneasy
ghost about a Yugoslav consulate cocktail party. A stranger was
introduced to him and observed, for want of something better,
that he had once been deeply moved by "He that a dream has
possessed."

"My God," said O'Sheel, "don't people think I wrote anything
else?"

The persons possessed by a dream are a minority in any time.
They are the ones who doubt neither that there is a good side and
a bad one nor that they are ready to die with the good. They are
moved, not by a mood, but by some inner compulsion.

It is these committed and these possessed who concern us here. They were not the people who read the new MacLeish or Strachey or Fischer with the eye of inquiry or mild approval; those were the drifters; some, in extreme cases, were fellow travelers of the Communist Party, and contributed to the myth of the thirties. But the dream was not their lives.

Most of my subjects were Communists, at one time or another, because the Communists were the dominant radicals of the thirties. Some were anti-Communists of the left. All were thus, by definition, creatures of a lonely impulse, because there have never been many convinced Marxists in America. They have traveled many different ways and some have ended strangers and enemies of the others, because, even if we accept the fact of dedication, man's course is dictated by chance and heart far more often than Marx's laws of historic necessity would seem to allow.

But all of them shared at one time or another the conviction that the most important thing in life was a remorseless effort to throw down the society which had raised and alienated most of them. In one form or another, the key and blazing issue of all their quarrels with world and self was which road would carry them to victory. And at one time, to one degree or another, they all spoke with the voice of history, a piece of temerity for which history had visited upon most of them its usual peculiar vengeance.

Most of them entered into the life of the society they hoped to outlive with the view of using as an instrument toward victory some special institution like the government, the trade unions, or the moving picture, all sunk in darkness, all bright with possible light. They changed these institutions a very little bit for a very little while; but far, far more were they changed by them.

Given their view of the matter, it might be expected that they would do society some damage. A few of them did. It might also be expected that, almost by chance and against their own judgment of what they were doing, some might do society a measure of good. A few of them did; we owe them, to a degree at least, the government planning and the strong unions which many people think are our best insurance against a repetition of the storm of 1932.

Some of them survive; others are dead in the sense that we are dead when our time is past us. The landscape upon which they once moved looks to the backward glance now like some bombed city in which the visitor passes through gutted streets to come upon some great monument still intact among the ruins. When they began, they could not have thought that it would end like this, because their time seemed to them as simple as a flame. We know now that it was a very complicated time and that they were more complicated people than they knew.

And it was never even the same time for all of them because for each there came that special moment, and not the least important one, when he was alone, choosing his own ground upon which to stand or surrender, suddenly aware that no law of history has been able to dispose of the pilgrim soul of man. We cannot then think of them as a whole, nor of their time as a unity, the way the myth said it was a unity. All the noise of the thirties— the march of their feet, the warping of their legends, the words they shouted, the songs they sang—was surface; what beat beneath, as it has always beaten, was a chorus of the hearts of so many different men. And man is a private and not a social animal.

It was the sense of the author of this book that the anatomy of any myth is the anatomy of the men who believed in it and suffered by it. To understand the thirties it is, of course, necessary to understand what the thirties themselves would have called their social forces. But it is far, far more important to try to understand the people who lived in that long-gone time. Whatever is permanent in the lesson of the thirties is permanent from these people.

And so what is to follow might perhaps be best described as a series of novellas which happen to be about real persons. Perhaps to my peril, I have tried to write about my people in dangerous depth; that much is borrowed from the craft of fiction. But they are real men and women, and their lives are facts of history.

I have my own stake in the thirties. I was in high school when Roosevelt was inaugurated; I belonged for a little while to the Young Communist League, and thereafter to the Socialist Party. The thirties were a part of my life like any other; I am aware that there are things in it for which I must apologize; I am also aware that in the whole of my life, there will be many things for which I must apologize, under what have to be compulsions stronger than a Congressional subpoena.

The eye which I bring to this inquiry is neither as cold nor as detached as I might wish it to be. I cannot conceal the sense that those of my subjects who became Communists were terribly flawed by their acceptance of a gospel which had no room in it for doubt or pity or mercy, and that, clutching its standard, it was inevitable that so many would set out to be redeemers and end up either policemen or the targets of policemen. It is my hope that mine will not be a crippling bias, and that I and any-one who wishes to join me on this backward journey will remem-ber that we are passing across a landscape which was blighted more than anything else by the absence of pity and mercy.

For in this study we are walking among the ruins of our own city, attempting to reconstruct it from the eye of memory and picking up those broken fragments which may be able to tell us what it was like better than conflicting myths or memories could.

1

ALGER HISS and Whittaker Chambers are two extraordinary men; yet it has been their fate, accepted by Chambers and forced upon Hiss, to be treated as typical of the decade through barely three years of which they were drawn together and so inextricably and fatally involved.

They are better known and the surface of their relationship has been more completely detailed for us than that of any two men who appear to have been Communists together in the thirties. One of them has written 799 pages interpreting their lives together; and there are at least three other books, conflicting in perspective, about their trial and their judgment. And yet reading all these words, the mind can more easily conjure up the image of the typewriter which conditioned society's formal verdict on the meaning of their relationship than it can define the faces of these two men at once so notorious and so shadowy.

The layman after all does not sit as judge in a formal court. The heart of any mystery for a judge or jury is the evidence before the court, which is so often, as it was in the Hiss case, old paper. The heart of the mystery for the rest of us is the life of man, and discussions of the paper seem to me an evasion of the far, far more difficult problem of the meaning, not of what men left behind in their past, but of the past itself.

Thinking about this, I commenced to wonder whether we might approach that inner mystery better if for a while we accepted the formal verdict of the Hiss jury. I confess that this is not so difficult for me as for some others; I believed very early that Chambers and Hiss were Communists together. But acceptance of a formal verdict of Hiss's guilt has left me too with a cloud of unresolved questions about the fatal emotional involvement of these two men who seemed so different from each other.

I grew up in a background very like Alger Hiss's. That may have drawn me to the idea that this background could tell us more than Marx could about the tragic flaw which has brought Hiss and Chambers down. A man's childhood can condition him more than a law of history or what he conceives as the logic of his time. Alger Hiss and Whittaker Chambers both grew up in shabby-genteel families, and each was framed inside the code of shabby gentility. That thought brought me back to Ellen Glasgow's *The Sheltered Life,* a novel about old Virginians gradually slipping down the scale. Miss Glasgow's Archbald and Birdsong families maintain a social position measurably above that into which Hiss and Chambers were born. But they too are declining and imperiled by new and alien passions; the middle-aged among them are encased in values which time has passed over and left either sterile or selfish; the young are imprisoned and longing, as Miss Glasgow's subheroine Jenny Blair Archbald says, to escape somewhere "out in the world."

By adherence to a special set of rules, the child of the shabby-genteel can sometimes leap across the time which has passed by his family and function in the real world without doing violence to the hopes his mother held out for him. But those who cannot live within this pattern are the freaks and the poets, and they travel a difficult road to peace.

Reading Miss Glasgow, I began to wonder whether Hiss and Chambers were not products of a private rather than a social passion. They were men of the thirties to be sure, and, if it had not been for their times, their lives might have been very much different and it is unlikely that they would ever have met or that they ever would have destroyed each other. But what if they were not the symbols of universal experience which simple history makes them but rather atypical fugitives from a narrow world like that of *The Sheltered Life*? I would like to think it the function of maturity to forgive the enemies, real and fancied, of one's childhood; and I wondered if it might not be the tragic flaw of Alger Hiss and Whittaker Chambers to have failed to achieve that reconciliation and to have been torn apart between love and hate for the tight little corners of the sheltered life in which they grew up.

The Sheltered Life

The Partnership of
Alger Hiss and Whittaker Chambers

> " 'The trouble with you, Jenny Blair, is that you do not
> know the first thing about life. It is only by knowing how
> little life has in store for us that we are able to look on the
> bright side and avoid disappointment.' "
>
> " 'Oh, grandfather, I didn't mean anything,' she cried, as
> she sank down into blackness. 'I didn't mean anything in
> the world.' "
>
> ELLEN GLASGOW, The Sheltered Life

THE WORLD of shabby gentility is like no other; its sacrifices
have less logic, its standards are harsher, its relation to reality
is dimmer than comfortable property or plain poverty can understand.

It is certainly better in the eyes of the world to be born one of
the shabby-genteel than one of the simply shabby. The product of
straitened gentility enters a society that flows upward or down-
ward but at least does not stand still for him. But that society has
its special rules for him and they leave their mark; he does not
have either the options or the margins for error other men have.

In its peculiar way, society is quite tolerant of the young man
of shabby gentility. It assumes that he comes of good, though not
fortunate, stock. It knows his father's name—recollects it at least
—and it has confidence in his mother's standards. For he is especially fortunate if he has a mother with the capacity to be
society's censor and to tell him with whom he can afford to play;
to remind him that he has been put into the world to better his

family; and that the price of fortune is unrelenting effort, and that he cannot be too careful.

"My impression was that his relations with his mother were affectionate but not too happy," Alger Hiss's friend, Whittaker Chambers, once said of him. "She was, perhaps, domineering."

Alger Hiss was the child of shabby gentility, and he and his mother made the best use of it they could. The Hisses were not a distinguished family run down. In his final tragedy, his friends and enemies would join in exaggerating the nobility of his origins. When disaster came to him, he was listed in the Washington *Social Register*, but his mother was not in its Baltimore edition.

Alger Hiss's father was a wholesale grocer; he committed suicide when Alger was nine. His older brother Bosley was a bohemian who died young. They lived near Lanvale Street, which is the heartland of shabby gentility in Baltimore. As he grew up, more substantial families around him were moving out into the suburbs. The Hisses stayed there in a neighborhood slowly running down. They were not a family of special social prestige, but the Baltimore in which Alger Hiss grew up was still enough of a Southern city to have its own corner for the sort of family that everyone had always known and which rested on that border between respectability and assured position. In the circumstances of her life, society felt a particular sympathy for Alger Hiss's mother; among the shabby-genteel, the women tend to be stronger than the men; the average runs alarmingly toward widows with promising sons. In a family like this one, as it was in China, it was better to be a boy than a girl, if only because Baltimore needed more boys than girls at debutante parties.

And Alger Hiss appears to have been the sort of boy who made a special impression on older people, and for the very good reason that he deserved to. Knowing him very young in the summertime left a lasting impression on Dean Acheson, a permanent affection which later exacerbated the critics of the Secretary of State, even though none of them appeared to argue that Hiss had been a Comsomol agent assigned to subvert the son of the Episcopal Bishop of Connecticut. But then, to the possessed cadre of the anti-Hiss brigade, good manners, charm, and the capacity for self-improvement have always appeared highly sinister qualities, except to the extent that they appertain to Vice President Nixon. Alger Hiss seemed to join engaging manners with moral worth, and his elders were Americans old-fashioned enough to appreciate the combination.

Whittaker Chambers once described Alger Hiss as "a man of great simplicity and a great gentleness and sweetness of character."

Whatever he had seemed to come to him very easily, because it was a piece of his grace never to show how hard at least some of it must have been. His education was substantially at the public schools; he moved on in 1923 to Baltimore's Johns Hopkins University, where the authors of *Seeds of Treason*, the first book on the great case, tell us that "he was a natural for Alpha Delta Phi, a fraternity which pledged only the wealthiest and most socially acceptable young men on the campus."

But it is also a matter of point that Alpha Delta Phi was the fraternity for those Baltimore boys at the Hopkins who would far rather have gone to Princeton or the University of Virginia and that in consequence most of its members had a feeling that the Hopkins was a little beneath them. But nothing appeared beneath Alger Hiss. He loped without noticeable strain down every visible avenue of undergraduate life; he was editor of the college paper, president of the Student Council, and Phi Beta Kappa in his junior year. No one had drives like his, and no one appeared to need them less.

Almost everyone who remembers him from those days can recall those particular qualities which Whittaker Chambers was later to recollect as "an unvarying mildness, a deep considerateness and gracious patience." But Chambers remembered something else which does not appear to have shown itself to those who knew him in that first blush of unshadowed promise.

Chambers said that he found in Hiss a "streak of wholly incongruous cruelty." The Chambers family had moved to Baltimore late in their friendship and Chambers was charmed by the cool and restful backwater in which they were resting. He was shocked once to hear Hiss call Baltimore "a city of dying old men and women."

Chambers commented that they seemed "to be pleasant and

harmless old people." "Yes," Hiss said, "the horrible old women of Baltimore."

This unexpected depth in Alger Hiss might better be described as morbid rather than cruel. He had the advantage of Chambers. He had grown up on this ground and knew its old women, sitting in their narrow, high-ceilinged rooms, remembering their dead, feeling the pinch of their little incomes, shivering before the invasion of Negroes moving eastward toward their shabby-genteel fortresses.

Chambers after all had small opportunity, as a retiring man, to press any of these harmless old people on the subject of the Jews. Baltimore then was a ghetto-ized city. Mrs. Whittaker Chambers, born Esther Shemitz, could hardly have used her maiden name and rented a house in Alger Hiss's old neighborhood.

But the tide of ethnic mongrels was beating against the Lanvale Street enclave with enough sweep to create its political disenfranchisement. Lanvale Street was in Baltimore's Fourth Assembly District; in one depression Democratic primary, its residents were confronted with a ballot bulging with Jewish names. In desperation they voted for an alternative candidate whose name was unfamiliar but indubitably old Virginia. They awoke to find they had helped nominate a Negro.

The threat of an alien scent against which no window is proof is inherent in the shabby-genteel tradition. The characters in *The Sheltered Life* lived on a hill above the Negro section; the invading hand of time had brought a chemical plant too near them and on the hot nights its odor hung over their gardens. "After living here all our lives," said George Birdsong, Miss Glasgow's flawed hero, "are we to be driven away at last by a smell?"

Whittaker Chambers, trembling on the brink of leaving the Communist Party, had been at war with Lanvale Street without ever knowing its face, and perhaps even then he was commencing to embrace it without taking time to look at its face. Alger Hiss had been at least superficially at peace with Lanvale Street all of his life; the harshness of his comment may indicate how much he longed for war. Unkind and extreme it certainly was to long for the extermination of these sick, frayed, and decaying old women; and "horrible" is a dangerous word to apply to your own kind.

They were after all harmless because they were so helpless. But a man raised by their standards and feeling their hands still upon him could not easily think of them as harmless.

Still, at the Hopkins, these old hands did not noticeably chafe Hiss; he seemed more than anxious to do what they were pushing him to do. His horizons were wider than theirs in just one, perhaps significant, particular. When he was graduated, he looked forward to a career in the private practice of law, but his dreams were not of Baltimore but of Boston and New York. In *The Sheltered Life*, Jenny Blair Archbald longed to bloom somewhere "out in the world."

And so he passed to Harvard Law School where what is left of Lanvale Street may still grasp at the assumption that Felix Frankfurter somehow corrupted him. But it is a measure of this young man's extraordinary grace that he seems to have touched Frankfurter as much as, and perhaps more than, Frankfurter touched him.

One of his classmates was Lee Pressman, a young man up from Brooklyn by way of Cornell University. A long time afterward, with his own world in ruins, Pressman sat in a bar and talked about how Alger Hiss had been in those days. What he said was something like this:

"I remember Alger Hiss best of all for a kind of distinction that had to be seen to be believed. If he were standing at the bar with the British Ambassador and you were told to give a package to the Ambassador's valet, you would give it to the Ambassador before you gave it to Alger.

"He gave you a sense of absolute command and absolute grace and I think Felix felt it more than anyone. He seemed to have a kind of awe of Alger."

Whether or not he had the capacity for becoming involved himself, Alger Hiss very plainly had something at once more precious and as dangerous—the capacity to make people feel involved with him. And yet in 1946, a long time after law school and just a little while before his disaster, a transient from Boston asked Justice Frankfurter who in Washington was worth cultivation.

He reported afterward that he had mentioned Alger Hiss and

that the Justice had declared a little sadly that Alger was a very
nice person but that somehow he had not quite come up to the
promise of his youth. The visitor was left with the sense that Justice Frankfurter felt that Alger Hiss had lost his focus somewhere
and had become just a model civil servant who had once seemed
pregnant with so much more. But, in the beginning, it had been
almost automatic for Frankfurter to recommend him for that
grand prize of the Harvard Law student, a year's graduate tenure
as secretary for Mr. Justice Holmes.

That December, he married Priscilla Hobson, who had been
Priscilla Fansler of Philadelphia, who had her year in New York
after Bryn Mawr and then an incongruous three years as the wife
of Thayer Hobson, a gay and casual embodiment of the myth of
the twenties. Priscilla Hiss seems to have come to her second
marriage with all illusions of casual gaiety behind her. She was a
person of the highest moral seriousness, uneasy and remote with
acquaintances, intense in a few attachments.

She must have been a trifle forbidding. One relic of the
twenties and a friend from her first marriage ran into Alger Hiss
after the war and was invited to stop by their apartment for a
drink. It was a dreadfully cold afternoon and he burst into the
refuge of the Hiss apartment to confront Priscilla alone with the
observation that he had been freezing all day.

He swears that her reply was a suggestion that he think of the
Okies. In these times, that story might be interpreted as evidence
that Priscilla Hiss was an iron Bolshevik. But it sounds rather like
a bruised outcry against the footling world of Thayer Hobson—
to be likened in its origins to Alger Hiss's more private savageries
against the horrible old women of Baltimore. Her guest's second
most painful memory was that Hiss called very graciously to
report himself ensnarled at the office and that he never did get
the drink.

Every mystery has its posse assigned to pursue skirts; and,
throughout the Hiss case, a body of private opinion held that
Priscilla Hiss was responsible for her husband's troubles. Thayer
Hobson held no such opinion. He observed that, in terms of individual character, it would be like expecting a rowboat to pull
the *Queen Mary*. Their life together, at its beginning at least,

showed no signs of departure from normal aspirations for achievement.

They completed their Holmes interlude and went to Boston and a law firm with the name Choate in it. After a year, they moved to New York and Cotton and Franklin, a firm of comparable distinction. And it was in New York, in 1931 and 1932, a very little while, that Alger Hiss first hinted at that difference from ordinary men which can either be a special distinction or a tragic flaw. The wreckage of the twenties lay all about him in those years. It was hard for anyone to escape the panhandlers on the streets or the uprooted men who choked the public parks. But there were very few of them, in spite of Archibald MacLeish, with the will to fight the police or anyone else; they were hopeless and defeated and each seemed gripped with what appeared to him more often a private than a social failure. And, in face of their apathy, it is possible to wonder what the storm in their lives had to do with Alger Hiss.

For most people could look at the wreckage without a compulsion to do anything about it. Alger Hiss was certainly no failure. His permanent emergence from shabby gentility needed no more for assurance than continued homage to shabby gentility's cardinal principle that it is impossible to be too careful. Most men can resist the temptation to lie awake over matters which do not immediately concern them. Only special people cannot.

But Priscilla Hiss began giving steady vocal evidence that the harsh world outside was all too much with her, and her husband began thinking much the same thing. In 1932 Priscilla Hiss voted for Norman Thomas and began to gravitate toward the Morningside Heights branch of the Socialist Party, whose membership included J. B. Matthews, Donald Henderson, Frederick Vanderbilt Field, and a cluster of other people then or subsequently afflicted with pan-Sovietism.

The Socialist Party was an attractive force for many uncertain people then. It was just beginning to be the sort of halfway house that it would be all through the thirties, a way station into which drifters came and then—after a short process of firming their temperaments—took more definite paths, some to the Communists, many more to the New Deal.

The Socialists, in New York at least, were a party proletarian at its base and normal and adjusted in its alienation from the American scene. Most of its members were children of the Eastern European Jewish tradition. Their liveliest intellectual activity was in the Yiddish language. They had built themselves a number of temples, notably the garment unions, and—even though the depression had been unkind to them—they had the outlook of men who were no longer young and combative and whose impulse was against glory and destruction. The revelation which was new and fresh to their 1932 recruits from the middle class was so old to them as to be wrinkled with commentaries and footnotes and ancient quarrels. There were anti-Communists among them who had distrusted Leon Trotsky when he had been a Socialist in Brooklyn before the war. They represented a great tradition, but one which seemed alien and hardly a refuge to the outsider. They had their passions and their inner conflicts, but it was a debate of scribes fingering worn parchment; in a way it was a debate between fathers and sons; there was little room in it for strangers.

But the Morningside Heights branch was different. Its members were immigrants of another sort, expatriates from the American scene. Socialism was fresh to them, and they were impatient of old quarrels. Very few of them stayed long and the drift of the most conspicuous of them was to the Communists.

Alger Hiss appears to have had no traffic with the indecisions of the Morningside Heights Socialists. By day he read law at Cotton and Franklin, at night he pursued interests odd for a junior in a safe old firm. He and Lee Pressman met again as members of the International Juridical Association, which Hiss later described as "an editorial group specializing in putting out notes on labor cases." The IJA has since been described as under Communist control. It would seem more accurate to think of it as an outlet for lawyers dissatisfied with their traditional role; young men who believed that the law must be a social instrument, aware of the rights and wrongs involved in the sort of thing Hiss thought of as a "labor" case. The IJA had a radical impulse; it was no place for the complacent.

On some evenings too, the Hisses studied sporadically at the

Socialist Party's night-time Rand School, a dusty, teeming heap
near Union Square. The Rand School faculty mingled sere and
shabby veterans of the class war with a sprinkling of Talmudic
young Socialists. Its most crowded attractions were its classes in
English for immigrants and a course on "The Road to Power" by
David Berenberg, a now forgotten revolutionary prophet. The
Rand School took its tone mainly from the Socialist Old Guard;
even its left instructors were more critical than enthusiastic about
the Bolsheviks, but they dreamed revolution.

The Hisses must have been a strange pair for the Rand School,
so neat, so quiet, so remote, moving past business agents for the
embroiderers' union on its stairs, sitting in its classrooms while
the young Robespierres and Dantons of the East Side fought the
old debate between reform and revolution. What did all this have
to do with the graceful young man from Cotton and Franklin?
He must certainly have been an alien at the Rand School; if he
had not been an alien even on Lanvale Street, in the days when
he shone there, what else could have brought him and Priscilla to
this grimy temple so many leagues out in the world? To think of
them there is to abandon any thought of these two as typical of
their time and their condition; the impulse which brought them
to this foreign colony almost cries out its loneliness and its
isolation.

For Alger Hiss was not like the young men who grew up with
him; if he had done no more than go to the Rand School, that
errantry in the step which seemed so sure and certain of its upward course would have marked the difference between him and
them. For the Hisses must have come to the Rand School searching for something very far from the sheltered life, carrying within
themselves, so well-contained, an obscure quarrel with Lanvale
Street.

Whatever they sought, they apparently did not find as strangers
at the Rand School. It was a brief association; in 1933, there came
the call to Washington and the new beginning. Alger Hiss went
down to become a legal assistant in the Agricultural Adjustment
Administration, then in its yeastiest and most exciting period. And
there, according to the testimony of Chambers and an anti-cli-

mactic late-starter named Nathaniel Weyl, Alger Hiss joined a Communist cell.

He departed AAA early in 1934 to become acting counsel of the Senate investigation of World War I munitions profits, a great war-crimes trial of the merchants of death, in the course of which Alger Hiss pan-fried the House of Morgan and other household gods of Lanvale Street with a cold savagery to which he was never again to give public display. For then he passed to the quiet little family of the State Department, there to proceed upward by routine and hardly spectacular steps until 1947.

Sometime in 1934, both of them agree, there slouched into his life an uneasy, unpressed man named Whittaker Chambers. Even the circumstances of their meeting are clouded by their conflict. These two men agree only that Alger Hiss did not know he was meeting Whittaker Chambers. Chambers says he was introduced to Hiss as "Carl" in a Washington restaurant in the company of J. Peters, the captain of the Communist underground. Hiss has always testified that he could remember only a free-lance writer who called himself George Crosley shambling into the Munitions Committee office in search of material for a never produced series of articles in the *American Magazine*.

Out of that meeting grew a relationship that was deeper, by Chambers' account, than the relationship customary among Communists, who are seldom either blessed or cursed with naked intimacy, and deeper, even by Hiss's account, than would be expected in a young careerist of high social standards with a man whom he has variously described as impecunious, a sponger, unproductive, and—to a fastidious person—almost repulsive in taste and appearance.

United States Senator Karl Mundt, a man realistic about the extent of sacrifice required for friends, let alone annoying strangers, summed up Hiss's account of their acquaintanceship this way:

"You knew this man . . . so well that you even trusted him with your apartment; you let him use your furniture; you let him use or gave him your automobile. You think you probably took him to New York. You bought him lunches in the Senate restaurant. You had him staying in your home when it was inconvenient for him to stay in the apartment and made him a series of loans. There seems no question about that."

To all this catalogue, Priscilla Hiss could only answer that she had found the Crosleys a distinct trial. Alger Hiss could only offer a single, repeated phrase to justify this tolerance of a man he otherwise described as a barnacle. The phrase would indicate that Hiss was touched by a quality in Crosley-Carl-Chambers that was unique in his careful existence—except perhaps with his brother Bosley—the rootless nonconformity, the bohemianism that terrified Lanvale Street:

"He told various stories that I recall of his escapades. He purported to be a cross between Jim Tully, the author, and Jack London. He had been everywhere."

There would thus appear, even from his own account, to be a pilgrim soul of romance buried in the compulsions of Alger Hiss's sheltered life, pushed outside the mold, unsatisfied by convention, unappeased by ordinary success. For Whittaker Chambers was a figure of romance; even as a Communist, he was plainly that special target of later Soviet inquisitions, the total cosmopolitan.

Alger Hiss's family had been a painfully held together rookery; Chambers' had been a total ruin. They had both been born into the Episcopal Church, that haven of the shabby-genteel. Hiss's mother had faithfully met society's standards for recovery; Chambers' mother had lamentably failed at them. Hiss had walked the road of custom; Chambers had traveled a wild, swarm-haunted route, an itinerant worker, a self-asserted veteran of the Industrial Workers of the World. He was unproductive as a writer because he had so much else to do. His art had been a weapon. His reputation as a writer rested on four short stories in the *New Masses,* which were celebrations of the myth of a Bolshevik, of a type rare in American fiction or reality. They were not so much stories as incantations; not so much fiction as heroic poetry. Their characters were Communists ready to die for what they believed; it is hardly accident that they did not seem like American stories at all, and that one of Chambers' admirers has described them as "reading almost like a skillful translation from the Russian."*

Lincoln Steffens read these stories and wrote Chambers that from now on "whenever I hear people talk about 'proletarian art and literature,' I'm going to ask them to shut their minds and look at you."

And these stories, barren though they are of exterior reality, do have that inner truth which comes when a man is consumed by the myth he is celebrating; Chambers believed in the obscure Bolshevik who dies in prison with no memorial but his triumphant defense of the human spirit. These were stories not of how it was, but how he wanted it so desperately to be. Then he had stopped writing and become an underground Communist, because it seems to have been the core of his literary fantasy that the actor was more important than the poet; he was a man who would rather do than write.

So Chambers was the image of dedication and adjustment to alienation. It seems odd that Hiss should accept him on his own terms as a Jim Tully or a Jack London, or that Chambers should present himself to the *New Masses* as a veteran of the Industrial Workers of the World, with which he seems to have no connection. For Chambers had never been an itinerant, except in his own soul; he had had some limited experience at manual labor, but he was no veteran of the barricades. He had been to Europe only as a tourist. He had suffered certainly and he had been desperately poor, but his experience as a revolutionary was largely on paper: he had been a city editor of the *Daily Worker*, a translator of novels, an editor of the *New Masses*. Alger Hiss's lawyers made a laborious effort to search his past for evidence of immoral activity, and all they really found was that he had been separated from Columbia University under suspicion of stealing books from the library; his only attempt at expropriating the capitalists was consistent in its literary character.

But all this does not mean that Chambers' posture was a lie. Even the little stories he told do not appear to have been untruths. Hiss mentioned just one example of what a four-flusher

* Ralph De Toledano in *Seeds of Treason*.

Chambers seemed to him: he told how "he had participated in laying the rails for the first Washington Street railway"—a story which appears to have been true. His posture was no less real than his short stories even though, like them, it was hardly the product of direct experience; he seems to have been, like Scott Fitzgerald's Jay Gatsby, the product of his own Platonic conception of himself.

Most human relationships involve certain misunderstandings; it is hard not to believe that Hiss and Chambers, when they met, were taken with each other because they misunderstood each other. Chambers must have sat in the Hiss apartment with all his scars upon him, a lowering symbol of power and experience and total revolt. All his life, without knowing it, he had been looking for a community. It would appear that Alger Hiss had been trying to get out of a community. Could Chambers have seen in Hiss the image of absolute security, absolute breeding, and absolute normality; could Hiss have seen in Chambers the image of absolute revolt and the breaking of the bands?

For what else could explain an involvement so confessedly passionate on Chambers' side, and so difficult to explain on Hiss's? To a career man in the State Department, to the rising son of Lanvale Street, Whittaker Chambers—whatever his guise—should carry a bell tinkling unsafe, unsafe. The cultural void between them was without limit. Chambers, by a steady process of alienation, had stopped even seeming like an American; he claims that Priscilla Hiss only warmed to him from the conviction that he was really a Russian. He could read a dozen languages; he is a man so incurably bookish that he can report spending hours outside a federal grand jury room reading Dante; you would expect almost anyone else to escape to Eric Ambler.

Fugitive hints of this cultural gap creep in and out of the stories both men were to tell later. Once the Un-American Activities Committee asked Chambers about the books in the Hiss apartment where he remembered spending so many days. "Very nondescript," Chambers answered. Once Chambers gave Hiss a present which he later asserted was a token of gratitude from the Russian secret police. Chambers went outside the Communist aesthetic orbit to ask Dr. Meyer Schapiro, a Columbia University art historian and an old acquaintance, to buy him four Bokhara rugs, one of which he gave to the Hisses. We may assume Schapiro's superior taste; later on, Alger Hiss referred to the rug as "that damned thing"; the Hisses put it in the nursery.

"I had the impression," Whittaker Chambers said once, "that the furniture in that house was kind of pulled together from here and there, maybe got it from their mother or something like that, nothing lavish about it, quite simple.

"Their food was in the same pattern, and they cared nothing about food. It was not a primary interest in their lives."

The Hisses' talk must have been in the same way free of frills and complications; Chambers indicates that he very soon lost any disposition to discuss revolutionary theory with Hiss. In his autobiography, he reports only Hiss's admiring comment on the Moscow trials: "Joe Stalin certainly plays for keeps." That was a view of things which could hardly offer much meat to an old Bolshevik who grew up in the Communist Party of the twenties when it had a less limited range of intellectual interests and a faint trace of skepticism about the hero in history.

Their bond seemed to be something much deeper—the strange, almost unconscious kinship of similar backgrounds. None of the other Communists in Washington, except perhaps Henry Collins, had a background like theirs. And Chambers seemed to reach out to the Hisses with some of that same passion for the ordinary and the normal which runs through his later odes to simple Americans who are no worse than the common mortal but hardly divine.

The best of the talk to him must have been of the small and the ordinary. Mrs. Chambers retained a vivid recollection, fifteen years later, of the "lovely linen towel" which Priscilla Hiss lent her once as an emergency diaper. Chambers pursued the background of the Hisses with the loving questions whose answers served him so well in court so much later. To read all that devoted detail is to wonder whether these people had ever known a real home before.

For all the apparent sleeping gypsy within him, Alger Hiss remained a very proper and fastidious person. As one of the less appealing consequences of a vagrant revolutionary's life, Chambers appears by common consent to have been somewhat gone in the teeth. He says that Hiss lectured him on the necessity of brushing twice a day with what Chambers felt was a barely concealed shudder. And, at the end, all Hiss said that he could remember was those bad teeth, as if the abyss before him then and now was somehow an ill-tended dental cavity.

But a whole part of Whittaker Chambers must have come fleeing to Alger Hiss, and this apartment, poor in imagination though it was, must have been for Chambers as close to peace as this man pursued by the furies could ever get. For, if the Hisses had consciously rejected the sheltered life, they still lived within it.

Shabby gentility grants its own degrees in the art of keeping up appearances. If we accept the notion of Alger Hiss's being a Communist, we still cannot disregard his childhood, a piece of irritated skin which none of us can tear away. A product of that childhood would certainly have felt a certain comfort in the party-dictated procedure which allowed him at once to be a private Communist and an entirely respectable public man.

But Chambers says that another part of Alger Hiss revolted against this shelter too. A dedicated man brings to the Communist movement a burning urgency which will never grant him assurance that he is doing well enough. Chambers described Hiss as such a dedicated man, who wanted to give his old Ford car, an object of sentiment, to some party organizer who could put it to more purposeful use.

"Mr. Hiss was a devoted and at that time rather romantic Communist," Chambers testified. "According to the organization and the underground, there should be no communication between the open Communist Party and the underground Communist Party, except through people delegated by either of those sections. Mr. Hiss, however, insisted that his old car should be given to the open Communist Party to be used by some poor Communist organizer in the West or elsewhere."

Somewhere "out in the world," as Jennie Blair Archbald wished.

If the sheltered life had produced an inner Alger Hiss at once in need of safety and hating it, he suffered most of all at the end from those rare occasions when he sought to break out into the world. Chambers' story of Hiss's desire to liberate his car to the cause of subversion was at once dubious to the innocent and persuasive to persons who had been unaffirmed Communists in the thirties and remembered the urge for self-expression which beat within that otherwise comfortable state of being. And, in the end, this strange story took on a fatal weight when the Un-American Activities Committee discovered that Hiss *had* transferred his car to a man who refused to affirm or deny whether he had ever been a Communist. And, for just that moment, it was possible to guess at what sort of person Alger Hiss had been in that time which had returned to pull him down.

For both of them remain such shadows, beneath all the paper of what they have said and of what has been said about them. The face of Alger Hiss, silent, is a mystery; the face of Whittaker Chambers, speaking, is hardly less of an enigma. If there was a moment in which he showed himself, it was in a New York courtroom on an August Monday in 1948, when the Un-American Activities Committee summoned him to identify a man called Alexander Stevens, more familiarly known as J. Peters.

The very pseudonym J. Peters, with its spare, self-effacing first initial, carries us back to the ancient internal bulletins of the underground Communists of Europe, their M. Ercoles, their P. Maximovs, their D. Manuilskys, and their N. Lenins, the last of whom used a single initial that did not stand for anything at all.

J. Peters had been the American representative of the Communist International. His manual on organization for the American party is a compendium of tested revolutionary tactics. Old Communists remembered him as the pleasant, self-contained tenant of the ninth floor of their New York headquarters, a man of indubitable importance but no precisely defined function. If any American Communist is a conspirator, he is one; if any is a guilty man, it is J. Peters.

That hot Monday, he stood up in Federal Court and looked at Chambers. His smile was enamel. He would not say whether he knew his accuser or not: to answer would tend to incriminate and degrade him. Chambers was afterward to remember a special accent on "degrade." Then Chambers rose to look at Peters. The smile remained enamel, and Chambers looked at the floor. His answers came in a voice lower than usual; they were terribly short and dry. Peters' was the face of assured innocence, and Chambers' was the face of guilt.

But what was this guilt of his? To answer that Chambers had known Peters as a Communist was simple truth; they had worked in the same Party office. His testimony against Peters was hardly defamation of an uncomplicated New Dealer. This was not Alger Hiss; Whittaker Chambers could not really damage the life of J. Peters, which after all is a life lived wherever the Party sends him; there are no good moments or bad in it; there are only assignments.

Chambers reports in his autobiography that, a little while after his break with the Communists, he attended a meeting of the CIO Newspaper Guild and "became aware that someone was staring at me." He turned to confront "the undisguised hatred" on the face of Nathan Witt, an old Washington comrade. We may assume, on the basis of the scene with Peters, that Chambers turned away from Witt too with something like the same shudder of embarrassment.

In Peters, he was looking, for the first time in ten years, straight at the open face of the Communist movement to whose service he had once offered his life. He was confronting the human embodiment of a vast company of men all over the world, which he had abandoned and fled. And Chambers, armed though he supposes himself with unseen powers, apparently could not look at that face without an infusion of weakness and guilt. And it is not the guilt of the renegade. It is the guilt of the man repossessed by the sense of sin looking at the man who is still free from it.

Men like Alger Hiss do not have to become Communists, at least in the West; it is an act of will. Membership in the Party is an inconvenience; its duties are much more material than its rewards. There are a variety of reasons that could impel a man toward this unattractive discipline. One of them may be the sense of guilt—the guilt of inaction in a time of action, the guilt of serving oneself first in the face of the knowledge that it is better to serve others, the guilt of unexpressed aspirations which are different from the aspirations of your own kind.

The men who became Communists out of that sense of guilt are spoiled priests.*

We have no more repetitive witness than Chambers to Alger Hiss's great sweetness and unselfishness of character. The rules of conduct for the young man of shabby gentility do not offer much public expression for those high qualities. He cannot be too careful; he is not granted time to waste himself in good works that do not bring tangible rewards. It is an endless shabby-genteel refrain that these things are not his business and when is he going to stop worrying about other people and start thinking about his own family?

Alger Hiss had never given shabby gentility any cause to ask that awful question. But the terrible conflict between his private self and his public conduct is the most compelling reason why he could have joined the Communist Party.

For the Communists offer one precious, fatal boon: they take away the sense of sin. It may or may not be debatable whether a man can live without God; but, if it were possible, we should pass a law forbidding a man to live without the sense of sin.

To be a Communist is to feel the thrill of fascination in recognizing that Joe Stalin plays for keeps, especially, as George Orwell said once, if one lives in an environment to which murder is at best a *word*. It is, and it has been in so many thousand cases, to have a very good friend and then cut him from your consciousness because he has left the Party. It is to give full play to your hates because they are necessary hates.

To be a Communist is to steal secrets from people who to some degree trust you. When Chambers describes the process by which he says he and Hiss entered into espionage, this man—usually so obsessed with moral discourse—suggests no interior quarrel in either case. We may assume that there would be none.

* This sentence seems to me a fair summary although subject to the peril of simplicity. My recollections of my own Communist experience, its beginning and its end, are not conspicuous for the memory of particular personal virtues. Ex-Communists tend to ascribe uncommonly lofty motives both to their fall and subsequent reclamation, which sometimes makes it faintly depressing to examine the current motives of a few of them. You would hope our society would be a little better equipped to preserve the moral purity of persons who claim to have kept it so intact from their entrance to their exit from the army of darkness.

And the conduct of Communists, which is at least as dreadful as that of ordinary men, is the conduct of people most of whom once had an active conscience and most of whom now feel a particular virtue. Until the dark falls upon them, they are immune to the insinuations of the sense of sin.

For Whittaker Chambers at least, his break brought back the sense of sin compounded by all the remembered, unatoned guilt of his life as a Bolshevik. We have to believe in all the baggage of his subsequent flight under what he considered a terror of Communist vengeance, if only because there exists a swarm of witnesses to the manner of that flight. But the fantasy that a Florida motel could be owned by a Communist determined to kill him, the long vigils with a gun on his lap, the idea that he was hiding out when he had his name in the Baltimore telephone book—these are not the actions of a man fleeing a simply material terror.

And so Chambers must have been fleeing as well the intangible, choking guilt, the overwhelming re-impulsion of that sense of sin from which the world was not wide enough to offer him shelter. Chambers once told Julian Wadleigh that he had known the trouble that keeps you awake all night at the window. A man can put a gun across his knees and know that the trouble which keeps him awake is not a physical thing. Men at peace in the mind can sleep on sentry duty; Whittaker Chambers never could.

He says that Alger Hiss cried on his doorstep on the night Whittaker Chambers told him that he had left the Communist Party and walked away. And that must have been not the lightest piece of his guilt too, sitting before the window and remembering this only true friend left behind in the darkness. And, as for that pale, lost, drowned friend, no one can say what Alger Hiss thought about in all those years. He was a success at the State Department, but his greatest achievements had about them a faintly ceremonial quality. He ended up, still looking very young, as president of the Carnegie Endowment for World Peace, a position which could take him very little farther.

His few published writings in that period have a hollow, foggy, airblown character; they do not read like products of that sharp young mind which impressed even Lee Pressman with its absolute control and absolute decision. Somewhere, it would appear, as Justice Frankfurter implied, that Alger Hiss had lost his focus. Or it may be that somewhere between 1937 and 1948 he had lost the Leninist sense of his place in history.

But, after that, he fought for his personal life with a coolness and decision which some persons saw as the face of innocence and in which Chambers found the half-conviction that Hiss must still be a Communist, because it is so hard for Chambers to believe that man can find within himself alone the strength to stand up against catastrophe.

Hiss maintained that strength, defiant against the evidence, long after most men gave up hope that he might be innocent of the formal charges and began to debate just what were the dimensions of his guilt. The source of that defiance is the last and deepest mystery about Alger Hiss. But his friends and enemies, as well as Whittaker Chambers, who came to the end thinking himself both, might wonder whether this too could be a private and not a social strength. They might remember that we are all what our background makes us and that the world of shabby gentility teaches the best of its sons that, when all else goes, empty though it is, they must fight to the death against losing the precious little they have won.

2

THE SUBJECTS of these studies seem to me to have been special sorts of people with peculiar rhythms of their own and with eyes that looked upon their time through a lens and with a focus very different from those of most of their contemporaries.

And, to understand them, I believe it is necessary to think of their lives as governed by a calendar of events different from the ordinary concerns of the American historian. Its red-letter days were not so much those of October, 1929, when the twenties perished with the stock market, as those of August, 1927, when Nicola Sacco and Bartolomeo Vanzetti were waiting for the executioner. For so many of these people, the myth of the thirties began at Charlestown Prison in Boston with Sacco and Vanzetti and not in lower Manhattan with Richard Whitney nor in Washington with Herbert Hoover. And for many of them the thirties ended, not with Pearl Harbor, but with the 1940 breach between Franklin D. Roosevelt and John L. Lewis, those two great, disparate allies of the revolution of that decade.

And the key image of their dreams was the working class, disarmed in the twenties and armed in the thirties. I am reminded of how deep that image is buried now whenever a young man of the fifties comes to me to talk about a future in the labor movement. His conversation is about the techniques of labor journalism, about training in labor law, about economic research, and pension statistics. He dreams, as St. Exupéry once complained of the young Frenchman, not of building a cathedral but of serving as its sexton. To yearn for a place in the labor movement in the thirties was to conceive yourself on the barricades. But, even then, it was to think of power; to enter the labor movement in the twenties was to think largely of protest.

The archetype of the worker of the twenties, by this special focus, was Bartolomeo Vanzetti, a conscious revolutionary, articulate in suffering, and doomed to die outnumbered and overpowered. The archetype of the worker of the thirties was John Llewellyn Lewis, an unconscious revolutionary, articulate in vengeance, a promise of power without limit. Vanzetti died affirming his sense of innocence; John Lewis went down unafflicted by a sense of sin. The transition from the worship of Vanzetti to the worship of Lewis was in its way the story of two generations of committed radicals in America.

I thought that to reach closer to the special time sense of these two generations, with their private calendar and particular set of saints' days, it might be best to take two men and play their lives against the stream of exterior events which were the critical moments in the lives of the committed. They would need to be men who had lived together in the great world and been close to the Vanzettis, the Lewises, the Philip Murrays, and others who were at once the icons and the chosen instruments of the committed. One of these men would be older than the other, and he would conceive of his impulse as an impulse of the heart; he would in other words see in his mirror the face of the innocent radical of the twenties. The other would conceive of his impulse as that of function; he would in other words see in his mirror the face of the radical of the thirties, sure of his purpose, impatient of pity or weakness.

Men are not often what they think they are, and no living person is ever an exact reproduction of a literary conception. Still I chose as my subjects Gardner Jackson, the secretary of the Sacco-Vanzetti Defense Committee, and a younger, sometime friend of his, Lee Pressman, who became general counsel of the CIO and was for years a symbol of the Communist influence within it. Jackson seemed the symbol of heart and Pressman the symbol of function; each in his way ended a very different man from the one he had thought himself.

Jackson has been a friend of mine for a long time, and it is perhaps natural that what he has told me has conditioned so much of the pattern of this story. I last saw Pressman some years ago, as I have left him here, at the moment of his fall; and it seemed only just not to search for him among the shadows, adjusting his rhythms to those of ordinary men. As for the gods in whose temples Pressman or Jackson—or both—moved, I am particularly grateful in the case of Vanzetti to *The Legacy of Sacco and Vanzetti* by G. Louis Joughin and Edmund M. Morgan, to Upton Sinclair's *Boston,* to Bernard De Voto's *We Accept With Pleasure,* and to John Dos Passos' *The Big Money,* all of which reflect the terrible crisis in faith which the case's final tragedy visited upon the older radicals. The legend of John Lewis is best embodied in Lewis himself and in Saul Alinsky's *John L. Lewis.*

The legend of Vanzetti has faded a little, but time has not affected its purity. The legend of John Lewis has faded more, and has been ravaged in some of its essentials, most of all in its aspect of infallibility. In somewhat the same way, Jackson, who seemed the weaker, has survived; and Pressman, the stronger, has gone under. I suppose that ironies of this sort are not uncommon for men whose pulses beat with a rhythm unfamiliar to their contemporaries and whose eyes have their own special focus. And I suppose, too, that time, if not fashion, is kinder to the older moralities.

The Dry Bones

Gardner Jackson and Lee Pressman

*"I am suffering because I am a radical and indeed I am
a radical; I have suffered because I am an Italian and indeed I am an Italian; I have suffered more for my family
and my beloved than for myself; but I am so convinced to
be right that you can only kill me once, but, if you could
execute me two times and I could be reborn two other
times, I would live again to do what I have already."*

> Bartolomeo Vanzetti, Statement
> upon receiving sentence, April 9,
> 1927

*"What was most in Hyacinth's mind was the idea, of
which every pulsation of his time was a syllable, that the
flood . . . was rising all over the world; that it would
sweep all the traditions of the past before it; that, whatever
it might fail to bring, it would at least carry in its bosom a
magnificent energy and that it might be trusted to look
after its own."*

> Henry James, The Princess Casamis-
> sima, p. 407

*"Beneath the spreading chestnut tree
I sold you and you sold me . . ."*

> George Orwell, 1984

NICOLA SACCO and Bartolomeo Vanzetti were brought to
trial in Dedham, Massachusetts, on May 31, 1921, in a courthouse across the street from the old Fisher Ames house and on an
island threatened by the encroaching lower orders of Boston.
They were held for an ordinary payroll murder; their case took

on a coloration of excitement because they were anarchists and because Boston journalism has always been devout in enlarging the routine into the sensational.

But even so the reports from Dedham sounded muffled in Boston, just a few miles away. No one could have believed that Sacco and Vanzetti were material to make Boston a name for execration in foreign tongues for marching thousands the world over in the next six years.

The Boston *Globe* sent Frank Palmer Sibley, New England's oldest trial reporter, down to Dedham. Sibley was a calm and careful man whose only concession to rhetorical adornment was his flowing Windsor tie, and he sent back careful, muted accounts of the proceedings. But shock and distaste must have broken through the surface of his reports, because they disturbed some citizens of Boston, not many, but enough to create a nuisance and a legend.

Gardner Jackson, a beginning reporter on the *Globe*, was too occupied with his own new duties to worry about the assignments of his elders; and at first he paid little attention to Sibley's Sacco-Vanzetti reportage. Then, one morning at breakfast, his wife Dorothy looked up from her *Globe* and said, "Pat, there's something strange about this trial down in Dedham. Why don't you see if you can find out something about it?"

A few days later, Pat Jackson ran into old Mr. Sibley and conquered his sense of the distance between them long enough to ask about Sacco and Vanzetti. "My God, I'm glad somebody asked me," Sibley replied. "I've never seen anything like it."

And this old man went on to talk with a sense of shock, which he thought he had outgrown, about a judge and a public prosecutor who conceived as their function the extirpation of the alien and the revolutionary, and about the two Italians who were objects of their fury. The trial had been an ordeal impelling him to break the pattern of years as a spectator and write a letter to the Attorney General of Massachusetts. But there had been no answer, and hardly anyone except young Pat Jackson had bothered to ask him about these obscure proceedings in a suburban courtroom. Sibley had no views on the innocence of Sacco and Vanzetti. But he was sure that theirs had not been a fair trial.

Then Sibley passed on to other courtrooms, but Pat Jackson could not forget Sacco and Vanzetti. They had been convicted and remitted to Charlestown Prison for the process of appeal. The agitation in their defense was in largely non-Boston tongues; Henry Mencken was the only American writer of distinction to give early public expression to disturbance over their case. Aldo Felicani, the anarchist who was the core of the Sacco-Vanzetti case, was straitened of means and cut off from Boston's mainstream when Pat Jackson found him in his printshop. Felicani glowed with the most romantic of social creeds. He had once been in prison with a young Socialist named Benito Mussolini, but his innocence remained unviolated. And in him, Pat Jackson discovered a soul unlike any in his experience, a man to follow to the farthest reaches.

Pat Jackson seemed so normal a young man that it was hard to understand the change which those two disparate instructors, Sibley and Felicani, had worked upon him. Afterward the *Globe* seemed more and more an empty vessel. He gave his evenings to Sacco and Vanzetti and, late in 1926, when their case was approaching its climax, he quit the *Globe* and joined Felicani as secretary of the Sacco-Vanzetti Defense Committee. Nicola Sacco always thought of Jackson as an ally from another world. Two months before his execution, he wrote Jackson to express his gratitude:

"We are one heart, but unfortunately we represent two different class . . . But, whenever the heart of one of the upper class join with the exploited workers for the struggle of the right in the human feeling is the feel of an spontaneous attraction and brotherly love to one another."

Sacco was fighting to conquer his sense of difference, for after all he came from a country where rich and poor seemed to him in armed camps. The road which had brought Pat Jackson to Charlestown Prison had not turned as sharply as Sacco thought; if the voices in his ear were not ancestral, they came at least from his family and his childhood. He had been born in the late nineties in Colorado Springs, that "City of Eternal Sunshine," whose rays shone on many fortunate young men and upon few with more kindness than upon Gardner Jackson. William S. Jackson, his father, had been variously a banker, promoter, and railroad owner and was altogether a capitalist of respectable dimensions even for Colorado Springs.

Gardner was the son of his father's old age, and he lived a safe and cushioned boyhood. Cripple Creek was very near; not long before his birth, striking miners were drilling there with guns, and Colorado Springs shook with rumors of imminent armed invasion. In 1904, the miners blew up one of William S. Jackson's railroad stations. But the echoes of this war—"massacre" is a recurring appellation from even its soberest historians—came very faintly to the Jackson home.

The Jackson property was, of course, a substantial segment of that challenged in the Cripple Creek skirmishers' lines. But the Jackson tradition was not one of pure aggrandizement. Little Gardner was the child of his father's third marriage; the second had been with Helen Hunt Jackson, a New England lady whose conscience had been an affliction to almost every citizen of Colorado except her worshiping husband.

The second Mrs. William Jackson was a forty-three-year-old widow when she came to Colorado Springs. In New England she had been a poetess and thus afflicted with turbulent sensibilities. This late marriage to a man of property might, in anyone else, have been taken as a prelude to a quiet and slightly stuffy old age. But Helen Hunt Jackson was no sooner settled as a queen in Colorado Springs than she was shaken by the condition of the American Indian. She prevailed upon the Interior Department to commission her to study the treatment of Indians throughout the West; the fruit of these researches was a catalogue of horror which she called *A Century of Dishonor*. In 1884, very ill, she wrote *Ramona*, an immense success as a novel and a close competitor to *Uncle Tom's Cabin* in the employment of fiction for inflammatory social comment.

In the West of the eighties, Mrs. Jackson could hardly have chosen a less respectable object of compassion than the Indian. Her endeavors in his behalf won her hardly a genuine non-Indian sympathizer in the state of Colorado. The Sacco-Vanzetti case in Boston in 1927 would be a popular enterprise beside this cause of Helen Hunt Jackson's. But William S. Jackson, whatever his limitations of identification, remained a loyal and devoted husband.

Helen Hunt Jackson died; her widower married again; and Gardner Jackson was born to this marriage. But Helen Hunt Jackson retained in the family the status of an ornament eclipsing the bank, the railroad, and the mines. And when he grew up, young Gardner was sent East to Amherst College where she had been a faculty daughter and had developed her iron New England conscience. He arrived there just before the war. Alexander Meiklejohn was then Amherst's president and busy shaking the dust off its Calvinism; before very long the epithet of anarchist would be hurled upon him as bitterly, if less accurately, as upon Nicola Sacco.

Gardner Jackson seemed as gay and careless as any of his fellows, and Meiklejohn's effect did not seem to sit heavy upon him. But, somehow, the real world managed to insinuate itself into one of those interior corners in which the sense of it can alter a man's life. On Sunday mornings, he would climb onto a trolley with nothing on his mind except the Smith girls in Northampton at the other end. But, before he had traveled very far, he would be involved in intense and ultimately self-subverting conversation with the Polish farm hands who alone failed to thrive in the flourishing Connecticut Valley.

The ideas of Alexander Meiklejohn and the mutterings of the Poles were alike a yeast to Pat Jackson. But at first they produced in him nothing more than the uneasy sense of something in life beyond the safety of Colorado Springs. The army took him away from Amherst and brought him home with the same unease. He tried Columbia; he tried a family enterprise in Denver; he tried selling bonds; he tried the *Globe*. But none of these things filled that vague sense of void. Nothing seemed to until he met Felicani.

The case of Sacco and Vanzetti was at once the glory and the tragedy, the triumph and the disaster, of American social protest in this century. No other cause would seem so pure; no other protagonists would glow so much like walking flames. And no other end would come so clean and sharp and so utterly annihilating to the souls of those who cared. To have been in the Sacco-Vanzetti death watch was, for one time in a man's life, to have walked almost alone among the heights. And that remains true, even though there is a Sacco-Vanzetti memorial plaque on Boston Common now, very near the spot where the police clubbed and chivvied fourteen pickets on an August Sunday in 1927. For it is not the least of a martyr's scourges to be canonized by the persons who burned him.

Sacco and Vanzetti live on in poems and plays and novels, and most of all in the words of the elder of them, who must certainly be the greatest writer of English in our century to learn his craft, do his work, and die all in the space of seven years. They are so much a piece of legend by now that very few of their enemies feel in a position any longer to dispute the major cantos of their epic—poverty, false witness, testament, and crucifixion. You might almost assume that no one in all Massachusetts really wanted them dead except one judge, one public prosecutor, twelve jurymen, and a governor—himself reluctant.

But it did not seem that way in the summer of 1927 when Bernard De Voto, then a Harvard instructor, walked about Boston and set down what he saw and heard in *We Accept With Pleasure,* a novel published seven years later. One of his characters is a defense lawyer who asks in the last hours:

"Who is it that is killing the poor wops? I wish I knew. Is it City or just the Hill? . . . Taxi drivers, newsboys, washerwomen, subway guards. . . . I ask them all. It's always 'Hang the bastards.' "

Another character wanders on execution night up to the police barricades near Charlestown Prison as a part of a formless, neutral crowd. He watches and reflects:

"They will couple up the hose and first they will use water. But, on the bridge, there are machine guns—Brownings to be used on people when they rise. Bodies twist screaming and blood mingles with oil in the gutter. Roar of many motorcycles. These have riot guns. I will die in the first wave."

But then the crowd stirs good-naturedly and his vision dissolves. He has learned that the people do not rise, that they do not even care; they are out to see the show while Nick and Bart die. He struggles alone with a policeman, and runs away sightless and in a trance. He passes a group of his friends. One of them looks after him and says:

"It must be painful to love the people and find the mob a whore."

The persons who died with Sacco and Vanzetti were thus cut off and isolated and surrounded by a mob that was hostile when it was not indifferent. But they had found, and they held, a fortress of the spirit. And, for a while, a few seemed utterly changed.

Edna St. Vincent Millay marched as a picket on the Common; when Sacco and Vanzetti died, she wrote that never again would a road through the wood or a stretch of shore bring her peace. "The beauty of these things can no longer make up to me for all the ugliness of man, his cruelty, his greed, his lying face."

John Dos Passos came home to Harvard to help the Defense Committee. In the case's last hours he heard "the old words of the haters of oppression made new in sweat and agony." And at the end he wrote:

"Our work is over the scribbled phrases the nights typing releases the smell of the printshop the sharp reek of newprinted leaflets the rush for Western Union stringing words into wires the search for stinging words to make you feel who are your oppressors america.

"America our nation has been beaten by strangers who have turned our language inside out who have taken the clean words our fathers spoke and made them slimy and foul.

"all right we are two nations."

Powers Hapgood, Harvard and Hasty Pudding before World War I, was arrested as a demonstrator on the Common four times, the last of them by the superintendent of police himself. As they were carrying him away, he turned his head and shouted: "Don't forget, comrades, keep it up—save the men!" He would marry Mary Donovan, a Boston Irish girl who had consumed herself in the case, and move on to be an organizer for the miners' union and the CIO, sick very soon and dying before his time twenty years later.

Powers Hapgood, dying; Edna Millay withdrawn to her interior terrors; Dos Passos, losing his powers, alone and embittered; so many left so much of themselves behind on a small green patch of Boston.

Gardner Jackson had changed too; in the spring of 1927 he found himself in the office of the Boston *Globe,* quarreling with his former managing editor and with Frank Sibley, both beings who had walked on clouds so far above him just five years before. Sibley had agreed to sign an affidavit detailing various expressions of prejudice against Sacco and Vanzetti in his presence by Judge Webster Thayer, who had presided at the Dedham trial. Now both Sibley and his editor argued that a reporter should not mix in maneuvers. Jackson found himself facing them both down with a toughness that was new to him and at last forced Sibley's signature on the affidavit.

On the day Sacco and Vanzetti were executed, the *Globe* very carefully sent Frank Sibley to cover a flower show. Pat Jackson was suffering at the Defense Committee's office on Hanover Street. Whatever the end, he could not go back to Boston family journalism again. None of them, even if they tried, could ever go back to what they had been. There were even a few who could almost feel envy for Sacco and Vanzetti, because their agony at least was ended.

In his *Boston,* Upton Sinclair makes Betty Alvin cry out a few minutes after the execution:

"You don't realize—it's all over. Stop and think what it means —Bart and Nick can't suffer anymore! Nobody can punish them, nobody can torture them, ever again! *They* aren't in jail! They're *free."*

There is, in these accounts of the last days, with their demonstrators stuffed into the Joy Street police station chanting their revolutionary songs, an illusion that these were glittering hours. And some may have thought them so, for there are always people who come to gape and thrill at any swelling pitch of existence. But they were not the persons to whom Boston, for the last two years, had meant only Bart and Nick and their tomb in Charlestown.

For them the stroke of midnight on August 21, 1927, sounded the knell of the life they had known and brought them to face a new life, unknown and terrible and without faith. They might be good citizens in this new life; some might even raise their heads and go out to win a new place in the world. But they could never have their innocence entire again.

They were not, even the most radical among them, the sort of people who deep down believed that it would come to this. Sacco and Vanzetti had assumed that it would, because they believed that the ruling class was implacable and that its instruments would kill them. A few writers, a lawyer or so, some ladies of New England, a segment of the Harvard faculty, a Gardner Jackson, had come forth to prove that Sacco and Vanzetti were wrong about American justice. Now they were failures.

Upton Sinclair's Betty Alvin, a revolutionary, could exult just before the execution: "Don't you see the glory of this case, it kills off the liberals! Before this, it was possible to argue that injustice was an accident, just an oversight—in a country that was busy making automobiles and bathtubs and books of etiquette. But now here's a test—we settle the question forever! We take our very best—not merely cheap politicians but great ones! Our biggest business man! Our most cultured university president! Our supreme court justices—even the liberal ones! We prove them all alike—they know what flag they serve under, who serves out their rations!"

But that was the exultation of the hard heart of youth and no consolation for the sensitive. How many of those who had begun the watch years before and had followed it to the cross could now write so pat a moral across the tomb? For they were people —at least Pat Jackson was certainly such a person—who believed that the most unpromising river flows somewhere to the sea, that darkness always breaks, and that the right always survives.

Vanzetti could say that an anarchist must expect to die like a soldier. Betty Alvin could say that every martyr was dynamite to the illusions which blocked the path to universal freedom. But what was a man to say when everything that God and his education made him has proclaimed so long that reason will prevail, now that he is confronted with the ultimate unreason of death?

Innocence, after all, is compounded, among other things, of the

absence of shattering experience. In their grief, the Gardner
Jacksons of the Sacco-Vanzetti Defense Committee had lost the
innocence which might have protected them in answering those
who said that, so long as the revolution was postponed, Saccos
and Vanzettis would have to die, and that their death after all
did have certain large social advantages.

The defense of Sacco and Vanzetti had been a cause in which
the Communists played little part beyond exterior nuisance. Their
party's chief theme was that, since the defense was in the hands
of a committee of liberals and anarchists rather than Communists,
Sacco and Vanzetti were being betrayed from within and Jackson and Felicani were as much their murderers as Judge Thayer
and prosecutor Katzman. The Party operated its own Sacco-
Vanzetti defense fund and raised a sum which defied accounta-
bility and no part of which was relayed to the Defense Committee or contributed to the case's towering legal costs.*

And, when Sacco and Vanzetti were dead, the Communists
continued to make the treason of the Defense Committee a
major theme at the Party's memorial meetings. At one early an-
niversary of the execution, the Defense Committee held a ceremony in Boston's Old South Meeting House. The Communists
announced a rival assemblage. As Gardner Jackson entered Old
South that night, he was stopped by Harry Canter, secretary of
the Communist Party of Boston. "I just wanted you to know,"
said Canter, "that tonight I'm going to call you one of the murderers of Sacco and Vanzetti. I hope you understand that inside
I don't really mean it."

But, after the final defeat, it was very hard for some of these
violated innocents not to believe that the Communists had been
right in one thing at least: If liberalism had not betrayed Sacco
and Vanzetti, liberalism had been blind at least in proclaiming
that they could hope for justice from peaceful appeal to the
conscience of established society.

* This summary of the Communist role in the Sacco-Vanzetti case is not
offered as evidence of this author's anxiety to be as patriotic in the flagella-
tion of dead horses as anyone else these days, but rather as background for
the irony that the Communists, whose chief contribution to the defense was
harassment of the defenders, were major political beneficiaries of the execution of Sacco and Vanzetti.

In the last days of the case, some two hundred persons of conscience, many of them writers, had been drawn to Boston to do something, however hopeless, to stand against the inevitable. They had picketed the Common and been thrown into jail, and they had all been pebbles in the churning tide. Some of them had been Communists before that terrible week; more sought the Communists afterward.

John Howard Lawson, no party man before, was to become the leader of the Hollywood Communist movement. Robert Benchley was to be so shaken that he could never function in politics again. Dorothy Parker, out of her own shock, was to drift more and more under Communist influence. William Patterson, a young Negro, walked from Boston Common into the Communist Party. Art Shields, who wrote the first Sacco-Vanzetti defense pamphlet, works for the *Daily Worker* now. Eugene Lyons, who wrote the committee's last press releases, went on to the Soviet Union and found there only the death of freedom which Vanzetti had recognized from a distance as early as 1921.

John Dos Passos, torn from his last illusions about the old America, would look for eight years into the faces of Communists for hope of a new nation and end so embittered that he would thereafter seek hope in the faces of anyone who was against them. Those who had been Communists would take a new, hard assurance from the fate of Sacco and Vanzetti. Most of those who had been liberals had only the loss of illusion and a sorrow without comfort.

Aldo Felicani had seen his old cell mate, Benito Mussolini, become the god of the first Fascist religion. He could hardly have been shaken from his moorings by a single disaster of justice. He went back to his printshop and the anti-Fascist publication which struggled and barely kept afloat against the stream of Boston's Italian community. Gardner Jackson carried on for two more years, holding the cooling ashes of the case, helping Felicani with his paper, keeping an office open, doing what he could to assure some stability for Sacco's family.

All this was a ceremonial of worship for the dead. It could not, of course, bring them back; after a while, it was clear to Pat Jackson that he must begin to live again. He could not, even if he had wanted to, return to the respectable Boston which had slain his dead, so, in 1930, he went to Washington. There he became once more a newspaperman with correspondent's credentials from a Canadian paper. Pat Jackson was not equipped by disposition to avoid causes of controversy, and there were a few such in those years. But, generally speaking, Herbert Hoover withered and passed and Franklin Roosevelt came, without giving Gardner Jackson any tug of recognition in the process.

Then one Sunday afternoon in 1933, while he was sitting on his porch in the country, he was visited by two strangers summoning him once more to commitment and involvement. They were young men and earnest ones, and they declared that they had come all this way to find Gardner Jackson, because he had been the hero of the Sacco-Vanzetti case and thus a figure in their dreams. They had themselves been Bostonians, although transiently, because they had begun quite poor and, by force of will and intelligence, had brought themselves to Harvard Law School from which they had both been graduated with honors.

One of the young visitors introduced himself as Lee Pressman; the other, and the more verbal, was Nathan Witt. They had just come to Washington from New York law firms because there was a great work to be done, and they were calling upon Gardner Jackson to join them. They both looked like what they were, the best sons and the focus of hopes for immigrant families. What they had, they had earned for themselves. Pressman had attended Cornell on a scholarship, and Witt had gone to New York University. They had come together in Felix Frankfurter's Harvard Law class of 1929, and they said they had caught from him the social gospel.

They had entered New York law firms above their stations; Jerome Frank had introduced Pressman into the secure precincts of Chadbourne, Stanchfield, and Levy. Both Pressman and Witt could have expected, with patience, to move on to substantial private success. But they had dreams of greater service. And when Jerome Frank came to Washington as general counsel for the Agricultural Adjustment Administration, it was with excitement that they joined the army of his assistants. This was, they said, a work that could change the face of America, and it needed Gardner Jackson.

Most of these expressions of inward gospel came from Witt, who seemed an enthusiast by nature and therefore an especially engaging guest for Gardner Jackson, who had a weakness for soft and enthusiastic persons. And Nathan Witt seemed soft and gentle and pouring forth enthusiasm.

The language of exaltation did not come easy to Lee Pressman, and he disdained to counterfeit it. "Sharp" was the word that came quickest to the mind in his presence. He had eyes like a squirrel's after a nut and a manner which even a friend would occasionally find too near arrogance. He was not patient with talk which proceeded to no decisive result; Felix Frankfurter, at once awed and charmed by Alger Hiss, is said to have always been a shade uncomfortable with Lee Pressman. Long after the summer day when Jackson met him, Pressman would be described by strangers as a smooth operator. But he never attempted the devices of inconsequential charm; he had a cool courtesy with the hostile but he never deferred to them.

Lee Pressman, there at the beginning, appears to have believed that there was a tide of history and that it would someday make men free. But his passion was with the journey and not the destination; the contemplation of a vision was not his line of thought. Much later, Gardner Jackson searched his memory for one moment in their years together when he could recall an act indicative of soft emotion in Lee Pressman. He could remember only that Pressman had sacrificed to send a younger brother to Yale Law School, and he decided that Pressman loved his own but was otherwise a stranger against the world.

He seemed like a naked sword. He did not make his way by charm and sympathy but because he was an instrument more serviceable than any other in the locker. His language was the language of operations; he burned not nor blazed about the goal; he offered only to tell you how to get there.

Now, the Sacco-Vanzetti case had terribly tried and almost destroyed the innocence of its Pat Jacksons. There had died in Charlestown Prison much of what had been the core of historic

American radicalism: the old, simple, undisciplined faith that every day was fresh and better than the one before it and that salvation was the inevitable end of a succession of good works. But this Pressman was a new breed of radical. He seemed blessed as though born without innocence; he looked pure function. To say that man has been born without innocence is not to say that he is wicked but only that he is enormously adaptive to circumstances, and that he cannot be bemused by second-level enthusiasms or diverted by reflective hesitations. And when he sets forth upon a wrong road, he will proceed straight to his secular hell without taking that wrong fork which leads only to a secular purgatory.

Lee Pressman had passions, but he appeared to display them only in discussions of tactics. As he went along in the world he always demanded the best fee he could get for his unquestionably valuable services. This bargaining streak, taken with his incapacity for the idle expression of idealism, made many of his enemies believe that he was a careerist with no real allegiance except to the main chance. And Lee Pressman does appear to have talked at least like a man who believed in the tide which would sweep all before it and would, above all, take care of its own. When he joined the Communist Party in 1934, it might have been in response to that tide.

He felt no other pull like it. Even though he says he left the Party a year after he joined it, he responded to its tug at every crisis except the very last one in his public life. And all those who argued so long that nothing but his career and his function was important to Lee Pressman will have to explain why, at the one moment in his life when he had to choose between his career and his vision of history, he chose to destroy, or at least badly wound, his career. So he must have been a believer somewhere very deep. When he lost his faith, he did not plunge after another. He was the kind who is constructed to love only once; when his heart was broken, he could not pick it up and pass it on to somebody else.

But none of those shadows was on Lee Pressman's young face that summer Sunday afternoon near Georgetown in 1933. And his promise did not at once reveal itself to Pat Jackson, who was much more fetched by Nathan Witt, glowing with exuberance and exhilaration. Jerome Frank and Felix Frankfurter had already been at Pat Jackson to assume his appointed place in the New Deal. But the sense that Nathan Witt, so much younger, remembered and revered him meant at least as much as any argument Frankfurter or Frank could offer. Jackson went to the Agricultural Adjustment Administration very proud and hopeful.

The Triple A was a great factory; in its early processes, Jackson did not see much of Pressman or Witt. He had become the AAA's assistant Consumers Counsel, an office which reflected the new administration's dim sense that, in rescuing the American farmer, certain protections were necessary for the American consumer. The Consumers Counsel was assigned to improve farm marketing methods and to raise farm labor standards. Fred Howe, an ancient reformer, was nominal Consumers Counsel. But it was understood that Jackson's youth and energy would make him the division's real force.

He remained with Triple A less than two years and was always a source of pain because his concerns had a tendency to stray over to the realm of the politically unacceptable. His earliest troubles involved Connecticut Valley farm laborers very like the ones he used to meet on the streetcars between Amherst and Smith. Early in his tenure, the Connecticut Commissioner of Labor came to Jackson's office with a report on the maltreatment of their hired hands by Connecticut Valley farmers who were beneficiaries of the AAA's bounty. Jackson took the problem first to Jerome Frank and then to Secretary of Agriculture Henry Wallace himself, with results only of apathy and inattention.

In the course of these intercessions, he chanced upon Lee Pressman, who took the Connecticut Valley report, incorporated a few legal touches, and converted it into a functioning instrument which was transmitted to Frank and Wallace and impressed them deeply. The department thereupon moved a little way in the direction of Pat Jackson's conscience. Then he began to sense Lee Pressman's special value. And, on his side, Pressman had discovered qualities he could appreciate in Pat Jackson; they were qualities he translated as usual into the language of function. Pressman thought they complemented one another.

"You are," he once told Jackson, "flat-faced and blue-eyed and blond, and I am sharp-faced and dark. You know everybody and you go into everybody's office and they are all your friends. We would make a very good team." For Lee Pressman could describe his own handicaps with total detachment and leave to his listener the appreciation of those fine-honed qualities of intelligence of which he was as conscious as anyone and which he did not feel it necessary to mention.

No one who thought as he did had ever talked to Gardner Jackson quite that way before. This was a new kind of radical ally, cool, assured, and so much the more valuable for freedom from the ancient inhibitions. Once Pressman suggested, as an instance, that Jackson make a habit of reading the Washington society pages, because there was no better index of who was important and who was not. Pat Jackson had been born to the society page. No one had ever suggested to him before that it could be a useful social instrument.

The team did not accomplish very much, partly because it was broken up in February, 1935, when the AAA resolved the feud between its conservatives and those radicals, like Frank, Jackson, and Pressman, who wanted to use the agency's conservation benefits to help tenant farmers.

The solution of the dispute was a lesson in reality for the committed. Henry Wallace himself did not comment on it until January of 1954; he made it plain that the best interest of the Democratic Party was the ultimate dictator of his decision.*

Wallace defined the two factions struggling over the sharecroppers as "those of us who had an agricultural background" and "those who had a city background."

"It seemed as though it were largely a question of speed of movement and the wisdom of moving rapidly to reform the agricultural customs of the South. It had to do with the handling of the sharecroppers in the South. . . . I had worked with some of the farm leaders of the South and representatives of the South on the hill and I knew their habits and customs and was convinced that, if we followed what I might call the extremist city

* Interview with the *U. S. News and World Report*, Jan. 26, 1954.

group, there would be such a break with the men on the hill that the agricultural program might be destroyed."

"The only thing," Wallace decided, "was to fire the extremist leaders." Frank and Jackson and Pressman departed; they were committed beyond compromise; and, whenever the politicians had a choice, Pressman and Jackson were alien and expendable.

Pressman, along with Nathan Witt and presumably Alger Hiss, was then a member of a Communist Party group in the Agricultural Adjustment Administration, an allegiance which, according to Party custom, he concealed from Jackson and Frank, his two most important allies in the agency. But he was not equipped to act as an underground man; and, largely as a consequence of his manner, the Department of Agriculture's conservative faction was already pointing to him as a security risk.

The first national reference to Pressman as a putative Communist arose out of the Triple A squabble and can be found in a *Saturday Evening Post* article of May 30, 1936, in which former AAA administrator, George Peek, described his disillusion with the New Deal. Peek said that, while he was in the AAA, Pressman had proposed that the government control milk marketing. Peek objected that this would mean either state socialism or communism and Pressman answered, "Call it what you may; this plan is failing, and government operation will have to come." Peek may not have known what communism was; but he was certain that it was a deplorable state and apt to be represented by ungracious and sharp-eyed young men, so he assumed thereafter that Pressman was a Communist.

Pressman, Hiss, and Witt were the only presumed members of the Agriculture Department Communist cell who reached policy positions in the government. And Hiss was the only one of those who survived long, perhaps because he was the only one who was careful in dissembling his views. Witt left the AAA to become General Counsel for the National Labor Relations Board, a position from which he was removed for shamelessly favoring the left-wing unions. After his ouster from Agriculture, Pressman worked briefly for the Federal Emergency Relief Administration and the Works Progress Administration, and left the government for good in less than a year. The New Deal, after all, had its moments of advance and retreat, and its radicals, as they had been in AAA, were often casualties of the retreat. Witt and Pressman concealed their Communist Party membership, but they always acted in public as advanced radicals and thus occupied outposts that were infrequently comfortable even under Roosevelt.

His departure from the AAA was the end of Pat Jackson's association with official authority; he had become the first of the displaced New Dealers. But he remained in Washington, still occupied with the problem of the small farmer. He became chairman of the National Committee for Rural Social Planning, a private organization. And this led him at length to an interest in the Southern Tenant Farmers' Union and then to John L. Lewis, who was taken with the dream of bringing the agricultural worker into his Committee for Industrial Organization.

Lee Pressman, for the time, was separated from all these fortunes. He had left Washington late in the winter of 1935 and returned to New York and the private practice of law. But, on occasion, he would come down for dinner at the Jacksons', for Pat Jackson, even out of government, was close to the main stream and, most important now, he was close to Lewis, who was beginning to be an electric magnet for the committed.

One night, Pressman wondered aloud whether Pat Jackson might introduce him to Lewis. He had always, he said, wanted to be a lawyer for labor. After a while, at the instance of Pat Jackson and other of his instruments, Lee Pressman came to the CIO, first as general counsel for its fledgling Steelworkers Organizing Committee and then as counsel for the CIO itself.

Pressman had never met a man like Lewis; there is only one. They understood each other because they understood that the price of power and victory is a man's innocence. John Lewis had once killed a mad mule in a mine with his bare fist; and, since in those days a mule's life was worth more than a miner's, he had saved his job by covering his victim's wound with mud and telling the superintendent that it died of heart failure. He was the two prime Homeric heroes in one mold, at once Achilles and Ulysses; he went as far as strength would take him and thereafter proceeded by guile. He respected force and cunning alike;

and he expected devotion. He was a worthy object for it, as he was a piece of awe and shock. Lee Pressman and Pat Jackson were entering a labor movement where men's entire lives would focus on John Lewis and where their course would be determined as much by hate as by love of him.

Lewis was marshaling his battalions to assault the great industries which had resisted unions throughout the history of America —the industries which were our national face to the world: steel, automobiles, rubber, and textiles. In less than five years, he brought them all to their knees, from Chevrolet in the winter of 1937 through Bethlehem Steel and Ford in the spring of 1941. He walked, in his own phrase, through the forest swinging a broadax to clear the way. He was not alone, of course; but what commander ever deployed his troops with care so infinite or went so far against the guns with them?

When the General Motors strike began in February of 1937, he dispatched Lee Pressman as his deputy to Detroit. Pressman met this test in a fashion which his commander could appreciate. The auto workers had sat down in General Motors' Flint and Chevrolet plants, and the company very quickly got an injunction to cast them out. It occurred to Pressman that a Michigan judge was as likely to own auto stocks as a Boston judge is to own textile stocks; and he had a friend in New York check the General Motors stockholders' list. The name of the judge who had signed the Flint injunction appeared on that roster as the owner of $219,000 worth of GM stock, and his injunction expired in the consequent public distemper. Lee Pressman had brought the sit-down strikers safely through their first peril.

But other menaces came so thick and fast that John Lewis himself left Washington to assume command in the field. He intoned at his departure that there should be no moaning at the bar as he put out to sea. For weeks he had played with Cabinet officers. He now commenced bending a governor of Michigan. And Lee Pressman watched him all the while. Whatever his later troubles, he is fortunate in that memory, because this was Lewis' great hour.

The Chevrolet strikers were shivering against the night in their fortresses when Lewis debarked in Detroit laughing with an assurance that reached across the police lines to raise their heads. And thereafter, he did not storm or bluster; his conduct with the officials of General Motors alternated cold arrogance with towering wrath. Never, while Pressman was watching, did he ring those changes false.

In those Detroit hotel rooms so far from Flint, there was a special majesty in Lewis because he was alone. Governor Frank Murphy wavered day after day between sympathy for the CIO and concern over the illegality of its conduct. One night he came to Lewis' room to announce that he could go no further and was calling out the troops to clear the factories. And Lewis answered on a swelling note of doom:

"I shall personally enter General Motors' Chevrolet Plant Number Four. I shall order the men to disregard your order, to stand fast. I shall then walk up to the largest window in the plant, open it, divest myself of my outer raiment, remove my shirt and bare my bosom. Then-n-n, when you order your troops to fire, mine will be the first breast that those bullets will strike." The great voice marched down near a hush. "And, as my body falls from that window to the ground, you listen to the voice of your grandfather as he whispers in your ear, 'Frank, are you sure you are doing the right thing?' "

It was Lewis' recollection that, upon this stroke, Frank Murphy went white and, shaking, left the room. The ouster order was never issued, because the governor could hardly doubt that this terrible giant would do exactly what he said he would and that the first shell would probably bounce off in any case. For it was the grandeur of John Lewis' posture that he could threaten you with a course of conduct heroic and outrageous beyond imagination and, looking at him, you could not hear the voice of common sense saying that no man could rise or stoop to this.

After the fall of General Motors, Lewis and Pressman moved on to settle the Chrysler sit-down strike. Hour after hour, Lewis sat silent while K. T. Keller, Chrysler's operational vice president, looked at him with an icecap of disdain which would have seemed excessive in the master himself. At last, while every CIO man present except Lewis shuddered under his stare, Keller turned to Lewis and said, with total contempt, "Mr. Lewis you haven't said a word about this situation. Do you happen to have any comment or contribution?"

Lewis arose and fixed his baleful eye and answered very quietly:

"Yes, Mr. Keller, yes, I have. I am ninety-nine per cent of a mind to come around this table right now and wipe that damn sneer off your face."

Both Pressman and Lewis affirm that Keller passed into an immediate state of shock, from which he emerged to totter over to Lewis and plead that he wasn't as bad as all that. This was, said Pressman long afterward, the high point of his life:

"It is impossible to put into words just what everyone felt at that moment. Lewis, the man, was not threatening Keller the man. Lewis' voice at that moment was in every sense the voice of millions of unorganized workers who were exploited by gigantic corporations. He was expressing at that instant their resentment, their hostility, and their passionate desire to strike back. There just was no question that Lewis' threat was not against Mr. Keller as a person, but against the Chrysler Corporation and every other giant, soulless corporation in the country. It was a moment of real greatness because Lewis transcended his own person and was speaking out of the deep yearning of millions to force a great, sneering, arrogant corporation to bend its knee to organized labor. I cannot remember when I have been so moved in my life. I have never before experienced anything so completely devoid of individual personality, for those two voices of Lewis and Keller were really the spokesmen of opposing fundamental forces."*

Lee Pressman never seems to have been voluble about what he believed, and this shining moment in his memory may speak volumes for him. He remembers Lewis best at a moment in history. History for Lee Pressman was not a personal thing and Lewis was not a personal figure. History was a war of contending classes, and its hero attained his peak when he transcended him-

* This anecdote, like the other Lewisiana which accompany it, is taken from Saul Alinsky's *John L. Lewis*, a biography which contains so much otherwise unpublished Lewis conversation and self-reportage as to amount almost to a memoir. Keller has denied that he was worsted in this encounter with anything like the finality implied by Lewis and Pressman, who, whatever their other virtues, are not necessarily unimpeachable witnesses.

self and became the impersonal embodiment of the class for which he spoke. It is the face and the imagery of combat between armies which give and ask no quarter, a war whose resolution is unforgiving violence and in which John Lewis was a great hammer and Lee Pressman a piece of steel. And its vision is without limit; for such a captain and his followers, there are no walls too high and frontiers too distant.

Bartolomeo Vanzetti and Nicola Sacco were very personal instruments. Their creed was the individual; they were victims and not conquerors of institutions. And, when they passed, men wept. John Lewis and Lee Pressman were the impersonal force of history; in them innocence did not die but history triumphed, and all material honors accrued to its representatives. As John Lewis said once, the strong move forward and the weak fall behind. But he who would be history's engine must move ahead without slackening or lesser men will tear him down. And when he goes, very few will mourn his fall, for men do not weep for an impersonal instrument.

John Lewis lived upon a mountaintop to which Lee Pressman did not often come in his early days with the CIO. He spent much more of his time in Pittsburgh with Philip Murray, a very different man, as counsel for the Steelworkers' Organizing Committee. Murray and Lewis had been together a long while; no one else in Lewis' panoply called him "Jack." But Philip Murray was not of the great world. He had come from Scotland when he was ten years old, and he had mined coal near Hazelkirk, Pennsylvania, which is hardly two hours from Pittsburgh, but remains a country town where cows still graze and where, when Philip Murray was a young man, he walked across a brook and through green fields to the tipple.

Organized unions in America began, after all, not in great cities in the fog of mill smoke but in little towns like Hazelkirk. Its gospel first touched the hearts of craftsmen in square caps— locomotive engineers, carpenters, and coal miners—the sort of men who swear and remain true to resounding oaths of obligation, who invoke the blessing of God upon their affairs, who call themselves Knights of the Footboard or of the T-square and are altogether representative of virtue sometimes wounded but always hopeful.

Like them, Philip Murray seemed in a state of original innocence. He had kept the manners of their old lost time; he seemed put together by handcraftsmen. The coal operators, to whom Lewis was a tiger, always said that Murray was a gentleman. But it was a piece of the guile of Lewis and Murray that the first would thunder his enemies into insensibility and that the second would approach and gently rub them back to consciousness and suggest in soft Scots accents that this terrible Welshman could be appeased with a little give here and somewhat more take there.

Murray hated the great world through which he moved so gracefully. He went to Washington only under sufferance; he was unhappy a day away from the dirty city he loved. His face still had a look of pain and soft patience which Lee Pressman could not know was as much a quality of the workingman as John Lewis' epic irritation. If Murray could have been happy when the miners weren't, his brightest days would have been during the mine union's long twilight in the twenties when Pittsburgh stood alone as a center of strength and loyalty to John Lewis and when the daily round was so undemanding that the union had a box at Forbes Field and there were no compulsions of routine to keep its leaders from going to watch the Pirates.

But when Pressman met him, Murray had forfeited all peace and leisure. The drive on steel had begun; and, having made himself a master of the economics of coal, Murray had to begin again on the economics of this greater industry. He had taken offices in the Grant Building where sat so many of the primates of Pittsburgh's old order. He would bow to them in the elevator with his ancient courtesy; and then he would go up to his office and gently impel the old miners who were his assistants to greater efforts for their destruction. His peace at an end, Murray both loved his old friends and longed for young men who walked quickstep. He was very glad to see Lee Pressman.

It was Murray's special quality to touch the love and not the fears of men. We do no special discredit to Pressman to say that he was only thirty-one and not yet of an age when men count that sort of love very high in the scale. John Lewis remained his personal icon, and nothing around Pittsburgh could match the thunder and lightning over Washington. Murray recognized in Pressman a new and valuable machine tooled for a changing labor movement, but he was otherwise not vastly popular. The men around Murray were not Pressman's sort. Pittsburgh was not like Washington; it was a divided city across whose barricades men did not move easily. Its nights would have been lonelier without the presence of a new friend named J. B. S. Hardman.

Hardman had been loaned by Sidney Hillman's Amalgamated Clothing Workers as a publicist in the steel campaign. Hardman, like Pressman, came to Murray from another world and one in which he was an ornament of social and intellectual history. As a teacher in Russia, he had led his students in the 1905 revolution; in America he was a labor economist and a prophet of the new industrial unionism with a reputation as scholar rare for union professionals.

Pressman attached himself to Hardman very soon and together they used to walk and talk for hours in the Pittsburgh night of 1937. Hardman remembers now that, one of those evenings in a drizzle, their conversation passed to the Soviet Union. Hardman said that he had often wondered about Lenin, who was a socialist and had lived in the West. Had there come a time, while he was signing the decrees ordering this man's death and that man's imprisonment, when he asked himself if the killing would ever stop?

At that, Pressman stopped walking; he was near the marquee of the Hotel William Penn, and, in the light, Hardman saw real shock on his hard young face.

"Do you mean, J. B.," he said at last, "that you reject the Terror?" Things were never the same between them.

Back in Washington, Pat Jackson sat with John Lewis and heard him say that the organization of the agricultural worker would be the crown of his life. The salvation of the sharecropper, Lewis rumbled, was the charge and duty of the labor movement. In July of 1937, the CIO chartered the United Cannery, Agricultural, Packing and Allied Workers as the engine of Lewis'

farm offensive. The miners opened their treasury for a large sub-
sidy and Pat Jackson was dispatched with John Brophy, the
CIO's director of organization, to Denver for the christening.

Jackson arrived to find the Communists his absolute masters,
and their appointed course so well-determined that all his mail
had been opened before he arrived there. John Brophy had announced his entry with a telegram to Pressman suggesting that
they meet at the Denver airport for a private strategy conference,
a message the union's new rulers solicitously opened and failed
to deliver to its addressee. Jackson and Brophy, once again victims of their innocence, thereafter sat helpless and watched the
convention elect as its president Donald Henderson, a displaced
Columbia University instructor, and set forth on the road to
deserts and disasters.

No word of all this appeared to disturb Lewis especially, so
Jackson took the story to Pressman, whom, he was beginning to
sense, he now needed more than Pressman needed him. When
next they met in Washington, Jackson told the entire story of how
the Communists had assumed control of the farm union, and his
mail had been rifled, and Brophy tricked. Pressman heard it out;
Jackson waited for a reply either of indignation or simple comment; it was a while before he understood that there was only
silence.

They were no longer the friends they had been, although the
distance between them went unmentioned. For one thing, the
farm campaign went badly, and Lewis soon lost interest in it.
Pat Jackson was not responsible for these failures, but some of
their shadow fell on him, and he did not see as much of John
Lewis as he had. By now Lee Pressman had become general
counsel of the CIO and the old team was out of balance. And so
there had come upon them one of those interludes between intimacy and estrangement which can last indefinitely among the
civilized. There were no lasting quarrels in it and few moments of
real coolness and only one when Lee Pressman revealed a sense
that Pat Jackson could no longer make the team.

But there was always, as their friendship died, an underlying
wedge between them. They did not agree on the surrender of the
innocence required in their common endeavor, which was a ques-

tion bound to recur among troops enlisted behind John L. Lewis. For Lewis lived somewhere beyond innocence. He could pin the class enemy to the wall with a glare that was a banner of the avenging oppressed; and afterward he would describe the scene as one in which "I summoned up my best frown" like a wizard showing his locker of potions. He simply fought without conscience. There was stature in his subordination of means, because it did not seem malignant for malignancy's sake. Lewis did not exalt trickery as a grace; he was believable and even admirable in his rascality because it was functional and directed at the peaks.

When Lee Pressman and Pat and Dorothy Jackson had their first quarrel in 1938, it did not involve a matter of conscience in Lewis' service but something as abstract as the conduct of a movie. Warner Brothers had just produced *Juarez,* a story of the Mexican revolution which had as its climax the execution of the deposed Emperor Maximilian by Benito Juarez's troops.

One night, the Jacksons met Pressman coming out of a preview of *Juarez.* They fell to talking about what they had seen, and Dorothy Jackson mentioned the unease which she and Pat shared over what seemed to them to be Juarez's unnecessarily cruel vengeance upon Maximilian and his family. And then Lee Pressman exploded as he had with Hardman in Pittsburgh a year and a half before. He read Dorothy Jackson a lecture on the real world and the necessities of social law, and then clicked his heels together and said he could not reduce himself to her intellectual level and got into his big car and drove away.

There is something almost ghostly about these sub-quarrels when one considers the life of Lee Pressman at the time he indulged them. He has said since that he joined the Communist Party in 1934 and left it in 1935. By his own account he was not even a Communist in these moments when he was so uncontained about the regrets and doubts of Hardman and the Jacksons. There is no evidence that Lee Pressman ever practiced the social ferocity he cherished so in his models. Still, these expressions have a Bolshevik source, and may be taken as evidence, not of good or evil in the character, but of an intellectual alteration of his own pattern to that of the Bolshevik hero who must

demonstrate strength even when it is cruel and unnecessary. It
was in this discipline to accept the Terror that Pressman marked
himself as different from old-fashioned radicals like Hardman
and Pat Jackson.

He would thus appear to have accepted Lenin as his model
with all the verbal consequences of that choice. The model was
rare in the experience of American social protest, because it was
an image of Christ inverted. The infant Christ confounded his
teachers; the boy Lenin received word of his brother's execution
for conspiracy against the Czar with the no-less-confounding observation: "Very well, we shall have to find more efficacious
means." Christ commanded his followers to love their enemies;
Lenin commanded his followers to hate their friends if they were
detected in the sin of being wrong. In peril of defeat, Lenin
chose, not his own death, but armed repression of his opponents.
He regarded the lie as a socially necessary weapon. He believed
that at least one scoundrel was a valuable asset among his
apostles; and, after all, even Judas was not a scoundrel. Christ
recruited sinners with the hope of reclaiming them; Lenin hoped
to turn their intact villainy to more useful pursuits. Both agreed
that the thought of sin was equivalent to the act of sin itself;
Christ forgave both and Lenin forgave neither. The disciplines
of both religions are rigorous for ordinary men, too rigorous perhaps for all but ritual celebration and execration by Lee Pressman.

But his shock at any dispute with the long-gone decisions of
foreign revolutionaries and his inclination to the Communist
line so long after he says he left the Party cannot be explained so
much by loyalty to the American Communists as by devotion to
the Soviet Union as the repository of the gospel in its highest
form. History was enthroned there. Its gravitational tug explains
better than anything else why Pressman could break with Lewis
and Murray and anyone else, even against his own best interests,
when the issue was adherence to them or adherence to the Soviet
temple of history. Nothing held him but his own religious
fantasy.

The wedge was not spoken of soon again, and Pressman and
Jackson lived together civilly enough even though both must

have been conscious that it lay between them. Jackson had by now moved over to Labor's Non-Partisan League, the CIO's political arm and John Lewis' foreign office in his relations with Congress, the Republicans, and Democrats and other minor principalities. It was a place bound before long to do violence to Jackson's innocence. Lewis, of course, had always regarded the labor movement as a solar system in which other men were petty planets revolving in an orbit determined by himself as sun, a concept which, without being excessively attractive, had at least some relation to reality.

But Lewis thought of the world too in something of the same image. And it was not easy to function in politics at the direction of a man who pictured Franklin Roosevelt, Wendell Willkie, and John Nance Garner as minor planets to be judged solely according to their degree of gravitation to himself as sun. Lewis had, after all, been a Republican as late as the 1932 electoral campaign. Through 1938 and 1939, he showed increasing outrage at the planet Roosevelt's tendency to shy off without regard to its appointed sun and was heard to talk more and more of returning to the Republicans. But his seemed a solitary tendency in the CIO. Its other leaders were warm New Dealers, none appearing more devout than the Communists, and they assumed that their chief was only bargaining.

Then, in September, 1939, the war broke out in Europe close upon the *rapprochement* between Nazi Germany and the Soviet Union. CIO leaders like Sidney Hillman regarded the war a major crisis of freedom; the CIO's Communists, but lately the loudest of anti-fascists, now accepted Molotov's new thesis that fascism was a matter of taste and that this was a struggle of equally perfidious imperialisms. The CIO right shared Roosevelt's obvious sympathy with Britain and France; the CIO left called him a warmonger.

The better half of John L. Lewis was convinced that war was wicked, that what he called "this imbroglio" was far away and that the uproar about it was a diversion from our domestic social miseries. The worse half of John Lewis regarded the war as an invention of Franklin Roosevelt to escape his responsibilities to the CIO. Both halves of John Lewis were implacably neutralist.

He commenced to thunder against aid to Britain and France in terms that seemed almost pro-Nazi to the inflamed sensibilities of the CIO right. Still Lee Pressman remained not merely loyal but enthusiastic. A CIO lawyer met him returning from the West Coast, where he had heard Lewis rake the allies and the Democrats with equal impartiality, and commented, "My God, what a speech." And Pressman answered, "Yes, wasn't it wonderful?"

All these things did not seem especially wonderful to Pat Jackson, a committed anti-Nazi. One day, early in 1940, his doubts were increased. The late Laurence Duggan, of the State Department's Office of Latin American Affairs, presented Jackson with a document indicating that an international wildcatter named William Rhodes Davis had used his friendship with Lewis and other CIO men to persuade the Mexican government to sell him crude oil subsequently refined for the Nazis in Davis' plant in Hamburg, Germany.

Davis was a peculiar companion for the Samson of American labor, and their friendship is an indication of Lewis' fine appreciation of anyone who appreciates him. Lewis had assisted Davis in getting pre-war oil leases from the Mexican government, which had some reason to prefer the CIO's advice to that of our own State Department. Davis' German holdings gave him a natural interest in international concord; after the fall of Poland in 1939, he persuaded Lewis to convey to the White House a "peace" offer from the Nazis. Subsequently Davis became a heavy contributor to the isolationist movements of the right and financed Lewis' 1940 broadcast for Willkie, the major theme of which was peace.

Jackson carried the story of Davis' exploitation of Lewis straight to a CIO board meeting. Lewis received it without comment. But afterward Lee Pressman came to Jackson and said something like:

"I never want to see you again. You care only for individuals and not for the movement. And you are, besides, too old. The movement belongs to the young."

Gardner Jackson went home, and, for most of that night, he could neither move nor speak. Pressman had ended for him as

Sacco and Vanzetti had ended—in death and darkness and viola-
tion of innocence. He was not long thereafter for the CIO; when
Lewis declared for Willkie in October, 1940, Pat Jackson had
already gone, leaving behind him these words:

"These are critical days when, more than ever, men seem to
become captives of their personal ambition for wealth, social
position and influence, and when their adventures in power politics and in finance politics, both at home and in the international
field, also make them captives."

It was the sad *envoi* of the old breed of radical to the new one.
And, having said his farewell, Pat Jackson picked himself up and
began again as a Washington correspondent for the newspaper
PM.

But Pressman went on in the CIO, endorsing Lewis' support
of the Republicans and more and more the old man's strong left
arm. In November, Lewis kept his promise to resign as president
of the CIO if Roosevelt should be re-elected. By now the mo-
mentum of his terrible engine had slackened. The CIO could
report very few gains for the year 1940; it was torn by the hardly
expressed but obvious rancor between its right and left factions.
Philip Murray, harassed and shrinking from the great world, took
Lewis' place as president of the CIO. But the shadows were not
yet for Lewis; his name was still the symbol of the CIO. For Lee
Pressman, as he escorted Murray to the great stage, there must
have been a longing backward glance at Lewis exiting to the
wings. But, even so, Murray found him useful as ever.

There was, for example, the occasion in February, 1941, when
Murray had to testify on President Roosevelt's Lend-Lease Bill
and was torn beyond the possibility of communication by the
cleavage between Lewis, who had offered his daughter to the
America First Committee, and Hillman, who was a government
defense administrator, two captains of armed camps from which
the Communists and their enemies glared across at one another.
Murray had campaigned for Roosevelt even after Lewis bolted
to Willkie. He was caught between loyalty to Lewis and his
natural disposition to help the British. It was a situation that
cried out for Pressman, who was a Lewis man at least in shield
and banner; and he helped Murray write a statement on Lend-

Lease which was sublimely everything to everyone. Pressman by now had mastered a language which managed at once to seem crystal clear and absolutely opaque, and was therefore equipped for that balance of irreconcilable ideas so conspicuous in resolutions on foreign policy adopted by every CIO convention between 1943 and 1947.

He had commenced that slow slide from his first image of himself which is for so many committed men the price of compromise and responsibility. He remained for the next six years as the quasi-official representative of the CIO's pro-Communist wing, its only figure who moved with equal authority into Philip Murray's office and into conferences with Roy Hudson, John Williamson, and others of the Party's labor consultants. And yet he was never safe, because he was after all only a technician representing no force but his own skill.

The daily routine of this man, who once seemed so dedicated to the Bolshevik model that he could not resist lashing out against its doubters even in social conversation, became a business of balancing forces in the CIO and in himself that were in terrible irreconcilable conflict. He became the author of convention resolutions which said nothing and only deferred the final decision. In Murray's office and in discussions with the Communists alike, he fought a rear-guard action to preserve that hopeless state of things which alone protected him in all his fantasies: in power that was no real power, in success that was empty and transient, in allegiance to the jade history, who is especially merciless to those who think they are her very own. For the next decade, his life became a matter of choosing between impossibles, until he chose the last, emptiest thing left to him and threw that away too. Looking back on that decade, we can only say that he began with his faith intact; no one can say, in the mass of his contradictions, when Lee Pressman began to lose it.

Lewis went first among Pressman's irreconcilables. He had remained Pressman's polestar until June 22, 1941, when the Nazis turned on the Soviets. The CIO's left and right were suddenly united in support of the war against fascism; before long John Lewis was alone, except for his miners. And Lee Pressman was not the last to leave. He knew the uses of argument with Lewis.

And so he went to him in August and told him flatly that he could go with him no farther:

"I had one conversation with Mr. Lewis and that was in August, very shortly after Mr. Lewis had signed a statement with Herbert Hoover and some other people demanding that this country stay out of war. I went in to see him and said to him, 'John, I can't go along with you when the logic of the situation puts you in the kind of company that you're in when you sign that document.' Lewis didn't say anything and I walked out and I just never came back."*

John Lewis and Lee Pressman had this much in common: their fires were cold. They neither bled nor winced at the touch of the knife. And they had a cold going of it. By now, Lewis had larger losses on his mind. For his talent for deception was never as large as when he was exercising it upon himself; he had always been an original, and he did not function in rhythm with other men. In 1934, he had leaped ahead of reality; by 1939, he had begun the process of falling behind it. He did not understand that the CIO was no longer the thing of passion it had been and that nothing flares and sinks so suddenly as the flames in men. The time had come when most of his armies would troop behind other banners and he who had seemed a little while ago to speak for an entire new class of Americans would now appear to speak for a private interest.

In that lonely guise, he did not merely lose the CIO and fall back to his old fortress in the coal fields, but he lost some of his best even there because old miners like Murray, Allan Haywood, and Van Bittner chose Roosevelt above him. They, after all, were

* Pressman offered this version of the end of the affair to Saul Alinsky on December 6, 1948 and it is a model of the disingenuous. Since December, 1940, Lewis' daughter Kathryn, whose notable personal capacities have never appeared to impel her to a single deviation from her father's whims, had been a member of the America First Committee, in company hardly more savory to Pressman than Herbert Hoover was. Until the Nazi invasion of the Soviet Union, Pressman had appeared thoroughly in concert with the Lewises. As a prior indication of difference with them, he has cited his part in Murray's February, 1941, statement on the Lend-Lease Bill, which might have been a happier selection if it had been his voice and not Murray's and if it had not been emasculated almost beyond communication, presumably by Pressman's own practiced hand. The statement was both weaker than Murray's real sympathy for aid-to-Britain and stronger than Lee Pressman's.

his own flesh. Pressman was only a piece of baggage, and this defection was one of the least of his losses. Roosevelt had beaten him on his own ground. Loyalty is the flag and the Bible of the miners' union; its contests of the spirit have always been conflicts of loyalties. Haywood, Bittner, and Murray had been loyal to Lewis in the twenties, when he was certainly as wrong as he was in 1941. But then he had been the symbol of the only union and the only community they had.

Now Lewis had extended his frontiers beyond the safe limit for an absolute monarch. The Murray who had been a viceroy had become an emperor on his own. His steel union had a stake in Roosevelt. And what went deeper, Murray had never before been faced with a conflict between his devotion to Lewis and his devotion to the idea of national self-interest. Even Lewis could not expect to hold "my Philip Murray" against the tug of the flag.

Lewis always had grandeur, and it remains the material of tragedy that this blinded Samson could change the face of America and unshackle three million families without understanding that independence is a communicable disease and that his revolution had overthrown himself along with so many other economic despots. As men no longer felt compelled to leap at the bark of a foreman, Philip Murray no longer leaped to John Lewis' growl in the United Mine Workers' building. Faced with that family disaster, Lewis would hardly open his veins at the departure of an in-law like Pressman. And if, on his side, Pressman felt a wound, it came much later when he looked back upon his life and wondered where he had taken the wrong step and then missed the old man far, far more than he had in the hour of departure.

The months to come were those when Pressman made his value plainest to a Murray tearing himself from what was almost a bond of flesh and learning to walk without Lewis. Pressman shored him up and guided him, giving him confidence and stiffening his back against Lewis' cudgels. And when, in 1943, the crisis was over and Lewis had expelled "my former friend" from the miners, Murray thought that Pressman was an irreplaceable treasure.

He moved thereafter to an increasingly lonely eminence. By

his own account, he was still meeting with envoys from the Communists. But they were envoys in a very real sense, and he dealt with them as an independent power. They, like their enemies, assumed that Pressman's primary allegiance was to them. But he was so far above and beyond the Communists now that some of them, left to assume without direct proof that he was theirs, called him, with a kind of awe, "Comrade Big."

The right detested him and did its best to reduce Murray's trust in him; the unvarying answer came back that Pressman had always done exactly what he was asked. He had come to that golden time for any man who has given himself as hostage to history, those moments when his own self-interest and the dictates of history seem to be running the same way. Pressman had by now smoothed over. His wrestler's figure slipped easily into his tweeds. He had gone far past the Jacksons and the Hardmans. Time appeared to have proved him right and them wrong; he seldom had occasion to lose his temper on theoretical issues.

By 1944, the memory of John Lewis in the CIO was either cursed or departed, and Philip Murray held there a power and authority greater than Lewis had ever known. Murray's was an influence compounded partly of strength and partly of moral suasion, and Lee Pressman was cloaked in its mantle. He was powerful, but he was not loved. Murray's associates cankered at every visible evidence of their new old man's affection for him, and Pressman's left allies were now too far beneath him for public fraternization. He could be seen at CIO conventions in those years, leaving one place and entering another with a sheaf of papers under his arm and his pipe in his mouth, sometimes with Murray but most often absolutely alone.

By now, Lee Pressman had achieved an unusually rancorous assemblage of detractors. For years they had been proclaiming him a Communist Party member assigned to subvert the CIO. The language of these assaults, assuming they were unjust, was slanderous, if not libelous, for a lawyer in a confidential relation with a client like Murray; but Pressman showed no disposition to sue his enemies. His silence lifted the pitch of their attacks. Still Murray trusted him, and behind this shield he appeared invulnerable.

But he did not hold that position without some cost to himself. It can be one of man's misfortunes to be remembered best for the things he did which were furthest from his own estimate of his character. And thus Pressman has left nothing behind him from his years of power except the resolutions he wrote for CIO conventions between the years 1943 and 1947. He managed there to contrive a rhetoric containing solace for both the Communists and their enemies in the CIO. He reached the apogee of this peculiar function in 1947, at his last CIO convention, when he constructed a foreign policy resolution which managed at once to endorse the Marshall Plan and not mention it by name. Pressman was against the Marshall Plan, but the situation had passed beyond his powers; the import of the resolution was unmistakable and it was a terrible blow to the Communists, because the Marshall Plan was their special target at the time.

These resolutions, the carefully oblique product of a hand once so sharp, are Lee Pressman's only monument, and it is a measure of his sense of reality that he must have sat up late over them and thought the degrees of their expression vastly important. In the reality of labor politics, nothing is less important than a resolution on national affairs passed by a union convention. At one miners' convention, John Lewis accepted the passage of a resolution inimical to his notions of the fit and the proper with the promise that it would go where all resolutions go. Murray regarded them as ritual offerings and was convinced that nobody read them.

We cannot say whether, in all those years, Lee Pressman had a vision of himself subtly molding Philip Murray to his designs. Certainly many of Pressman's critics thought he was. But there is a sense in which power assures its possessor against making mistakes; Murray had great power, and Pressman had little. And it may be that, in this his zenith, Pressman was more Murray's instrument than Murray was Pressman's. This was a period at whose beginning the Communists might have destroyed Murray by mass secession of the unions they controlled. We have Pressman's own word that he counseled frequently with the CIO's left-wing leaders from 1943 through 1947. We may assume that his advice to the Communists was to contain themselves and depend on him to win Murray over. Whatever his intention, Pressman's advice was so bad that, in the end, the Communists were thrown out of the CIO with only a fraction of their former strength.

For the happy coincidence between guiding dream and personal self-interest is seldom permitted any long life for the truly passionate. And, by 1947, Pressman's dream and the realities of the CIO were in hopeless conflict. The Soviet Union was challenging the United States all over the world. The CIO was moving with increasing definition behind its government. Inside the CIO, the Communists were dropping back. They had lost all influence in the huge auto workers' union. Their smaller bases were either fragmenting or casting off their influence. After the 1947 CIO convention, only one of the CIO's eight vice presidents could be described as susceptible to left influence; the CIO itself was all the way over to support of President Truman's foreign policy.

For just a little while longer Lee Pressman carried on, silent, invaluable as always, but invaluable in a function in which he had ceased to believe, his image and the reality having come so dreadfully in conflict. By now the Communists were seceding from American political reality. They had declared war on the Democrats, and they had convinced former Vice President Wallace—the same Wallace who had fired Pressman from the AAA— to run for President on the Progressive Party ticket. In the spring of 1948, Philip Murray chose to make Wallace the test of loyalty to the CIO. He told Pressman that he was welcome to stay if he would abstain from supporting the Progressives, but that otherwise he would have to go. Pressman was ready for that choice; he very quickly said good-by to Murray and went forth to join the Communists in their last fight to survive as a political force.

Before he went, he talked to the reporters in Pittsburgh. For the first time in his public life, he displayed an emotion besides anger or cool confidence; he was crying and it could not have been entirely because he had lost his shield. Murray held no press conference; those who saw him during the first few days afterward found him unusually detached and inattentive and somehow as though what he had lost was important to him too.

Murray sent Pressman off with the parting gift of a $15,000-a-year retainer from the little Marine Engineers Beneficial Association and an assignment to handle the briefs for the CIO's legal challenge to one minor clause of the Taft-Hartley Act. It was a routine case, but Pressman and his co-counsel sent the CIO a bill for $83,000, which Murray paid with pain. In all save the big things, Lee Pressman still seemed to know how to take care of himself.

Pat Jackson was still in Washington. After Sacco-Vanzetti and after Lee Pressman, he had a hard time finding the assurance of a permanent commitment. He was a journalist; he worked with the co-operatives; he spent himself in causes ranging from civil liberties to the American Indian. And most of what he did, he did for nothing. In the small things Pat Jackson had never known how to take care of himself.

Nat Witt had been in New York since the late thirties, still a Communist and practicing labor law. He and Pressman had been friends a long time, and theirs seemed a natural partnership. The pro-Communist unions appeared to welcome Pressman; he was, after all, their "gray eminence," although he was at first too occupied with Wallace's fortunes to practice much law. For a while, there was the illusion that the new life would be fruitful and important. The men around Wallace were less than first-class, and Pressman soon became a titan among them, a tennis partner for Wallace, and secretary of the resolutions committee of the 1948 Progressive Party convention, where he performed his old, now empty, function of bridging the gap between the Communists and the remaining innocents who were with them on an increasingly lonely plain. He ran for Congress in Brooklyn, a wild campaign of hate against America, counterfeiting emotions he could hardly have felt, and losing badly.

When it was over, Wallace had barely a million votes. Truman had been re-elected; bleat though it would, the Progressive Party could not disguise its end in dank disaster. In November of 1948, Lee Pressman awoke to find that he had fallen out of history. He had begun the private practice of law a little late; it was a contracting field for pro-Communist practitioners; his fellow left-wing lawyers paid their homage to economic determinism by sabotaging his career as best they could. He was not what he had been. This was a narrow world at the end of its tether, and no rational man could convince himself that it was related to the future.

In December of 1948, Saul Alinsky, Lewis' biographer, came to see Pressman in his office. Very late in the interview, Pressman commenced to talk about how much Lewis had meant in his life and how much he would delight in seeing him again. That early in his new life, Lee Pressman was throwing lines across the wet deck and nobody would catch them. In November of 1949, he and Nat Witt dissolved their partnership; absolute silence surrounded the end of their long friendship, but it was obviously not amicable. There were rumors that Pressman had sought reconciliation with Philip Murray.

Then the night covered him again until August of 1950, when he announced his resignation from the Progressive Party because he had discovered that it was under Communist control. This announcement had the peculiar cast of many of Lee Pressman's public utterances, which had a tendency to sound like Tallulah Bankhead essaying Little Eva; and it did not of course prevent the House Committee on Un-American Activities from swiftly visiting upon him its subpoena.

One afternoon, just before he went to run his course before the committee, Pressman sat and talked about the meaning of his life. Who could have believed that it would come to this, he said, and that he of all men would guess so wrong? Henry Wallace was a former vice president of the United States. Truman was on the run. Who could have believed that the Progressives would get only a million votes? In hindsight, men have a deplorable tendency to excuse their mistakes by resorting to their enemies' image of themselves. Pressman's many enemies had always said that he served only his own advantage. After the Wallace disaster he might have argued that, in leaving the CIO, he had taken the chance of destroying his career for a principle. But he preferred to say that he had made the choice because he believed that the Wallace movement was great and powerful and that he was leaving the dying side for the living one. Even at the end, he wanted to think of himself as the victim of a bad guess rather than of a sacrifice to principle.

He would stand henceforth, he said, for America and the United Nations in Korea. He said it flatly and with all the passion of a school child reciting the flag oath. But the tone was no indication of unbelief. He was drained. He had lost the great dream of his life, and he could bring no passion to the dreams of other men. There were mines planted all along this new untraveled road of his choice; whatever guideposts there were had to come from within himself, where so little remained. And so he knew that this was a time, like so many other times, requiring economy of emotion. Once he spoke of Whittaker Chambers and he looked at the floor as though it were a thousand feet deep and a pit gaping for him as it had for so many others.

Between the abyss of the right and the left, he set forth on the course prescribed by the House Committee on Un-American Activities, coolly and carefully and with terrible lacerations of his pride. There seemed somewhere back in his mind the notion that, if he could run it safely, things might be as they were when he was young and could tell Pat Jackson that he was too old. He had lived, after all, without sense of guilt or innocence; the one was not there to rouse, the other was not there to violate. He told the committee that he knew little which would assist it. He himself had joined the Communist Party in 1934; there had been three other members of his group; they had studied the Marxist primers together. And, after a year, he had departed, Lee Pressman said, because he wanted freedom from all baggage.

But he remained a fellow traveler until the Korean War began. He had never discussed this lingering Bolshevik bent with either Murray or Lewis; he saw no reason why he should have.

The committee received this story with the visible dissatisfaction of men who had anticipated prodigies of new material or corroboration, and there was about it a certain lack of amplitude even for persons not so involved as the committee. It had an incomplete sound, as though Pressman knew that respectability has its rituals, but that, if he must pay its price, the bones he would throw the dogs would be dry as dust.

Alger Hiss was not one of those bones: Pressman declared that he had never known Hiss as a Communist when he himself belonged to the Party cell in the AAA. This was a piece of information in which everyone seemed peculiarly uninterested. The Hiss case was on appeal, but it might ordinarily seem a trump for the defense to cite a witness who was there and hadn't seen Hiss. Yet the Hiss defense was silent on Pressman's testimony. Since then, another witness besides Chambers has put Pressman and Hiss together at Communist meetings in their Triple A period. But the committee on its side has made no suggestion that Pressman be indicted for perjury.

No one could gain much pleasure if it had because, if Pressman's memory had failed him in this particular, it was not to serve his own advantage. For Pressman to have confirmed Chambers on Hiss might have restored his own fortunes if his fortunes were all he cared about. But, whether by chance or not, all the faces from that long-dissolved cell about which Pressman professed himself unable to confirm Chambers still had some slight, tenuous tie to the outside world. And the three men Pressman named as Communists were politically dead beyond any resuscitation except by their own recantation or a world victory of the Soviets.

The bones he threw were his own bones. One was Charles Kramer, an economist, who had apparently meant little in Pressman's life. But another was John Abt, a Communist lawyer who had been his friend; and the last was Nathan Witt. They had been at Harvard together; Pressman had brought Witt to Washington. Most men are capable of just one great friend. If there had been any such friend not of his blood in Lee Pressman's life, it must have been Nathan Witt. Witt accepted the news of Pressman's testimony with the comment that he had no comment at all. To him, it seemed as though Lee Pressman no longer existed; Pressman had lived by that standard and now he was perishing by that standard. There was the thought in some quarters that, after these formalities, the outward things might be as they had been for Lee Pressman. But if he waited for a call from Philip Murray, it never came.

Not too long afterward, in fact, Philip Murray called Pat Jackson and asked him to come back to work for the CIO. Pat had waited eleven years, a little too long for any absolute triumph of justice; but it seemed somehow a sign and a symbol, as though the old breed of radical must wait outside the door for years on end, but, if he waited long enough, it would open to him.

Lee Pressman went on through what must have been for him the unchanging days, practicing law with his customary skill, far, far out of the main stream. Rumor still hung around his head; but his name came up, if it came up at all, more from old memory than from recent association. There were reports that Pressman was interested in Israeli real estate; an old enemy commented that he was still seeking history and a solid six per cent.

Pat Jackson was the old breed of radical. It was a breed that knew disaster and pain and bereavement. But after all they were the disasters of others, and they had passed; and there were new endeavors and fresh disasters, because they are the way of life, and the art of life is to save enough of yourself from every disaster to begin again in something like your old image.

Lee Pressman was, or thought he was, the new breed of radical. His image was of the foreign revolutionary: all decision, all function, without pity or hesitation. Yet he could not live by that image; the reality of his life was a conflict with his dream. He was always a man in between. And so his disasters were his own; they were total, final, and irredeemable. They cost him not just a friend but his only friend, not just a dream but his only dream, and not just the sale of something dear but the sale of himself. And when the disaster had come to him, he could not even summon up the memory of his past and say that, if it were all before him, he would live again to do what he had done.

3

SHERWOOD ANDERSON wrote once about two mill girls whose life was so bare and whose environment so constricted that even the characters on a movie screen seemed alien to them. One of the girls wished that a Communist union would come to her mill. She had heard that Communist unions were the worst and she wanted the worst.

Such were the people anointed to inherit the triumphant dream of Lee Pressman and Whittaker Chambers. Zola in his *Germinal* thought of them as a black, avenging army which would come to overthrow the earth. Most of the persons in this book were not like this faceless god they worshiped. They responded as I have said to a music different from the rhythms heard by ordinary men. And still they thought themselves aware of every heartbeat of their time, and they read and discussed every interior short paragraph of the *New York Times*.

But the avenging proletarian who was the protagonist of their dreams was often a man who knew the *Times* best in the moments when it was most serviceable to clothe his body through a cold night on a park bench. His rhythms were not so much different from those of ordinary men as buried almost below his own level of consciousness. If he became a Communist, it was by coincidence; and less through commitment than from being essentially unconscious of what the Communist Party was. At the particular moment of his contact with the Party he wanted only destruction, and that made him a symbol of hope to some and of terror to others. But the time came when he had something he wanted to preserve and then he became a person neither those who hoped nor those who feared could have imagined. For he was a fickle god, who wanted something very different from what his votaries wanted.

There were never very many proletarian Communists who affected the social history of the thirties, and most of them were uneasy allies soon to depart. For they could not wipe out the past which they had brought to the Communists, a past to which almost any doctrine was alien and whose wounds and memories they would carry with them all their lives.

To tell their story, I have chosen a group of sailors who became Communists or near-Communists, and, under that fancied unity of impulse, built the CIO National Maritime Union. They were largely untutored men, they were wanderers, and they came to the Communists as young sailors come to each fresh port—with the dim hope that it might become home. They took the sea with them wherever they went. The sea is treacherous, it is pitiless, and it is alien to the land around it. It is not a place for strong loyalties and berths of long duration. The word shipmate does not mean the same thing as the word comrade. Men cooped up at sea begin on occasion to hate each other beyond reason before the voyage is over. And they can say good-by without a pang.

I went to sea briefly in the thirties and was a transient member of the Communist fraction of the sailors' union on the East Coast, which went under the very perceptive name of the Travelers Club. I had joined among other reasons because the Travelers Club ran the union and was at the heart of things; I do not think I would have joined at any other time or any other place. And I was thus, like so many of my shipmates on this brief voyage, a Communist partly by coincidence and accident.

The Communist sailors ended their brief hitch ashore as seamen so often do, fighting with their fists in a little room. For a while the Communists ran the National Maritime Union, and then they were thrown overboard. The sea has accepted them and left very few traces behind. In searching for them and their story, I have talked to many remnants of those days and have read through the raw material of their national conventions and the records of their internal quarrels, a literature in which passion cries forth louder than is customary in documents of labor history.

I am especially grateful to two secondary sources. The first is *The Dark Ship*, by Richard Boyer, a profile of the National Maritime Union in 1945 when the Party still ruled the sailors; its author was a Communist, but it is a warm book, and there is a relevant irony in Boyer's faith that becoming Communists had wrought some moral rebirth in these bitter, rough, and alienated men. The other is Emile Zola's *Germinal*, which has its own special, ironic picture of the deep, conflicting passions of the men who would lead the working class and of the capricious army they hope to command.

Most of all, this is a story of men who had learned to live without pity. And its primary figure is Joseph Curran, a boatswain and the kind of man who survives wrecks; and how he shipped out with the Communists until they changed the sailing orders and then said good-by with a curse.

"It's Time to Go, I Heard Them Say . . ."

Joe Curran and His Shipmates

" 'Down with the traitor,' repeated a thousand voices, while stones began to whistle by.

"Then he turned pale and despair filled his eyes with tears. His whole existence was crumbling down; twenty years of ambitious comradeship were breaking down beneath the ingratitude of the crowd. He came down from the tree-trunk with no strength to go on, struck to the heart.

" 'That makes me laugh,' he stammered, addressing the triumphant Etienne. 'Good! I hope your time will come. It will come, I tell you!' "

EMILE ZOLA, Germinal

"I was not afraid because the membership is going to see. When the executive committee of the old ISU expelled me, the membership reinstated me; when the Mariners Club expelled me, the membership reinstated me. Now the Communist Party is trying to get me expelled from the union, and I will get back the same way.

"I have been a seaman only. I don't know what else to do. I will be back."

HARRY ALEXANDER, remarks at a meeting
of the National Maritime Union, April 3,
1947

JOSEPH CURRAN is by nature a creature of habit and so it was his custom when shipping was slow—and it was iced over in the early thirties—to settle down schooner-rigged on the streets of lower Manhattan.

He spent his days around South Street, touring the offices of the shipping masters or washing dishes for a dollar a day; and his nights, if he had the thirty-five cents, at the Seamen's Church Institute or, if he hadn't, on his bench in Battery Park. He became, especially on the cold nights, a connoisseur of the public prints. Men reduced to the custom of sleeping on park benches soon learn to stuff newspapers inside their coats as a weather-break. For all purposes, even this simple utility, the *New York Times* was well ahead of its competitors. That made Joe Curran a *Times* man.

But nothing shoreside could have reached his inner self, neither the homilies at the Institute nor the leaflets the Communists passed out. Any printed word that touched him was in a manual on seamanship. At a time when the craft of the sea was worth less in America than ever before, Joe Curran was a seaman by profession.

His father had died before he was born. He was an orphan in that word's ultimate sense. By 1936, for fourteen of his thirty years, he had been shipping on deck, a world with no room in it for woman or child or friend, for the seaman was alone among strangers. It was a world whose survivors, if they were soft, became crying drunks and, if they were hard, were harsh and piti-less by necessity, never again with ordinary people's doubts, quavers, and regrets.

Joe Curran was not one of the soft ones. He was six feet two inches tall and weighed 220 pounds. One of his biographers has compared the sound of his voice to the ripping of canvas; his craggy head was already bald from a strange Pacific fever. His nose was seamed from unfriendly blows; his fingers looked the width of hawsers. His back still had its moment of unease from one wild and terrible night at sea when a crazed sailor had hit him with an ax.

And he knew the consequences of command; in size and skills he was the sort of hand a master would pray for in those days, and he sailed most often as boatswain or deck-gang foreman. As he remembers himself then, Joe Curran was not an easy straw boss and he did not allow a sloppy deck. The crews under his command ran abnormally to drifters and floaters, sodden with defeat and contemptuous of their calling. Curran could handle the performers among them; far, far more he hated the talkers and the sea lawyers.

In those days, the Industrial Workers of the World still maintained a vocal, if non-functional, influence in the merchant marine, and some of Curran's least pleasant recollections of the boatswain-seaman relationship arose from the disparity between his own and a Wobbly's conception of a fair day's work.

One verbally active but otherwise somnolent syndicalist so tortured Curran with his unabashed malingering on one trip that Joe finally told him that he couldn't do a sailor's job if he wanted to. This touched the Wobbly in some submerged class-conscious deep, and he replied that he was a better seaman than Curran would ever be. Curran at once challenged him to execute a simple splice and had the satisfaction of returning an hour later to find his tormenter still struggling with the rope.

But then, Joe Curran's notion of a simple splice would be less minimal than that of most of us. At a time when most sailors crammed for the elementary ropework required for an able-bodied seamen's ticket and let the rest go, he was a tier and splicer of such virtuosity that he is still occasionally called upon to lecture on the art of knotmaking. Ever since then, the IWW has persisted in citing Curran as a backbreaking straw boss in his sailing days, a derogation he blames on that old quarrel. The Wobblies hung on Curran the nickname "No-Coffee-Time Joe" to indicate that he was a boatswain so disdainful of employee relations as to deny the crew even its traditional right to knock off fifteen minutes for coffee twice a day.*

But all this special strength and these special skills were worth no more to Joe Curran than at most an infrequent sixty-five dol-

* The fact that Curran was a boatswain before he became a union leader might impel the careless reflection that, in times when management is uninhibited by unions, the finest sons of the working class begin by larruping their mates across the back. Actually most labor leaders are drawn from superior workers in their craft; unions have a rough merit system. Walter Reuther was a diemaker; Philip Murray was offered a place in management before he became a figure in the miners' union; David Dubinsky was a skilled garment cutter. Curran made boatswain because he was a man of capacity; most persons who achieve anything of substance bring a certain pride of performance to the worst calling they fall into.

lars a month. There were seamen who were half vagrants and there were sailors like him. The end, for the fit and the unfit, was a bench in Battery Park. He had made all the formations. He was a worthy young man. And he had no more to show for his virtues than any old piece of salvage grifting in a South Street gin mill.

The sense of all this came to him, if it came at all, filtered dimly through the stiffness of his limbs and the compulsions of the meal he had skipped and the meal he had to get. Joe Curran stands for every seaman; and, twenty years ago, he was an individual of massive truculence accepting the pattern of a group which seemed committed to an habitual, almost hereditary, submission. To work on a ship, it was assumed that the sailor accepted the shipowner's terms. Those terms included food just above the Maritime Commission's minimum standards for the avoidance of scurvy; average wages of a little under two dollars a day; a corn-cob mattress if it was a good ship; and a twenty-eight-man forecastle unless it was a very good one. And, for all this, the seaman had to bribe or crawl before the shipping agent he called the crimp or stand at the pierheads in all weathers trusting some mate to pick him from the herd.

The sailor had no sense of the community and the community had no sense of the sailor. Down in those depths, a different sort of man was being created, rootless, kinless, and unforgiving, to whom words like mercy and gratitude were from another language, never to be translated because never experienced. He was off limits to all save the dedicated, remembered by no one from the outside world except the artist and the evangelist, clerical or revolutionary. The attitude of ordinary society was nowhere better indicated than in the American Federation of Labor's International Seamen's Union (ISU), which had perhaps 800 members and an even smaller perspective of its possibilities.

The Communists came to the waterfront very early, and, for a long while, what they did and what they said seemed to make very little difference. When Joe Curran was washing dishes for his supper, the Communists held out as his salvation the Marine Workers Industrial Union, which said very flatly that he could hope for nothing else under capitalism and that his solitary escape was to follow "the path beaten out by the Russian workers."

More than anyone else in America, the depression seamen might have been expected to accept this unvarnished doctrine, but in the mass they paid it no attention. If they listened at all, it was to agree with the AFL that the Marine Workers were Communists and with the Marine Workers that the AFL was larcenous. They stayed away from both. The Communists, by mere activity, managed to arouse a little more interest than the AFL did, but, between them, these rival unions never before 1934 attained a membership embracing more than five per cent of the seamen.

Joe Curran, that Everyseaman, does not appear to have maintained any consistent connection with either. But there were a precious few who joined the Marine Workers and almost automatically passed over to the Communist Party, and they were to be the fathers of a revolution. The first among them was Thomas Ray, a spare, silent, already gray man, who had made his trip to Moscow and returned with plenipotentiary powers as American seamen's representative to the Red Federation of Trade Unions.

Ray sat among the infidels, a starveling ambassador of a great, faraway presence, failing with the many but succeeding with he did not know how important a few. For all his credentials, Moscow appears to have forgotten Ray very soon; he had to do with the little he had. It has been a very long time since Tommy Ray believed that he and his few comrades were any vanguard of the black army that would overthrow the earth, and the loss of that belief is a great one for any man. But he knows something he did not know then: who he was and who they were and why they became Communists.

"Nobody," said Tommy Ray a few years ago, "has ever written the story of the maritime industry—of why they go to sea and why they come back to it, of why they drink and the life they live in port. You can go to sea with a man for twenty years and never know where he comes from. He doesn't tell you. There's no place for a sailor to go. Even now, if you go through West Street or South Street, you see kids doing what we did, gassed up with no place to go. Then along comes somebody and takes an interest in you.

"You find a home, you find other people, your life seems to

get a purpose, you get a religion. In a sense you are a new man. But I suppose you're not really a new man, not really."

Any insurgent religion, good or bad, makes its first converts among people capable of large feelings of love or hate. And there were not many sailors, granted the life they lived, who could bring to this particular religion the capacity for universal love. There were more who understood universal hate.

Hedley Stone, a scrawny, thirty-eight-year-old able-bodied seaman, already older than most of his shipmates after twenty years on and off the decks, came off the North Atlantic run of a luxury ship in the winter of 1934 with just $34.75 in his pocket and joined the Communist Party.

"I was alone and I was single and I was full of hate and up to my neck with the rottenness of things. No one had to tell me I was treated badly or paid too little. All the guy had to say to me was, 'Look at what the shipowners made and what you made.'"

Harry Alexander, engine-room watertender, became a Communist too; to this squat man with a mouth like a catfish, there was no other place where people even talked about the conditions of his trade that were his single obsession. Harry Alexander was a Communist for nearly thirteen years; there is no evidence that he ever read the Party's prophets. His world was bounded by the bulkheads of his engine-room; his mind was a cavernous receptacle for every detail of what it was to work on a ship. Always he was a seaman only; not long ago he quit his union office to go back to sea.

The Marine Workers Union won few and meager victories, but Harry Alexander was responsible for the greatest of them. In Baltimore, in February of 1934, he called together 700 beached seamen and pledged them not to sign aboard any ship except through what he called the Centralized Shipping Bureau. For that little while, Alexander ran the only union hiring hall on the East Coast waterfront. Negroes and Filipinos were admitted as equals with no test for shipping berths except the length of their waiting time on its roster. Wages were raised fifteen dollars a month. Then the shipping companies began boycotting the port of Baltimore and starved out Alexander's first experiment with the system that is the backbone of the sailors' unions today.

Alexander and Stone were the apostles of the here and now, enlisted by default in the army of the future. There were others to whom Lenin was to be eternal sacred writ. Messman Charles Keith became for the waterfront Communists a kind of wandering evangelist, living on roots and bark; he would sign on a ship in Baltimore and jump it in New York after one night's prayer for the social salvation of his shipmates. He followed his dream to be wounded in the Spanish Civil War and came back to the ships, and was driven eventually from the Communist Party, never, never to be reconciled to his loss.

They were all different men, but they shared awhile the same impulse, every sailor's common search for a harbor he can carry with him wherever he goes. And their great strength was neither in doctrine nor tactic; it was the fact that they were a very few people who knew each other in an industry where every man was a stranger to the bunk beneath him.

"An organization," says Tommy Ray, "is people who know one another," presumably in a world of strangers.

But their time was not yet upon them, and the world of their dreams was not a real one. They marched in May Day parades and turned out for hunger demonstrations and hurled imprecations upon the treason of the AFL, but only the very few listened. For only the very few, even in the trough of depression, even among its worst victims, ever listen to the dream of revolution.

In triumph, men polish their early defeats into epic conflicts. After the ascendancy of the National Maritime Union in 1937, the Communists who were writing its history gilded over the largely rhetorical struggles of the Marine Workers and presented them as a revolutionary precursor of the NMU, with wider influence and victories more glorious than they had ever known in real life. The veterans of the Marine Workers Union carried the scars of heroic old Bolsheviks, a status which did not protect most of them from expulsion from the Communist Party in 1945.

A revolution requires of its leaders a record of unbroken infallibility; if they do not possess it, they are expected to invent it. Joe Curran never claimed to be any pillar of the Marine Workers, so the Communists claimed it for him. A Communist NMU vice president named Joe Stack cited himself on no visible evidence as a veteran both of the Marine Workers and of six months in a Nazi concentration camp. Ferdinand Smith and Blackie Myers, for years the NMU's two highest Communist officials, both professed to have been stalwarts of the Marine Workers.

"Smith and Myers weren't members of the Marine Workers," says Ray. "They all claim it. I don't know why. I guess it's a badge of honor. So what do you do with a badge of honor?"

But, in the early thirties it was a badge neither of honor nor of power. These lonely shipmates struggled on until first Moscow and then Washington permitted them a grasp at the real world. By 1934, Hitler had come to power and the Soviet Union was searching the West for allies. The Communist International began indicating the discovery of certain virtues in democratic capitalism, and it was no longer necessary for every good Communist to begin by asserting that the revolutionary path of the Russians was the only one possible. The Roosevelt administration had passed the National Recovery Act, with its asserted guarantee of the right to form unions. The West Coast sailors and longshoremen had already erupted in a violent and successful strike. The Marine Workers had stood outside society bombarding it with Bolshevik paper; they were now permitted to set aside the slogans of revolution and seek unity with the AFL to reform the here and now. Tommy Ray invited the AFL International Seamen's Union (ISU) to join with the Marine Workers to rescue the East Coast. The response was silence.

For the ISU was near the end of its career of poverty and neglect and its leaders felt no need for assistance from inconvenient quarters. In December, 1934, the East Coast shipping companies, hearing the rumble of the West Coast drums, called in the ISU and conferred upon it nominal control of their crews. The ISU's leaders set the initiation fee at ten dollars and battened their hatches against any destructive effects from the incoming golden tide by voting themselves power to expel any disturber of the peace. Joe Curran and some 13,000 other seamen came in.

Their dues entitled them to watch union meetings over which Dave Grange, an Oxonian West Indian who was the ISU's *de facto* president, kept order with a .45 pistol as his gavel. Otherwise, nothing was changed; an able-bodied seaman still earned fifty-five dollars a month and still begged his berth from a ship-ping agent. Nothing seemed likely to change.

By now, Tommy Ray seemed forgotten by Moscow and almost everyone else. There was no choice for him and his few com-rades except to dissolve the Marine Workers and go into the ISU. So Ray did the only thing he knew how to do; he left San Pedro, cadged a little office on Irving Place in New York, borrowed twelve dollars and put out a leaflet. He called it the ISU *Pilot;* it ran to eight mimeographed pages, and it cost a nickel when he could sell it. He composed it all by himself, and, across the top of its first issue, he wrote:

"IT'S TIME TO GO I HEARD THEM SAY; I HEARD THEM SAY IT'S TIME TO GO."

The old slogans were gone, and in their place Tommy Ray had put an ancient chant rooted in lost time, the sailor's half-sad, half-relieved farewell to the harbor just before the heaving of the lines. Maybe for the first time, Joe Curran could pick up a piece of paper and see himself. For Tommy Ray was writing about grievances he did not have to manufacture and he was on his way. But he was still moving only the very few. No wall was ever thrown down by a piece of mimeograph paper; Ray's *Pilot* began with only 400 readers and it would be almost a year be-fore enough people would give him the fifty dollars he needed to print it every week.

Still, the *Pilot* held the Communists together. They took the short runs to the coastwise cities to argue all night in the fore-castles. They caucused together before every ISU meeting, and they turned those normally soporific sessions into nightmares of parliamentary sabotage and resolutions inimical to the public safety. But, beyond those few gaudy nights and one short strike in Philadelphia, they had nothing of substance to show all through 1935. There were only a few rumbles, very far away, when Grange went to Washington in February of 1936 to ne-gotiate a new contract to fix the wages of able-bodied seamen at $57.50 a month.

Grange was still in Washington when word came that there was trouble in San Pedro: the 250-man crew of the SS *California* had refused to cast off without a five-dollar-a-month raise. For a while, Grange couldn't even find these rebels; he finally reached them at a telephone in a butcher shop a mile and a half from their pier. Grange told the voice so far away and in a state of mutiny to go back to work, and it rasped back, "Go to hell; you sold us out." It was the voice of boatswain Joe Curran.

So Dave Grange turned to the White House and induced Secretary of Labor Frances Perkins to come out from a Cabinet dinner and reason with the distant voice of the avenging army. Joe Curran was having his first experience with the exalted of the earth. There is no public record that his truculence was abated by the contact. Madame Perkins promised her good offices, and Joe Curran let her stand holding the phone in her evening dress for thirty minutes while he and his mates argued in the butcher shop for half an hour before deciding to accept her pledge and take the ship back home.

They brought the *California* back to New York, where sixty-four of them were fired, and Joe Curran walked off in his black stocking cap with no pause except to stammer a few words to the movie cameras. They all moved up to Ninth Avenue and announced a general seamen's strike. The ISU replied by calling them all Communists and expelling Ray, Curran, Alexander, and ten others. No more than fifty ships followed Curran's lead; they were not enough. The strike was broken.

Three years later, Joseph P. Ryan, president of the AFL longshoremen, was to provide his own history of that first defeat:

"We got some money from the shipowners. . . . We said 'Give us money; we are going to fight them.' We got the money and we drove them back with baseball bats where they belonged. Then they called the strike off."

Joe Ryan's bats had driven Curran to the only corner where he could find friends. The shoreside Communist Party awoke to find that this field it had neglected was burgeoning with fruit; it enticed Bob Hope and a cluster of other actors to a Madison Square Garden strike-fund rally, and its fronts gave all they could. In the spring of 1936, Joe Curran marched in the Communist May Day parade; he was walking with the committed.

And he was back that October fomenting another East Coast shipping strike. The crews began pouring off. Dave Grange

called them to Cooper Union, near Skid Row, on October 30, for
the last time to preach to them care and caution and moderation.
He had lost some of the imperial edge by now; he had been
caught $144,000 short in his accounts, and it seemed more politic
to leave the .45 at home.

They sat there, 1,500 of them, hour after hour and roared at
him and pitched pennies at him, until at last Grange turned out
the lights and went home. Then, while the sailors sat hushed in
the chill and the dark, flashlights began going on all over the
hall, the doors were opened and Curran and Ray and Alexander
and the rest of the strike committee came in with their coats
buttoned to their chins and their faces lit up by those sweeping
torches. Curran moved the strike; Hedley Stone, leaning against
a pillar, called out the second and the affirmative voices of their
army rolled back at them.

After that, the seamen came up out of the avenging earth for
a strike that lasted ninety-nine days and killed twenty-seven men
before it was over. We do not have strikes like that any longer.
The old soldiers of this one remember their feats in it with advantages, stripping their sleeves and showing their scars, half-
believed and themselves almost unbelieving after all the quiet
years in between.

They struggled with policemen on horseback; they scrounged
for food around the markets; they slept in flophouses and they
were beaten by AFL professionals who hunted them like rabbits
around the piers. They hung on through days of cold, hungry
battle when each was prouder of himself than he could ever be
again, days he could recall as successive cantos of an epic where
he and all the others were heroes. Joe Curran's head acquired
another spike wound and was hit once by a billiard cue; but all
those strokes had the ineffectuality of the intermittent shots from
a beaten rearguard. At the end the seamen had destroyed the
ISU and set up the National Maritime Union.

They joined the CIO at their first convention; Joe Curran was
chairman and Tommy Ray was secretary. The revolution was
achieved but still the Communists held together, caucusing before every meeting, united on the floor, writing, presenting, and

passing the resolutions the Party expected from a mass organization. And the Party's fraction ran the NMU.

There was a period, in the early days, when Curran and the other seamen swung back and forth between the Communist fraction and a right-wing group which called itself the Mariners Club. That hesitation ended in 1938 when Curran swung to the Communists under the impact of evidence that the Mariners were financing their activities with shipowners' money. Most of the Mariners had been active in the 1936 strike; they were apparently accepting assistance from the same companies they had fought so desperately just two years before.

The Communists explained the Mariners' defection with the assumption that these first fallen heroes had been in the pay of the enemy all along. Curran believed that explanation and the sailors agreed with him. But life is never that simple; sailors in a bar will take their help wherever they can find it. There is a moment in *Germinal* where Zola discovers two rivals for leadership of the striking miners suddenly surprised by a chill dislike deeper than any disagreement over doctrine:

"The two men no longer shouted, having become bitter and spiteful, conquered by the coldness of their rivalry. It is at bottom that which always strains systems, making one man revolutionary in the extreme, pushing the other to an affectation of prudence, carrying them in spite of themselves beyond their true ideas into those parts men do not choose for themselves."

That is so often the fate of the committed, to swirl and hate past reason before a host of bystanders. The Mariners were stoned out, as Grange had been stoned out. The Communists and Curran closed ranks for eight uneasy years and then the process began again.

The years to come were quiet on the surface, but slowly these men, Curran and the Communists, were becoming a little different from what they had been. Charlie Keith came back from his Spanish hospital to find fresh and unremembered faces filling the waterfront section of the Party he had left behind him. Half unconsciously, the Party had become the vehicle for the young man of conventional ambition. The Communists made the decisions and assigned the offices. Membership in the waterfront section of the Party had become more necessary for the careerist in the NMU than the Rotary Club could ever hope to be in more ordinary societies. Even in 1937, there were ports whose waterfront Communist section included every local official of the NMU and not a single rank-and-file seaman.

And these were Communists of a different sort. Tommy Ray was known all over the coast as a symbol of the Party. For reasons of discretion, it seemed best for him to avoid high union office. He went into the shadows, thin and fading in his shabby black suit, unnoticed by the newcomers and kept on for research assignments because Curran trusted him above all others. And there were other veterans uneasy in peacetime; Harry Alexander dropped lower in the hierarchy, turning more and more often back to the sea, happier out of headquarters.

Paddy Whelan, one of the oldest of them, a Communist and the son of a Wobbly, built the union in Baltimore almost by himself; and, when it was done, he commenced to drink and growl and drifted back to the boiler room to die at length on the Murmansk run in World War II and regain a posthumous glory from his old comrades. The government named a Liberty Ship after Patrick Whelan during the war. It became a staple Communist legend that he had died of machine-gun wounds snarling at the Stukas, "I'll get those krauts yet." His friends preferred a report that Paddy had gone out riding a piece of driftwood shouting "Hi-yo, Silver," the old unhousebroken Adam to the last.

They were not weak men or soft ones, those ground breakers for what was now a temple, but they were not conformists either; they had no real wish to be sextons; they consumed themselves because essentially they were without personal ambition.

They were fading away, and the shoreside Communist Party was very happy to deal with their less complicated successors. The NMU had by now become an edifice of heroic proletarian myth; with the war, John Howard Lawson, Hollywood's leading Communist, wrote a movie about the sailors on the North Atlantic. Richard Boyer completed a book on the National Maritime Union, its major thesis the idea that being a union leader and a

Communist can transform an ordinary man into an early Christian.

By now, there was a new kind of waterfront Communist, home from the sea and with no special urge to return. In that way, he was unlike the sailors he led; the mass of them never became Communists and few of them really cared about running for union office, because their wants were either too large or too small to be satisfied in any permanent berth. There were only 500 Communists in the National Maritime Union even when it had 90,000 members; most of them held union offices; the Party had become the commitment of bureaucrats.

NMU Secretary-Treasurer Ferdinand Smith became the ornament of a hundred Communist fronts, a graceful, ineffably superior West Indian, adorning the boards of dinner after dinner. NMU Vice President Blackie Myers, a jaunty veteran of innumerable gallantries in the 1936 strike, was made a member of the Communist Party's National Committee; he took to coming late to the office with the excuse of meetings of high policy with Earl Browder; and his expense accounts got bigger and bigger.

The NMU was building a $350,000 headquarters on the West Side of Manhattan. It was wartime; society needed the seamen now. Their pay and their bonuses went onward and upward with no semblance of the old harsh combat. And nobody noticed that, somewhere at the core, people were going soft and that it was harder and harder even to pay men to go out and organize what ships remained outside the union. For there were things you could not buy. Blackie Myers spent $170,000 to unionize the Isthmian Steamship Line and ended up with nothing. A reformed and resurgent AFL sailors' union was shaming the NMU wherever there was a contest.

Joe Curran had grown up now. He was married and had a son. He moved to Riverside Drive and was off on that road to domestic stability which would take him from Long Island up to a farm in Westchester County. He was becoming part of the community. For him, as for all sailors, today had become far better than he had ever expected it to be.

Curran worked at his job as few of the others did. The Communists still held him up as a stately monument of the proletarian.

But in those years, he must have felt that his office as president of the NMU had about it aspects of reign without rule and that it was Myers' union more and more. Hedley Stone was still treasurer of the union; the rest of the old Bolsheviks slipped farther and farther down the scale. Curran could not know how much these half-captors of him and all the other seamen had come to hate one another.

But then there came a time, out of the blue, one morning in the fall of 1943, when Blackie Myers walked into Curran's office and announced that Stone, Alexander, and Tommy Ray were fascists and Hitler lovers plotting a strike to sabotage the war and destroy the union. The surface of his charge was Stone's conduct of a minor quarrel with a shipping line, but its root was much deeper. Myers said then that he was a patriot and Stone an enemy of national unity, but that was hardly what he meant. Stone, Ray, and Alexander were the old and he was the new, and they were quarreling in the deeps of spiteful rivalry. In other times they would call *him* a Communist and he would call *them* agents of the shipowners, for the issue was buried far below doctrine.

That first morning Stone looked back at Myers and said at last, slowly and softly, "You know, Blackie, I would as soon kill you as look at you." Their voyage together had come to this sudden, hate-swarming end. They could not even say why; they could only look at each other, these two sworn comrades, across an infinite distance with nothing between them but the word fascist.

And then, the five top officers of the National Maritime Union, all of them Communists but Curran, sat in that locked office and fought for six hours. Afterward the thing most of them remembered best was the long minutes when they sat silent and looked at the floor. At the end, Myers began to cry and say that his nerves were unstrung and that he wasn't himself. Then they all went out to a gin mill, and for a while there was peace without forgiveness.

They remained nearly two more years, inextricably tied together in that embrace of hate, which can be as strong as love and which can take longer to resolve. They carried out their quarrel away from Curran and the other sailors, inside the waterfront section of the Communist Party, to the death of all fraternity. Land-based Communists like William Z. Foster and Eugene Dennis came around to mumble irrelevancies about the necessity for a new program. But these were sailors fighting in the forecastle, and you could not quiet them with a lecture on navigation. They had passed to those reaches where a man does not know what he is doing, from which no doctrine or appeal to brotherhood can call him back. And there they chewed one another up and spit one another out. At the end, in 1945, NMU Vice President Jack Lawrenson, Stone, Keith, Ray, and Alexander had all been expelled from the Communist Party; the revolution had devoured its parents.

Stone was to say later that he could never again think of a Communist without thinking of a cockroach. He and Alexander and Ray turned on the ashes and never looked back with longing again. But Keith and Lawrenson, perhaps as long as they lived, could not help looking back, because they were the committed and they had become Communists because they dreamed of the perfect.

A year after his expulsion, Keith arose at an NMU meeting and began to talk about what it had once meant to be a Communist in the long-gone shadows of the forecastles, remembering all alone and grieving his loss.

"But these people," he finished, "violate the principles of the union and the principles of communism. They are betraying the traditions of Communists on the waterfront." Keith paused and his eye fell on Howard McKenzie, one of the NMU's Communist vice presidents: ". . . and men like McKenzie cannot even come to work on time."

Keith was longing for a tradition that was alien to Curran and to most of the other sailors; this was a quarrel that few of them understood. Both the Communists and those they had cast out continued to exalt Curran as a symbol; in 1946, the sailors re-elected Curran, Stone, Lawrenson, and all the Communists to their old union posts. The passion of their quarrel had not yet destroyed the habit patterns of the NMU's membership.

But then Curran threw in with the apostates, and together

they threw the waterfront section out. For the time had come for Joe Curran when he had the world he wanted, and the dreams of his old Communist shipmates seemed to him irrelevant when they were not destructive of that world. They thought of themselves as his creators, and he became their destroyer. Roaring, rasping, and unsleeping, he fought them and beat them in union meetings month after month up and down the coast. The sailors could look uncaring at a brawl between Communists and ex-Communists, but they looked at Curran and saw a mirror of themselves, and his passion became their passion. And after their last long fight there arrived for the Communists in the NMU the moment that had come to Grange, to the Mariners, and to so many others, when they looked upon the seamen, row on tossing row, and saw no pity.

And none was more pitiless than Joe Curran, who had been their symbol and was now their master. By the summer of 1948, the National Maritime Union did not have a single officer who was a Communist, and only Lawrenson and Keith remained to remember the old lost flame with anything except disgust.

In the end, Keith and Lawrenson had to go too, because they were not men comfortable in peace and order. Curran, by now implacable, put through an amendment to the union constitution ordering the expulsion of all present and future Communists. Keith and Lawrenson fought against it and were never reconciled. On Thanksgiving of 1949, they rallied their followers for one more battle in the streets and seized the union headquarters. For one more night, Joe Curran came back to stand unmoved on a platform while the sailors roared him down too, smoking a cigarette and smiling a cold smile with bits and splinters of the woodwork flying about his head as they had flown around so many others'.

But Curran did not walk away and, before very long, he beat them too. Then Keith went and Lawrenson was defeated and with them passed the last organized segments of the army of the future. They had been shipmates for a very long time, but there is no record that anyone said good-by to anyone else.

There were never very many Communists in the National Maritime Union. Their departure did not leave any special void;

if you did not know that they had been there, there would be no way of telling now. Keith was a house painter when last heard from; most of the orthodox Communists have been blacklisted out of the merchant marine, although a very few still buffet around the waterfront for occasional berths with non-union or foreign lines, because they do not know what else to do.

It is very peaceful at the NMU's great hall on Seventeenth Street these days. The men in charge of its New York port headquarters seem too young even to lie about their wounds from 1936. Every now and then one of the old performers has himself a ball around headquarters, drunk but orderly, and his juniors treat him with a certain deference because he is, after all, an old hulk with a glorious history.

The sailors fall out no more to picket selective enemies of peace and progress; they march no longer in May Day parades. By night the crowds are thinner than they used to be in the gin mills around the hall, because so many have family responsibilities and are the normal, uncomplicated people most men prefer to be. They can earn a base pay of $250 a month with more for overtime; their vacations are paid for; they have linen on their beds and fresh milk on their tables and innerspring mattresses in their forecastles. There are months when shipping is slow; but if an old hand has to sleep in a flophouse, it is likely to be his own fault.

Joe Curran is a man of moderate substance, a vice president of the Congress of Industrial Organizations, an articulate and respected figure, almost indeed a statesman in his industry. The wild dreams are very far behind him; he is not one to ask for the moon either now or in the future; he takes a comparatively small salary and he works a long day.

Joe Curran loves his family; he is very gracious to visitors; he left the faculty of pity after all somewhere in the Western Ocean, and you cannot ask him to mourn the old shipmates who have left him and are overboard. All his wounds and all his voyages and all his memories caught up with Joe Curran in the summer of 1953, and he had a desperate heart attack. He arose still huge and craggy but with a black-gang pallor and the look of a man whose wars were past him. But the old hatreds would not leave him, and, if they had, his destiny seemed to be new hatreds with each new trip.

Civil war had come to Curran's crew too. NMU Vice President Hulbert Warner and Secretary Neal Hanley were fighting to oust Joe Curran's old friend Hedley Stone as treasurer. They were all veterans of the 1936 strike and the quarrels of the water-front section of the Communist Party. Now the word "psycho-path" and the word "liar" fell like a stone between them too, as it had so often with so many others before. Their wounds were once more too great for fraternity, and they were not yet too tired for fratricide. And Joe Curran, sick, summoned himself for one more quarrel, his final outlet for passion, and went forth to fight for Hedley Stone, almost the last of his old shipmates remaining to him. He beat those mutineers too, and he and Stone were all that remained of the old crew.

All those shipmates are gone now except Curran, because Curran was only a sailor. There had been a time when he was hungry, and the Communists had fed him when no one else would. But it had been enough for him, as for most of the other seamen, to be fed and to win for himself a place in the here and now. The black, avenging army had not come to overthrow the earth; it asked no more than a place in the sun. Curran had come from too deep down and he had seen too many men put in a sack and thrown overboard. He was almost the sole survivor; he was again an orphan.

Still, Tommy Ray lives on as research director of the National Maritime Union, wearing the old black suit, girt round by volume upon volume of shipping industry data, apparently detached from any recollection of that day Moscow appointed him an agent of history. One of his abiding interests is in the actuarial statistics of a pension plan for old sailors. He could not have thought twenty years ago that it would end quite like this, but he could not say looking back that it had ended badly.

The dead were dead; the drowned were drowned. And Harry Alexander, NMU book number 12, old voyager, squats in his boiler room, scowling at his water gauge, a little harsh with the new third engineer. He has survived. He had been a seaman only.

4

OLIVER WENDELL HOLMES, JR., said once that every man should take part in the actions and passions of his time or else risk being judged not to have lived. A serious writer has less choice about that risk than the rest of us. To take responsibility for expression is to accept many perils but at least to escape that detachment from the passions of one's time which Holmes thought was the worst fate in life.

A serious writer cannot ignore the myths around him, because they may be the stuff with which he must work. Perhaps for that reason, to search among those caught up in the social myth of the thirties is to be confronted with a number of literary men of a dimension and stature plainly superior to the average of the committed. In no other group did the myth find so many votaries approaching the first class as among its writers.

They were moved by many different impulses. The best of them, so far as we can judge them two decades later, found it wanting very early and departed. Some of the lesser ones who remained behind held to their fantasy until they lost their powers and disappeared. Others found the myth a short way station along the road to the cheap, the trivial, and the commercial.

The writers came to the myth in waves, and the first wave was different from the last. The pioneers included many established figures of the twenties who had been alienated from the business culture of that decade and were both shaken and grimly satisfied by its collapse in 1929. Some of them had sat up too long with the gospel of art which was one escape for the committed of the twenties and which now seemed cold and broken to them. They came to the social myth of the thirties in the best instances because it seemed to them to promise the destruction of a botched civilization. The word hope recurs in their comments on their conversion. For most of them, the myth did not bear close examination and they left it quite soon. I have taken Edmund Wilson, Sherwood Anderson, and to a lesser extent John Dos Passos, as models of their impulse.

They were succeeded as literary celebrants of the myth by a younger and more plastic group. These were beginning writers, narrower, with far less sophistication and with different impulses. The new group tended to be plebeian. In the case of most of them, the mere process of becoming writers had been the triumph of an alienated spirit, and they were very lonely. They were no less vain than other writers and no less desirous of appreciation, and their hopes were a little more personal than those entertained by the first wave. They thought of themselves as poets laureate-elect of the emerging proletariat. And some of the more respected of their elders remained a little while to tell them that the revolutionary inspiration of the social myth could of itself give them immortality as artists.

A few of them were glad to pay the stated price of this immortality, which was allegiance to communism and the practice of the proletarian novel. Even in the thirties, they were neither fashionable nor successful. Their work is buried now, and to discuss them is to catalogue the names on tombstones. James T. Farrell and Richard Wright, who fought against the idea of art as a weapon even when they were committed to the social myth, are almost their only survivors.

I think the story of the left-wing writers of the thirties is like its subjects: it promises more than it can fulfill. Those literary men of the first class who were involved in the myth had a transient association with it; the experience for them was impermanent. And those more intensely involved and finally destroyed by the myth were themselves, I am afraid, impermanent people, and to discuss their works is more an act of exhumation than of rediscovery. It seems to me to have been one of the tragedies of the thirties that so many people substituted an exterior for an interior passion, and nowhere is this process more damaging than to literature.

The very mortality of so many of its subjects seems to me to demand a focus at once wider and less precise than I have attempted in the rest of these studies. It would be distortion to segregate a few persons and treat them as typical of the left writers of the thirties; the individual impulses of writers are too variegated to make that practical.

The thirties did not, of course, change the writer's responsibility, which is at best a lonely one, or his primary concern, which is his attitude toward his craft. You cannot play the subjects of these chapters against their time, because the writer's problems are almost timeless, I think. Some of the writers who supported the Communist ticket in 1932 were gentlemen who detested the values of a commercial civilization; Edmund Wilson, for example, writing in 1931, sounds oddly like Henry Adams describing Washington after the Civil War. Many of the authors of proletarian novels were plebeians shooting at the genteel tradition, and at the latest their ancestors were Theodore Dreiser and Sherwood Anderson. These were very old literary quarrels.

The revolutionary myth of the thirties was part of the passion of their time, and very few writers were entirely unaffected by it. As a group, writers more than most persons believed that it was the stream of their time; Robert Penn Warren, Sinclair Lewis, and Thomas Wolfe accepted it by writing against it. Dreiser solved the problem by intermittently joining the Communist Party and by consistently writing as though it did not exist. The subjects of this chapter were different even from most of their colleagues because, for a time at least, they thought of themselves as revolutionaries and made some effort to adjust their craft to revolutionary disciplines.

The transitory impulse of its first-rate subjects and the imperfect talent of its second-rate ones make this the most archeological chapter in this book and do violence to my hope that I could avoid paper and other dead matter. The faces of many of my subjects have disappeared and they have left only paper behind. In studying them, I read a great number of the novels consciously inspired by the revolutionary concept, many of which are cited in what follows. Among veterans of that period, I am most grateful for the recollections of James T. Farrell and Joseph Freeman, who was editor of the communist *New Masses* in the thirties. I have also rested heavily upon two men rather unfashionable in the period—William Butler Yeats and Gustave Flaubert. Both of them, of course, consumed themselves for their craft alone, and theirs seemed a cold and inhuman preoccupation to many of my subjects. But it was, I think, the preoccupation behind most of what has been permanent in literature, and in the disparate and cluttered literary wreckage of the thirties, Yeats and Flaubert seemed to me to be necessary adjuncts to play the permanent against the transient.

There are enough names in this chapter to risk the loss of perspective and to invite the conclusion that an entire literary generation sacrificed itself to the social muse. It certainly appears at short range to have been no golden period in our literature;

but it is worth remembering that William Faulkner's *The Sound and the Fury* and Scott Fitzgerald's *Tender is the Night*, two novels which have best survived the early thirties, were written entirely independent of the influences which concern us here.

Yeats said once that out of the quarrel with others we make rhetoric and out of the quarrel with ourselves we make poetry. The subjects of this chapter, the buried ones at least, had a different view; they believed that to be a great writer one needed simply to be on the side of the future and to substitute outer reconciliation for interior quarrel. The lesson of their failure is literary and not moral. For the writer is lonely even in fantasy and, try though he will, it is very often his fate to damage no one but himself.

The Social Muse

"What artists we should be if we had never read, seen or loved anything that was not beautiful; if from the outset some guardian angel of the purity of our pens had kept us from all contamination; if we had never known fools or read newspapers."

GUSTAVE FLAUBERT, letter to Louise Colet

"To me a strike bulletin or an impassioned leaflet are of more moment than 300 prettily and falsely written pages about the private woes of a gigolo or the biological woes of a society dame as useful to society as the buck brush which infests Missouri cow pastures and takes all the sustenance out of the soil."

JACK CONROY, speech to the American Writers Congress, 1935

"Evil comes to us men of imagination wearing as its mask all the virtues."

WILLIAM BUTLER YEATS, Dramatis Personae

"I remember a fellow expatriate opening a letter from a mutual friend of ours, urging him to come home and be revitalized by the hardy, bracing qualities of the native soil. It was a strong letter and affected us both deeply until we noticed that it was headed from a nerve sanitarium in Pennsylvania."

SCOTT FITZGERALD, Echoes of the Jazz Age

FOR AMERICA, the year 1931 was one in which it began to look as though the center could not hold and the ceremony of innocence had been drowned; and Mr. Edmund Wilson turned from his vastly admired studies of Yeats, Joyce, and Eliot to watch hunger demonstrations and coal strikes.

He stood as near as he could get to New York's City Hall in January of 1931, and heard the Communists shout, "We want bread, not horses' hoofs" at the police. Before the afternoon was over, he watched a Communist demonstrator snatch the apples from an unemployed vendor, cast them all at the police and crown the occasion by breaking the empty crate over a bluecoat's head.

Wilson set down that scene without allusion to its double shades of meaning as symbol for the writer in the next decade. In the universities, graduate students were opening up his *Axel's Castle* like Keats over Chapman's *Homer* and marveling at Wilson's sense of the symbolic. But he himself cared only for the real. His old world had torn loose; he called next year's book *The American Jitters.*

When Edmund Wilson was at Princeton, his schoolmate Scott Fitzgerald called him "the shy little scholar of Holder Court." He had been literary editor of the *New Republic;* now he was tearing himself from his library to watch the storm over his country. In March of 1931, he went to Washington for a press conference conducted by that "great pulpy ectoplasm," Herbert Hoover. "One hardly expected to find him a real man." He sat in on a conference of progressive politicians at the Hotel Carlton and heard old George Norris make the old speech against the House of Morgan. Watching Norris, Wilson was at once charmed and appalled at a nature "so essentially sweet" and by that "defiant look of pride" that was passing more and more into a "look of pain."

"Why," he asked himself, "do the American progressives have to be so tongue-tied with inhibitions? . . . The surest way to shake an American reformer and make him back down has always been to accuse him of socialism." Someone at the Carlton had seen Lincoln Steffens glowing with satisfaction at the sight of the reformers backed to the wall with no idea what to do about

it. Wilson left the progressives and went to a meeting of the
Taylor Society to hear the report of an engineer just back from
the Soviet Union. "He seems to have ended . . . in catching the
fervor of their faith."

Then he rode back to New York on an airliner, which sounded
as doomed and as asthmatic as the American system itself. He
looked down at the black wasteland around Trenton and reflected
that he could not even see his beloved Princeton. They do not
care, they do not care, the rachitic engines of his plane kept beating in his ear:

"The trouble is that neither the politicians nor the intellectuals
have really been hit by the depression—the people that ought to
supply the ideas—I've done unusually well myself this winter—
I suppose that nobody at the conference was in anything but
very comfortable circumstances."

The guilt of his own material comfort was with Wilson all that
terrible year. A week later he was in Brooklyn, piecing together
the histories of three different persons who had tried to kill themselves in separate dustbins of that borough on March 25, 1931.
All were unemployed. The widow of one of them told Wilson
that "the Italians who come to America and go in for racketeer-
ing have wonderful opportunities, but there is no place for a
skilled machinist."

Edmund Wilson spent May Day of 1931 at the opening of the
new Empire State building. He observed that business was so
bad that only a quarter of the Empire State's office space was
rented and that this monument had no function "in the hour
when the planless competitive society, the dehumanized urban
community, of which it represents the culmination, was bankrupt." Death was all about him that year. Wilson counted
forty-eight corpses, one a suicide, which had gone into the construction of the Empire State. The next day, he went over to
Buchanan, New York, to write about a bankrupt storekeeper who
had shot himself and his three sons. He returned to Washington
again with a Socialist delegation to see Mr. Hoover, and was
snubbed even by the President's secretary; he came home to
write about a man on Second Avenue who had shot his landlord.

He watched a strike at Kelly's Creek colliery in West Virginia.

A Vassar girl was teaching the miners the words of "Solidarity Forever" by chalking them on a blackboard in a schoolroom. He saw in people like her, none of them Communists, "the conviction, the courage and the will . . . which makes them do thankless work and take chances which few *middle-class* people care to face." And, in the face of this girl's purity of purpose, American businessmen seemed to Wilson "such half-baked and half-educated people that they are no longer capable of giving any kind of leadership." A new generation of radicals was marching to capture their power, "convinced and cool-headed revolutionaries, with a clear idea of their relation to society and of America's relation to the rest of the world."

For Edmund Wilson saw a terrible beauty struggling to be born, the hand of a great cleanser preparing to sweep away the rubble and the dross of a dying civilization. The depression's consequences touched his pity, but its possibilities raised his hopes. He could not avoid a certain satisfaction at the ruined lives of so many of the "fatuous"—brokers, bankers, and bond salesmen. "The money-making period of American history has come to an end."

To Wilson, Herbert Hoover was "stupid and timid"; the Russian Communist leaders seemed by distant contrast "men of superior brains who have triumphed over the ignorance, the stupidity, and the short-sighted selfishness of the mass." For he was, after all, primarily a writer, and he felt "a special interest in the success of the intellectual kind of brains as opposed to the acquisitive kind." And, Edmund Wilson concluded at the end of his year with reality, "we shan't know what morals and manners or science or art can be till we have seen them in a society of sound people run for the common good."

One reason why the serious writer is apt to be an alien is because he thinks he is passionate and so many other people seem to him apathetic. That was a problem of Edmund Wilson's in the twenties when the rule of commerce appeared invulnerable; it remained his problem as he rode the ruins of America at the onset of the thirties. He was overwhelmed by the conviction that we hung over the abyss and that nobody cared. His was a journey into the American brush very different from the joyous forays

Henry Mencken used to take in search of boobs in the twenties. At this moment, Mencken's old enemies were losing even the illusion of control; they were jumping out of windows and they were postponing the dance at the Country Club; they seemed unable to assert even the excuse of capacity for command. Now Wilson was journeying in search of hope. He found it in a very few places and among a very few people, dedicated and committed revolutionaries.

Mencken did not ask for hope; he needed only amusement. He had, as he affirmed with pride, no more social conscience than a cat. He sat in Baltimore all through Edmund Wilson's rootless, desperate voyage into the storm and, in 1932, he went to the national political conventions, in Chicago, interested in nothing except legal beer—the one issue, by the way, which stirred the common people in the galleries to any show of passion. And, as he sat there heaving beer bottles at the Republican platform committee, Mencken was in his twilight as a god to many of those who had been his acolytes ten years before.

In the twenties, Mencken had been a great shield to Sherwood Anderson, a lost and groping man like the persons in his stories. In the summer of 1932, Anderson came to New York looking for hope as Wilson had sought it across the country the year before. Anderson thought he had found his reward in the faces of the young Communists talking on street corners:

"Among these fighting young Communists," he wrote to the *New Masses*, "I found poverty, youth and no gloom. . . . If the movement to free all men from the rule of money means the submerging of our class, let us be submerged. Down with us. Let's have no starving workers to save us."

Anderson's cry of "Down with us" was in key with Wilson's guilty reflection on his own comparative immunity from the prevailing chaos. Only a poet could have proclaimed himself so consciously ready to be submerged if man could be saved in the process. The poet accepts oblivion; his lessers seek survival.

The hope which Anderson and Wilson found in the faces of the Communists was a very fleeting one. Even in 1930, Wilson looked at the Communists with an eye less dazzled than Anderson's. That October, he had watched Congressman Hamilton

Fish questioning William Z. Foster, the Communist leader, and was distressed to see creeping into the speech of the militant American workingman the "idiom of Russian Communism." Foster seemed to Wilson then unpleasantly aware "of the awful eye of the Third International upon him—itself a secular church that rivals the sacred ones." But at the end, matching Foster against Ham Fish, Wilson decided:

"In the presence of the Communists today, the representatives of our 'Republican form of government' seem conspicuously lacking in either moral force or intellectual integrity."

And so, in the 1932 election, Edmund Wilson could only throw his vote to William Z. Foster, now the Communist candidate for President. Even at the time Foster was a strange choice for Wilson, who had such close ties with the more gradualist progressives who had joined the *New Republic* in supporting the Socialist Norman Thomas. But a moment had come when none of the elements of the old American order, including its historic progressive opposition—so earnest, so often defeated a part of it—seemed to Wilson even tolerable. The Socialists, after all, were part of the established order; they had elected mayors in such cities as Milwaukee, Reading, and Bridgeport, Connecticut; and the storm across America blew over these islands as unabated as anywhere else.

In this transient period in Edmund Wilson's life, Foster seems to have represented total alienation and revolt against established society. To support him was to accept an onrush of the will to subversion more rooted in the will to create than any Committee on Un-American Activities could ever understand.

This impulse to destroy was not a new one to American writers, and it had less relation to the depression than Edmund Wilson thought. Right near the end of the boom, James T. Farrell, apprentice novelist, was living in a New York YMCA, ragged by choice, raging by alienation, an affliction to his fellow tenants, all earnest volunteers in the army of commerce. Even the best of these Christian young men were to Farrell only "philistines with tolerance." And, one night, before a table full of them, he flung out the words of Mikhail Bakunin, the nineteenth century anarchist:

"The urge to destroy is a creative urge."

The urge to destroy which at once shook Edmund Wilson of Princeton and James T. Farrell of De Pauw ran all through the twenties. Mencken was, after all, a gloriously destructive force. In his assaults upon the *booboisie* he must be considered as one of the prime creators of the New Deal he hated. And the proletarian novelists of the thirties were his children too, however deformed. Their revolt into literary conformity was just one more chapter in the writer's response to alienation. And their John Reed Clubs, their immolation into the May Day parades of the early thirties, their fugitive creations, seem after twenty years like one more version of those fortresses of the spirit of Greenwich Village in the twenties, the "art and love warrens," over which Mencken laughed so loud and whose occupants he cherished with a tenderness no later American critic would show.

*   *   *

As a Foster supporter, Wilson was asked by the *New Masses* to give his reasons for moving left. His answer was simply that he had always had the same general tendencies. Like many other writers who were at once the best and the most fleeting recruits to the concept of a Soviet America, Edmund Wilson's revolt had been born in the twenties and not in the depression.

Even before 1929, John Dos Passos was well along into *U.S.A.*, the loving fabrication of legend that ran below the façade of the American dream, a kind of substratum of rebellion and defeat, with a major character who carried the red card of the Industrial Workers of the World and with intermittent portraits of men against the stream, of Big Bill Haywood and Robert M. La Follette, of Randolph Bourne and Jack Reed, of their West against John Dos Passos' East. The committed of the thirties would cherish *U.S.A.* as their epic, but the twenties created it. Dos Passos' rebellion, like Wilson's, was an aristocratic one. Dos Passos, sooner than most of the literary rebels of the twenties, had reached out to the working class as an ally against the rulers of society. But he had learned enough about the workers to know that theirs, by his standard, was an existence as empty of true poetry as that of other Americans. He celebrated them but he was not really fond of them. The only really attractive proletarians in *U.S.A.* are immigrant anarchists.

U.S.A. is the hardiest survivor of the social literature published in the thirties. In that context, there may be something revealing in Dos Passos' choice of the historic heroes whose portraits he scatters through it. There is a sketch of John Reed, a member of the Harvard Club who was buried in the Kremlin, and another of Paxton Hibben, Princeton 1903, who laid a wreath on Reed's grave and, as a consequence of this and other social outrages, was subject to a mock lynching at his twentieth class reunion. To the outsider, this may appear a slightly disproportionate representation from the Big Three. But Dos Passos was a Harvard man who both hated and loved the old school. He had a special sympathy for the aristocratic rebel because he was one himself. The aristocratic rebel is, of course, performing an act that is no less commendable for having an aesthetic character; he is not always comfortable with ill-bred people. *U.S.A.* is unusual for the thirties, not merely for its depth, but for the expression of special feeling for the sort of radical who feels drawn back to Old Nassau.

Dos Passos supported the Communist ticket in 1932. But, just before the election, he sat in Madison Square Garden at a rally celebrating the October Bolshevik Revolution and felt even in this audience "the old sense of loneliness and abandonment." There were just a few moments when he could catch "the tremendous intoxication with history that is the great achievement of communist solidarity." Most of the time Dos Passos, like Wilson, longed to believe; but the evidence for belief was somehow lacking.

Never again would the Communists find as many men of real creative substance ready to declare themselves for the Party's entire program as came forward for Foster in 1932. He got fewer than 100,000 votes, but that was no measure of quality. The Communists failed with ordinary Americans, but they had succeeded for a time with some extraordinary ones.

"Culture and the Crisis," the manifesto issued by artists and writers supporting the Communist ticket in 1932, declared without equivocation "for the overthrow of the system which is responsible for all crises . . . the conquest of political power, and the establishment of a workers' and farmers' government." The Communists, narrow in so many other matters, have always been tolerant of the motives of their recruits, and this was a mixed bag indeed. It included plebeian writers, new and raw, who hated the middle class from below, and it included intellectual aristocrats like Wilson and Dos Passos who hate the middle class from above.

Next to those of Sidney Howard, the playwright, Sherwood Anderson, and Dos Passos, the names that shone brightest on Foster's shield were those of persons who had not before been conspicuous for political concern and whose affirmation of revolutionary impulse might easily have been mistaken for the final entombment of the gospel of art of the twenties.

There were the poets Léonie Adams, Horace Gregory, and Alfred Kreymborg. There was Slater Brown, who had gone to France in World War I as a volunteer ambulance driver and had been interned by the French with e.e. cummings in *The Enormous Room*. There was Waldo Frank, once editor of *The Seven Arts*, who had been occupied with Spain since the middle twenties and had emerged into the future in 1931 with *Dawn in Russia*. There was Matthew Josephson, the playboy of the revolution of the word in the twenties, who had previously been identified with movements with names like *secession, transition,* and Dada. And there was Malcolm Cowley, who had also driven an ambulance, and been a friend of Dada in Paris and a model in New York for Ernest Boyd's unfriendly composite *Portrait of an Aesthete* in the old *American Mercury.* *

---

* Dada was the most extreme of all post-World War I Europe's attacks on the conventional in art. Malcolm Cowley's *Exile's Return* contains the best summary of Dada—a word deliberately without meaning which united a group of artists and writers who aimed to "outdo the politicians in lunacy." The Dadaist manifesto declared that "any work of art that can be understood is the product of a journalist." The Dadaists thought that men have so little in common that they cannot even expect to communicate with one another. The world is round; after Dadaism's collapse, many of its leaders took their impulse for total destruction into the Communist movement—Louis Aragon as a Stalinist and André Breton as a Trotskyite. Aragon submitted a paper to the 1935 American Writers Congress under the title: *From Dada to Red Front*. He described himself then as a factory worker reporting to his

For Cowley and his friends social rebellion was a new turn and the passion they brought to it seems more rhetorical now than they knew then. Cowley was the most articulate historian of their highly complicated state of mind, and his *Exile's Return*, published in 1934 and revised in 1951, is their best testament.

That segment of his generation for which Cowley speaks tended, by his own account, to have been spectatorial by disposition and uninvolved by choice. Their youth had been very unlike that of the anarchist generation which fled to Greenwich Village before World War I. Cowley and his friends "had never broken with our parents, never walked stormily out of church, never been expelled from school for writing essays on anarchism. We had avoided issues and got what we wanted in a quiet way, simply by taking it.

"We had lost all our ideals at a very early age and painlessly. . . . We believed that we had fought for an empty cause, that the Germans were no worse than the allies, no better, that the world consisted of fools and scoundrels ruled by scoundrels and fools, that everybody was selfish and could be bought for a price, that we were as bad as the others. . . . Either we thought of our real home as existing in the insubstantial world of art, or else we were simply young men on the make."

This conscious farewell to banners had brought no special happiness in the twenties. It was a time when "hardly anyone seemed to believe in what he was doing." Cowley tried to place himself in the outer spaces reached by Joyce, Eliot, and Paul Valéry; the word "cold" is recurrent in his recollections of his days at their worship. His own country was in the hands of persons to whom, as a writer, "he felt a professional hostility. . . . The same social mechanism that fed and clothed the body was starving the emotions, was closing every path toward creativeness and self-expression."

"Some of us had accepted too much from publishers and Wall Street plungers—too many invitations to parties and week-ends, too many commissions for work we really didn't want to do, but it

---

comrades. Frank, Cowley, and Josephson, who had been sympathetic spectators at the Dada circus had, by 1932, become sympathetic spectators of the Communists.

paid well. . . . We became part of the system we were trying to evade and it defeated us from within, not from without; our hearts beat to its tempo."

They had felt no compulsion for an affirmative stand against this state of things in the twenties; of all his generation, Cowley remembers only John Dos Passos as a political radical then; the others had been indifferent to politics. Cowley and Allen Tate and Hart Crane used to sit in a Village restaurant matching poems while the *New Masses* board burned and glowed unattended at another table.

Now, the early thirties looked to Cowley and some of his friends like "a wildly hopeful time." He was writing *Exile's Return*, a literary autobiography embodying his decision that communism in the thirties was the logical terminus of the wandering course he had described in the twenties. But, even then, Cowley's was a commitment primarily literary. He remained a spectator and he confessed in 1934 that, as "a petty bourgeois critic," he was debarred from complete involvement.

But the conversion of Frank, Cowley, and Josephson was no less important for being only partial and fleeting. Each of the succession of myths which have sometimes comforted and sometimes afflicted our national life appears to require a ritual burning of the myth which preceded it. And one of the regular attendants upon this ceremony is a witness to the cold and empty character of the myth to be cremated and the grandeur of the myth to be elevated in its place. Whittaker Chambers has been such a witness against the thirties to the fifties; and Malcolm Cowley, however less intense and however less involved, was a witness against the twenties to the thirties.

Cowley and Josephson represented a cluster of less fortunate young men, intellectuals *manqué, declassé,* and *de trop,* and torn between past and future. These were persons of primarily literary disposition; by a defect of quality or a defect of fortune, they had not yet made their way as well as Cowley or Josephson, and their sense of failure and personal impotence carried a note of desperation into their conversion. They were advertising men who both hated their jobs and feared to lose them, college instructors struggling in the second division of academia, and writers who had followed the fashion of the casual and the uninvolved and now felt the future turning toward the rhetorically intense and enmeshed.

The interior storm of persons like these, who differed from Cowley and Josephson in want of success and degree of hysteria, is best preserved in Tess Slesinger's almost forgotten *The Unpossessed*, a novel about a desperate little corner of New York culture in 1932. Its three prime male characters are graduates of the class of 1921 at a university which sounds like Columbia. One teaches English there, another is a starveling copywriter, the third is the author of indifferent novels whose indifference has been especially marked by the critics of late because they are barren of social content. Each in his way is a failure at love. All three are sterile by choice. None are Communist Party members, but all feel a compulsion to sympathize. They hope for escape by establishing a magazine, that most timeless of exits: this project is timely because it will celebrate at once the religion of art and the religion of the Soviets.

As their angel, they fix upon a vacuous doll of a lady of quality, who agrees to launch their project with a dance, its guests the New York gentry, its purpose to solicit funds both for the magazine and a Communist hunger march on Washington. The witches' Sabbath of this wassail is the grand climax of *The Unpossessed*. At its height, Bruno Leonard, the academician, rises to read the manifesto of his magazine to the assembled Philistines, loses his notes and his self-possession, and is carried away into a haunted exposition of the desperation of some intellectuals in the year 1932:

"For too long, we have wandered unorganized, unwitting members of the lost tribe, the missing generation, the forgotten regiment, outcasts, miscast, professional expatriates . . . we are scared until the blood in our veins runs thin, and we hop from one faith to the next because to believe is too unbearably exactly what we want. . . . We have no class; our tastes incline us to the left, our habits to the right; the left distrusts, the right despises us. . . . Have you read today's assignment in Pushkin, young man? 'Strike me dead, the track is vanished, well, what now? We've lost the way . . .' "

Upon that note, the society orchestra breaks forth; the guests commence to dance on uncaring, and Bruno seizes one of his Communist students and implores him:

"Go west, young man, go south, go north—go anywhere out of our god-damned city. . . . My friends and myself are sick men if we are not already dead. . . . Listen you kids, get out of it, get out of it while you can, leave us rotting in our blind alley, we've lost the way, we've dug ourselves in . . ."

And so Bruno's acolyte goes off to the healthy air of the hunger march; his love whirls off with the newest of her other men; and, in a final triumph of the stone over the flower, the wife of his comrade, the copywriter, has a stillborn child.

The Unpossessed is almost our only surviving document on a group of intellectuals who were drawn to the Communists early in the thirties and left them very soon. Its models are chiefly interesting because persons like them were in the vanguard of that literary counterrevolution which in 1936 saw a number of *New Masses* contributors resolve the dilemma between art and propaganda by leaping most of the way to art with *Partisan Review*. Most of them thought of themselves for a while as left socialists, varyingly appreciative of Leon Trotsky, a particularly unfashionable position at the time. Since their political views were hardly viable, they became by force of circumstance purely literary men. From this position, they carried on an offensive against various communist debasements of culture in the thirties. It was a noble and valuable work, although, now that Howard Fast is almost the only surviving exemplar of Communist culture, one sometimes wishes they would direct their attention elsewhere.

The characters in *The Unpossessed* are quite possibly the most unattractive specimens in American literature prior to the works of Mary McCarthy, who visited her savagery on a group very like them sixteen years later in *The Oasis*. Miss Slesinger was in the process of divorcing herself from the set and removing to Hollywood. *The Unpossessed* is accurate enough to be considered still a *roman à clef;* the putative model for one of its major characters is now an editor of *Fortune,* another a critic of notable powers, and the third the editor of a monthly magazine. All are anti-Communists, and it would be surprising if any could recognize himself in Miss Slesinger's portrait of his storms in 1932.

But they, rather than Cowley, are typical of a special sort of intellectual who thought of dedicating his capacities to communism in 1932. Cowley was calm and they were hysterical. But they represented the mass of that group of the elite which formed the first significant American writer-type to move toward the Communists. It was an elite not of origin so much as of attitude; like Wilson, its members hated the middle class from above. Its motives were disgust and alienation; it sounded most rhetorical when it spoke of "hope," and emptiest when it spoke of identification with the working class. It represented an aesthetic rather than a social tendency. Its members were valuable as adornment, but they had the good fortune to be barred by the Communist Party's attitude toward aesthetics from long or total enlistment in its cause. Wilson, who had been almost the first of the intellectual elite to attempt a serious self-conversion, was almost the first to leave; after 1932, he returned to his library and began a decade-long critical study of the Bolshevik prophets which bore important fruit in *To the Finland Station*. Cowley remained as guide and counselor to a number of younger writers more formally committed to the Communists. But, by 1936, most of the aesthetic rebels had gone; what remained behind were social rebels practicing aesthetics as a revolutionary weapon.

*   *   *

For the impulse of Wilson, Cowley, and the less controlled spirits of *The Unpossessed* had very little to do with what was to be the largest, and promised to be the most important, segment of writers who moved toward the Communists during the depression. For the truly involved of the Party's literary recruits were not expatriates coming home with luggage empty of Dada; they were not teaching in universities or in touch with angels unaware of the implications of supporting them. Many had not even been to college. They were plebeians; their Mermaid Tavern was a cafeteria on Fourteenth Street in New York or the John Reed Club in a loft in the Loop in Chicago or the office of the *New Masses*. All other doors seemed closed to them.

The American literary tradition has never been especially tolerant of the plebeian writer; to think of established literary figures who fought his battles is to remember William Dean Howells and Mencken almost alone. The plebeian has felt otherwise condemned to beat his wings against what he considers a barrier of Eastern literary snobbery; he feels afflicted alike with sparseness of material and harshness of expression; he makes his critics uncomfortable.

Sherwood Anderson, to take one instance, was held by New York literary society throughout the twenties in grudging, often flagging, esteem. But he was always a god to the plebeian writers of the midlands, because his loneliness expressed their own. Even Dreiser wrote very often about the great world; his characters move through a fluid society. Anderson cannot conceive of any such fluidity. His characters are bound by circumstance. Their search is for an escape; their world is a large, empty room, its walls covered with representations of doors, each labeled "Exit" and each false.

In the early thirties, Anderson, Waldo Frank, and Dos Passos were each at work on his own novel of social protest. Each thought of his design as at least loosely informed with revolutionary prophecy; they had all voted for William Z. Foster in 1932. It is perhaps a measure of the impermanent stamp of any exterior influence on the serious writer that the three books they wrote each differed so profoundly from the others. Dos Passos' *U.S.A.* was up to his best work; Anderson's *Beyond Desire* and Frank's *The Death and Birth of David Markand* are generally inferior to their standards; yet all three bore a characteristic individual impress that was at war with what they intended to do.

The characters in *U.S.A.* are in the main humbly born; they move into the great world so swiftly that they prefer to forget the existence of their parents. The experience of the climber is central to Dos Passos; in *U.S.A.*, his ascent is an act of patricide so unconscious as to be almost peaceful. He is seldom trapped by love or hatred for his roots; in a number of cases he is at most ashamed of them. *U.S.A.* accepts the tradition of equality of opportunity in America; it is most savage in its expression of how hollow and mocking are the rewards of opportunity grasped. Dos

Passos' social conscience is most passionate when he is an aristo-crat protesting the rule of commerce. His quarrel with liberals and advertising men alike is a poet's quarrel: they have sold themselves to convention, comfort, and conformity.

Waldo Frank published *The Death and Birth of David Mar-kand* in 1934. He dedicated it to "the American worker, who will understand" and could hardly have been expected to. David Mar-kand is a businessman living before World War I and afflicted with an emptiness which drives him to leave his family to search for truth. His search lasts four years and carries him all over the country; it is largely interior reverie and sexual fog ending with an acceptance of revolutionary socialism. David Markand re-flects Frank's own search for some promise in the American jun-gle. He comes closest to peace teaching the children of factory hands and finding in them "a race of buried dreamers." Waldo Frank was in search of a substitute for God. Near the end of his pilgrimage, Markand meets John Byrne, a revolutionary, who tells him: "If I did not have faith in men, I'd be a Christian like my father. You must . . . while you live . . . have faith in something." Frank, like Dos Passos, had remained true to his consistent impulse. *The Death and Birth of David Markand,* whatever its original design, was a tract for the wandering, cere-bral man; it had nothing to say to the anchored, acting proletarian whose search was not for reconciliation with himself but comfort for his kind.

But Anderson's *Beyond Desire* was rooted in the plebeian tra-dition. Its hero, Red Oliver, is typical of Anderson: he does not know what he is doing. He is a town boy working as a textile hand in Georgia, alienated from town and mill village alike. Dur-ing a textile strike, Red joins a riot on the side of the workers; in the confusion both sides assume that he is fighting for the com-pany. As he sits in the town library and is drawn to the Com-munist prophets, Red Oliver wonders: "How do I know that I give a damn for people in general . . . for their suffering . . . it may be all bunk."

Beyond Desire, like so much of Anderson, was written at a buried level of consciousness. For his characters as for him, com-munism could be a new religion, only they do not know just what it is. His mill girls wonder about communism with minds to whose area of experience even the characters on a movie screen seem alien. One of them longs for Communists to come to the mill only because she wants the worst. Red reflects that the trouble with being a Communist is that even there you get blocked.

Beyond Desire closes when Red Oliver is killed by the state militia in a strikers' camp in North Carolina, to which he has wandered a stranger. Just before he dies, he thinks: "I'm a silly ass." And the lieutenant who kills him thinks: "I'm a silly ass," and pulls the trigger. The doctrine toward which Anderson was groping and from which he soon wandered away could not remove him even for a little while from those depths of doubt, fear, and loneliness in which he worked and which are the habitation of the plebeian writer.

Dos Passos' Richard Ellsworth Savage, a spoiled poet in an advertising agency, and Frank's David Markand, a regenerated businessman, both played against the great world: the first was corrupted by it; the second saved his soul by escaping it. Each had a choice. But Anderson's Red Oliver had no real choice; he felt blocked whatever he did; his world was almost too narrow for decision. Of the established literary figures who essayed the revolutionary novel, only Anderson wrote as a plebeian, with the plebeian's loneliness and sense of entrapment.

But most of the young novelists who turned to the Communists in the depression had an impulse like Anderson's. In 1932, Richard Wright, who was not only a plebeian but a Negro and thus under a double curse, was living in Chicago with his mother, who could not have lived farther from his longings if she had been wearing a handkerchief on her head somewhere outside Natchez. One day, one of his white friends announced with pride that he had sold a story to *Anvil*, the Communist literary magazine. Wright ought to meet the people around *Anvil*, his friend said; they would teach him how to write. Richard Wright answered that no one could tell him how or what to write. Still he took *Anvil, Left Front,* and a few other little magazines of the left home with him, and that night Richard Wright found that he was not alone:

"Out of the magazines I read came a passionate call for the experiences of the disinherited, and there were none of the lame lispings of the missionary in it. It did not say: 'Be like us and we will like you maybe.' It said: 'If you possess enough courage to speak out what you are, you will find that you are not alone.' It urged life to believe in life.

"I read on into the night; then toward dawn, I swung from bed and inserted paper into the typewriter. Feeling for the first time that I could speak to listening ears, I wrote a wild, crude poem in free verse, coining images of black hands, playing, working, holding bayonets, stiffening finally in death. I felt that, in a clumsy way, it linked white life with black, merged two streams of common experience."

The phrases, "call for the experiences of the disinherited," "you are not alone," "I could speak to listening ears," all express the loneliness inherent in the beginnings of the plebeian writer. The most important thing after all was to feel that you were not alone and hunched over your feeble candle in the night. No one owed Richard Wright a living, but somebody owed him a home. Mencken, the great fostering father of so many inglorious Miltons in the twenties, had departed. Only the Communists seemed to take his place.

The new plebeian writers were so largely unknown in 1932 that few had the prestige to earn listing on the elite roster of writers for Foster. But they were young and could believe that they were the future. They did not feel lost or tired or bankrupt. Some of them felt that they were the precursors of a new kind of American realism that would open up subjects and explore a side of life neglected in the literature of their country. They would find their poetry in the world of urban poverty from which so many of them had come and which only the sociologists and the census takers had penetrated before them.

Success at that search alone might have given them an important, if moderate, place in American letters. But they dreamed of more. The past had been destroyed for Cowley and Josephson; these their juniors thought of themselves as legatees of the future. Most of them assumed that plebeian realism would in the end come to dominate American literature and that the proletarian poem and the proletarian novel would outlive James and Joyce and Yeats and Eliot, because history was on its side.

They crossed under that impulse into the Communist movement. To some of them, this passage did not mean joining the Party; but, for all of them, it meant writing for the *New Masses*, marching at May Day parades, and joining the American Writers Congress, which was proudly revolutionary in the early thirties. All of them thought of themselves as revolutionary writers and as Communists, even such of them as did not join the Party. All of them, for various periods, felt themselves, if not subject to party discipline, at least subject to the Communist aesthetic concept.

They were novelists like James T. Farrell, Richard Wright, Nelson Algren, Edward Newhouse, Robert Cantwell, Henry Roth, Edwin Seaver, Edward Dahlberg, Edward Rollins, Myra Page, Clara Weatherwax, William Cunningham, and Jack Conroy; and poets like Isidor Schneider, Alfred Hayes, and Sol Funaroff. Except for Algren and Farrell, all were able at one stage in their lives to believe that art is a weapon or it is nothing and that its first test is whether it is on the side of history.

Farrell, as one of their survivors, is perhaps the most articulate witness to the impulse which had made them writers and revolutionaries. Farrell had been rooted in a world harsher even than Anderson's; the process by which he had broken with his family had not been the forgetting and moving on so characteristic of Dos Passos' plebeians, but rather a savage tearing of the manacles and consequent wounds that took a long while to heal.

The poverty of the plebeian writer's environment follows him wherever he goes. Farrell once said that a writer's style is his childhood; in middle age, he chose to put on the title page of his *Bernard Carr*, a terrible reflection of Anton Chekhov's:

"What writers belonging to the upper class have received from nature for nothing, plebeians acquire at the cost of their youth."

When Farrell went to the University of Chicago, he had seriously described his entrance as a confrontation of the Torch of Learning. There were ways in which he was the best-educated young writer of his time. He had read philosophers well outside the realm of discourse of conventional critics; he was a deep, though perhaps narrow, student of history; he had great resources in the European tradition. He was a perceptive enough critic to argue for William Faulkner in the early thirties, when Faulkner was at his peak of creation and his nadir of reputation. He was certainly better educated than Hemingway and Fitzgerald, who in many areas were not educated at all.

Yet he was, and always would be, received as a barbarian in the genteel world of the literary supplements, just as Theodore Dreiser had been, because poverty had blunted his fingertips and left his work heavy with passion and deficient of charm. A distinguished journalist once heard Farrell speak at a literary forum and came to him afterward in honest wonderment that he could speak English.

The plebeian's survival was an act of the will almost from the nursery. When Dreiser died, Farrell wrote him a farewell that would have seemed bathos from anyone else; in Farrell, it had some of the majesty of Dreiser's own mastery of the cumulative cliché: "We have lost a man who made the way easier for many of us. . . . His work encourages us to struggle. . . . Farewell, Theodore Dreiser, you, creator of titans, were a greater titan yourself." Farrell's world, like Dreiser's, was one whose inhabitants understood the price the artist pays. They looked at the New York literary world and thought it commercial, supercilious, logrolling, and absolutely alien.

The plebeian writer had to talk about the world in which he grew up; he had to write about a drab and barren existence; he did not after all feel qualified to write about any other kind. He could not write romance, because there was so little romance in his life; he could not write with easy grace because there was so little grace in his life.

All that circumstance and environment qualified the plebeian to write, in his apprenticeship at least, was what Edward Dahlberg called "bottom dog" literature. Dahlberg, a close friend of Farrell's and like him a short-time friend of the Communists, was the author of *Bottom Dogs,* a depression novel written before the depression and a kind of vanguard stab into the new naturalism. Its protagonist was a vagabond and its last line was:

"Something had to happen; and he knew nothing would. . . ." Dahlberg had been himself "a vagabond everywhere"; he had been born in a charity ward, been weaned in two orphanages, spent his adolescence in the slums of the labor market, and, by a kind of miracle, escaped to Columbia University.

D. H. Lawrence wrote an introduction to *Bottom Dogs* that was at once a salute and a warning to the plebeian writer. Dahlberg's style, said Lawrence, was "the bottom-dog mind expressing itself direct, almost as if it barked. . . . This is a genuine, if objectionable book. . . . I don't want to read any more books like this. But I am glad I read this one, just to know what is the last word in repulsive consciousness."

But the Marxist critics were less guarded. Michael Gold, a Communist and a plebeian writer of the twenties, hailed the first novel of Jack Conroy, one of the new naturalists of the thirties, as "a significant class portent . . . a victory over capitalism. Out of the despair, mindlessness, and violence of the proletarian life, thinkers and leaders arise." Gold was celebrating the struggle out of which a plebeian comes; it was an understanding which seemed to his juniors unique among critics, and it kept many plebeians with the Communists long after the association brought them any assistance as writers or rewards of the spirit.

Among all the enemies of the plebeian writer's promise, none lasts longer than self-pity. In 1934, Dashiell Hammett brushed off Clifford Odets' *Awake and Sing* with the observation that the arts had little to hope for in a man still weeping because he did not have a bicycle when he was twelve years old.

Farrell was of different clay, and his recollections of his colleagues in the first days of the new naturalism are always recollections of self-pity and forced emotion. In 1932, he came back from Paris deep in debt and stopped around at the *New Masses* to tell Whittaker Chambers that his child had been stillborn. Farrell remembers best of all from that conversation Chambers' brooding impassivity. Eighteen years later, Farrell again met Chambers, who said he had never forgotten that day because Farrell's story seemed to him the essence of tragedy. "And what was tragic about it?" said Farrell. "I was young; it was life."

When the thirties began, there was a flowering of low-born

realists and their work did not go entirely without appreciation in established literary society. Mencken opened the *American Mercury* to Jack Conroy, Michael Gold, Albert Halper, and Farrell. *Hound and Horn* bought Ben Field's *Cow*, a still-vivid portrait of a Communist farmhand, and *Story* published Nelson Algren's *So Help Me*, which was about hobos. But the new and the subtalented had no home except in the little magazines of the left—*Blast*, *Dynamo*, and *Anvil*—those now still, and always small, voices of revolution, which held out the same shelter to the incompetent socialist realist that the fleeting flimsies of the *avant-garde* had offered the incompetent imagist of the twenties.

The Communists offered a man a place in print; they would help him write, or help him not to write, a form of assistance cherished by some sorts of writers. They offered the plebeians a community. The standards of a calling are somewhat the same in all classes; and so, Alexander Trachtenberg, of International Publishers, the Communist imprint, was an enormous figure with the young left writers of the early thirties. After all, he controlled a printing press.

By 1934, Edmund Wilson's jitters were over, and he had gone. His successors were young and raw; they felt something like surety that the future was on the side of the forces of revolution. The so-called depression novel appeared to be flourishing. A congeries of John Reed clubs was issuing little magazines where young writers sang the stirrings and movings of the toilers. The new literature had attained a volume, if not a quality, to justify the issuance of an anthology of *Proletarian Literature in the United States*. Joseph Freeman, who had carried on through the lonely twenties at the *New Masses*, could exult in its introduction, "Revolutionary literature is no longer a sect but a leaven in American culture."

After the depression, Freeman wrote, "Writers and artists, like other members of the educated classes, began to read revolutionary books, pamphlets and newspapers; they came to workers' meetings; they discovered a new America, the land of the masses whose existence they had ignored. They saw these masses as the motive power of modern history, as the hope for a superior social system, for a revival and extension of culture."

Freeman thought he was describing an experience universal to his craft. But, even in 1934, the interest of the elite he was describing was ebbing, as it had ebbed for Wilson. With the exception of a few of their elders, most of the writers who remained as the hope of socialist art were themselves from the masses of which Freeman spoke. They were plebeian in origin; they had started as naturalists by disposition. Now they had become revolutionaries, and had turned to the practice of that "socialist realism" which was the Communist critic's name for his own special brand of romantic fiction.

The Communists believed and sometimes said frankly that agitation was the writer's main function. When a writer came to them, he was expected to recognize that his craft was secondary to a number of more compelling considerations. It could be argued, as an instance, that Whittaker Chambers, who is remembered for something much different, was the purest Bolshevik writer ever to function in the United States. Chambers was the author of a few short stories, formalist invocations of revolutionary epic, which had been hailed in the Soviet Union as models of Communist literature. He had then put off his mantle of high priest to become an underground Party activist in 1933. Chambers was one of the most public underground recruits in history. The revolutionary poets around the *New Masses* office debated his choice; it appears to have been their consensus that he had taken a path more important than literature.

Chambers' commitment was already imminent when he had his talk with James Farrell in the *New Masses* office that afternoon in 1932. They talked about art as a weapon, and Farrell said that it was his intention to write and think about writing in other terms. Chambers replied that writers like Farrell would be forgotten in ten years. Farrell said that he was not afraid of oblivion and went home to his basement apartment in the Village, leaving history behind him.

The Communist view that the writer was a recruit into the army of history carried with it the traditional Communist faith in empty celebration and rhetorical posture. By its rules, the writer must be a member of a community of the orthodox; he must belong to an organization of writers and it must unfurl banners like those of the army's other regiments. This special barracks was the American Writers Congress, which began in 1935 as the annual convention of the League of American Writers and which expired in 1941 after wriggling through the Nazi-Soviet pact.

When the Writers Congress convened in 1935, there remained a few men of standing in the old world of letters who could arise and tell the plebeians that they were the new world of letters; it appears to be a function of middle age to tell youth that the water is fine even though middle age hangs back from jumping in itself.

Malcolm Cowley and Matthew Josephson were not Communists, but they believed that the young writer was wise to be one and could give him better reasons than he could give himself. Josephson told what it meant to create in the Soviet Union:

"Writers address a colossal public; cheap editions are circulated by the State Publishing House in amounts of six or more millions, at literally a few pennies a copy; and, as a consequence, writers, being paid on a royalty basis, enjoy a peculiarly favorable position. The security, the prosperity that I noted in Russian writers offered a striking contrast to the condition of writers in my own country, where a very few may succeed in earning somewhat meager livings, establishing them among the lower-paid workers in the community, while the majority starve in garrets still.

"It seems," Josephson ended, "that there is only one way out, that, before we can raise the status of workers in the field of literature, there must be a social revolution."

This must have been a glowing dream to all the madly hopeful young men there present, because, even in the presumed height of the proletarian fashion, very few of them were selling their stuff. Very few indeed were even writing it. The delegates to the first American Writers Congress included a high quotient of Party and left-wing union professionals, whose major works were even then preserved, if at all, on mimeograph stencils. At one session of the Congress, Merle Colby, a transient visitor, deplored the low rate of production of his colleagues. "There are," he said, "about 300 writers here, and perhaps we produce an average of ten or twelve books a year. Let us stick to our lasts."

But then their prime function was service to the revolution;

the best-selling live author in the Soviet Union, as Josephson did not have to say, was a politician named Joseph Stalin. And the revolution was, as Cowley said, a "new source of strength" for a writer. To join its army was to enter a movement which "allies the interest of writers with a class that is rising, instead of the interests of a confused, futile and decayed class."

And Cowley turned and surveyed the vast history of man's creation and fetched up the bones of writers who had blazed when they were radicals and been gutted when they lost that faith. Arthur Rimbaud was a major poet "when he caught the energy of the French working class" and nothing when he lost it. Wordsworth's decline is traceable to disenchantment with the French revolution. Blake was immortal when he called himself a Jacobin; then he "too became disillusioned, he decided that the first revolution must be in 'the soul of man' and he wrote those prophetic books which nobody reads precisely because they are not worth reading."

The revolution could give a man, Cowley indicated, the gift of prophecy. "It gives the sense of human life, not as a medley of accidents, but as a connected and continuing process . . . it gives the values, the unified interpretation, without which one can neither write good history nor good tragedy."*

Cowley was not one of the committed and he was there mainly as ornament. He confessed himself unable by condition and vestiges of class heritage to contest for the glories of this vision; they belonged to the young and the plebeian. And it was a vision whose canons required of a serious writer actions and passions unusual in literature. Its ideal was the writer at once conformist and activist; its heroes were Alexei Tolstoy, so attuned to the Soviet temper as to pass the test of sweeping success with the builders of socialism in factory and farm, and André Malraux,

---

* The notion that the Marxists-Leninists alone knew what they were doing exercised a special temporary fascination for a number of persons like Cowley who otherwise described themselves in his words as "highly class-conscious petty bourgeois critics." In September, 1932, Clifton Fadiman wrote the New Masses that he had turned left because he had found his "old point of view inadequate for the interpretation of events, particularly cultural events." The deadline was the beast in the jungle of Fadiman's critical existence; this was a brief clutch at certitude by a man professionally required to display a measure of assurance in a time of total doubt.

an intimate of history whose works were composed in the intervals allowed him between Shanghai and Madrid and the other frontiers of revolution.

And, when we think what the image of the revolutionary writer was, we may understand why so many of the young expected too much for themselves or even why some of them felt a kind of contempt for their craft. There were very minor protests among the delegates to the American Writers Congress of 1935, when Jack Conroy, author of *The Disinherited*, stated his aesthetic credo:

"To me a strike bulletin or an impassioned leaflet are of more moment than 300 prettily and falsely written pages about the private woes of a gigolo or the biological woes of a society dame about as useful to society as the buck brush which infests Missouri cow pastures and takes all the sustenance out of the soil."

Jack Conroy had begun, like so many of the other plebeians, writing the depression novel. It was an unvarnished kind of literature and one without much grace; but it had certainly not been uncompelling in Farrell's *Studs Lonigan*, Dahlberg's *Bottom Dogs*, Nelson Algren's *So Help Me*, or Henry Roth's *Call It Sleep*. At its best, plebeian naturalism held the hope of a fiction describing life in those buried portions of society which American literature had generally neglected in the past. This was a respectable and even exciting concept. But now hope had come to these younger naturalists as the Communist Party—a sort of overlay of fantasy upon reality—and the shift of fashion for them was to the Party novel.

In essence, their new source of inspiration was the Party of Struggle and Liberation introduced into the life of bottom dog as an element containing within itself absolutes of art and truth above the limitations of the literature of the past. That impassioned leaflet which Jack Conroy found of such transcendent moment was a Party handbill. A politician does not violate the meaning of his life by declaring that a handbill is more important than a novel, but a writer has larger problems. If he makes history the judge of his work, it is enough for him that his interior quarrels be set aside and the correct analysis of an historical situation put in their place. Literature is after all the product of doubt and self-quarrel; when Cowley spoke of the overriding inspiration of the revolutionary temper of the working class, he could not be blamed if some in his audience heard his words only as an argument for Conroy's scorn of careful writing and Chambers' desertion of literature for the career of a professional Bolshevik.

By 1935 and for just a little while thereafter, the prescribed form of revolutionary expression was the novel of Communist Party struggle to free the working class. The Communist Party habitually generalized from the particular, and its new art form was called the proletarian novel. It was, of course, the Party novel, which is something very different.

One of the myths of the fifties is that the proletarian novel dominated the literature of the early thirties. It did have some fashion as a notion; there was a sense that, after all, this might be the future. William Faulkner, then in his greatest period, was dismissed with more assurance than many nonpolitical critics could bring to Jack Conroy.

But, in point of fact, even while the proletarian novel was being discussed with most intensity, very few writers were producing it. Its canons were as sharp, rigid, and enclosed as any prescribed by older traditions; a disenchanted Cowley once compared it in structure to a Petrarchan sonnet. The story line was basic and always reiterated. The novel began with a community of workers, on factory and farm, at first divided and unaware, then opening their eyes, hesitant and afraid, being broken and at last regrouping for final combat, having learned from defeat that there are no halfway houses, that the Party is their only ally, the owning class their only enemy, and that they have a world to win.

The proletarian novel was thus rooted in the American tradition of bad literature. Its formula was: boy sees vision of exploitation, boy goes on strike, boy finds vision of freedom. It stood the popular short story on its head, but, like that story, it preached that success is material and that its rewards are to the strong and the assured, not the weak and the doubtful. The proletarian novel's hero was an Alger boy who had learned that the road upward is blocked and that the future is with him who looks to his own class. On occasion, he has his chance to live with the daughter of the bourgeoisie and chooses to die with the daughter of the toilers.

The standards of the proletarian novel were so demanding as to amount almost to a conspiracy against the writer. That may be why the sum of its product in pure form is so much smaller than the accepted recollection might believe. It attained its full flower, indeed, near the moment of its death in Clara Weatherwax's *Marching-Marching*, winner of the *New Masses* prize in 1935, an award never to be repeated, because there were no further orthodox adventures into "the novel on a proletarian theme."

Marching-Marching met the canons with a fidelity approaching parody. Its working-class characters are unexceptionably developed and intelligent Communists. One, a crippled old lady, is a Bolshevik bibliophile: she collects Party pamphlets. The nonworking-class characters are all fascists; the vigilante band signs its warning notes with the swastika.

One young hero is the putative illegitimate son of the mill owner and a wage slave; his proletarian blood turns out to be pure. He is a bastard, but a working-class bastard; his mother's last words were: "Live poor and fight." He became a Communist in college after picketing a fascist banquet in Seattle with 1,500 workers under the red flag and hearing them shout "Free Thaelmann."

The girls in *Marching-Marching* are uniformly uninterested in such distractions from the struggle as personal adornment; one of them reads in a fashion column: "Styles this year will be soldierly," and thinks, "Making people war-minded." They understand: "Capitalist society makes suicides"; "Whatever happens to us, the movement will go right on; no matter what they do to us —beat us, kill us, jail us—they can't stop the working class"; "only the workers stand by the workers." The lumber workers' union unanimously boos down its AFL "mis-leader" and deliriously applauds a speaker who addresses the audience as "comrades" and bawls out, "You've got to know who you can trust: the Communist Party . . ."

Marching-Marching offers in sequence: the accidental death of a lumberman; the slugging of Pete, the boss's putative bastard by a group of workers who think he is a spy; Pete's affirmation of his class by assaulting his supposed father; the kidnaping and beating of Mario, a Mexican Communist; the suicide of a displaced old peddler; a successful gang-up on Filipino strikers by Filipino scabs (the use of Caucasians on this mission would be "bad from the racial split angle"); a raid on workers' homes by the Vigilantes who beat their occupants and destroy "pianos, books, literature and household furniture"; and a final march on the militia by an unarmed body of strikers which closes the book upon a note of imminent massacre. Such was the proletarian novel's prescribed quota of violence.

Miss Weatherwax, an amateur, had attained a perfection never reached by professionals who essayed the proletarian form. Proletarian novels almost as faithful to the canons as *Marching-Marching* and thus of interest as curios include Jack Conroy's *The Disinherited* and *A World to Win,* Grace Lumpkin's *To Make My Bread,* Fielding Burke's *Call Home the Heart,* and Leane Zugsmith's *A Time to Remember.* Edwin Seaver's *Between the Hammer and the Anvil* offered characters so deliberately faceless that they were even named Mr. and Mrs. John Doe.

But all in all, the sum total of proletarian fiction was very small and very fleeting; the entire movement was conceived in 1932 and interred with Miss Weatherwax in 1935; and, by any standards of orthodoxy, it cannot be said to have produced as many as ten published works. Certain widely admired novels of the period, which are sometimes described as being in the form, did in fact such violence to its canons as to be not proletarian novels at all when we consider the degree of fantasy required in the genuine article. Steinbeck's *In Dubious Battle* was, for example, so detached in its treatment of a Communist as to bring upon its author's head the Party's curse for anarcho-syndicalist deviations. Robert Cantwell's *The Land of Plenty* was most effective in its closely observed account of the process of labor; it is an echo of Zola's *Germinal* without an identifiable Communist character.

James Farrell, Richard Wright, and Nelson Algren, three still-functioning social realists who were close to the Communists in the early thirties, never even essayed the proletarian novel. For the Party, after all, asked too much of its young plebeians, who of all people may have been least qualified to bring conviction to the celebration of the myth inherent in a novel like *Marching-Marching.* The writer's impulse is one which develops with some degree af alienation and isolation. Most of the Party's writers had been bottom dogs themselves. They knew the working class too well to expect any miracles from it; they might think of themselves as Marxist-Leninists and still remain disqualified from inner conviction that the people with whom they grew up were capable of that seizure of light which would transform them into the creatures of revolutionary epic.

No writer can carry on very long until he has assimilated his own environment. The myth of the moral superiority of the proletarian was a barrier to that assimilation by any plebeian. Later on, when the canons of Communist art became more flexible, a number of apprentices to the proletarian form were able to move easily into radio or Hollywood and the presentation of an image of the common man so one-dimensional, so hyperbolic, and so contrived as to be totally removed from reality. The proletarian novel was a training school in the manipulation of stiff cardboard dolls.

*   *   *

If the proletarian movement was never really a writer's revolution, it was even less of one for readers. Even in 1935, Henry Hart wailed to the American Writers Congress that very few proletarian novels made any money. The problem was something more than the "conscious and unconscious fascism of book and magazine publishers." There was no detectable audience for the new fiction.

"It requires a sale of 2000 copies for a publisher to get back what he has invested—before he can make anything," said Hart. "Cantwell's *Land of Plenty* had the largest sale—3000 copies. Jack Conroy's *The Disinherited* sold 2700, but of these, 1000 were sold at a considerably reduced discount. William Rollins' fine novel, *The Shadow Before*, has not sold anything. Novels which you all know and have read and admired have sold less than 1000 copies.

"Sales such as these mean that the bourgeois publishers are going to refuse to publish our novels. At the moment it is still possible for a publisher to say, as one of them said recently, 'It's smart to be a Communist.' But, and I have heard it already said, proletarian novels don't sell."

The wait for the revolutionary future was no great problem for Cowley or Josephson or Dos Passos, who were established literary men. But the plebeians had no place to go. The Party continued to hold out the promise that it would open some broad channel to make the proletarian artist a popular success, but it never found one. They did not search; they only sat and waited, those of them who did not go to Hollywood, reciting their litanies; and, whether in Hollywood or New York, the sap went out of them.

They sat in a school where the instructors were cheer leaders and where the students could expect exemption from classes any time they agreed to join the band or scrimmage with the varsity. It was not their fault that the faculty was so inadequate; Cowley was a guest lecturer on infrequent occasions; Wilson came not at all; Dos Passos was on a perpetual sabbatical; and those who remained were either academic hacks or men so torn within themselves that they had no strength to help others.

These young men had taken fire originally from the promise that the literature of a new class could convey a special strength and feeling impossible in the literature of a dying society. They had felt outside society and blocked by what they considered the *snobisme* of literary gentility. They had thought they were entering a world where log-rolling, back-scratching, and politics would give way to Bolshevik self-criticism, and that, with such inspiration, there were no limits for them. And they had come to a narrow little corner whose canons were tight, whose prescriptions were harsh, and whose orthodoxy had hardened to a degree unapproached by the literary society it promised to displace.

When James Farrell began his association with the revolutionary writers, almost the first thing Edwin Rolfe told him was that it was wise to be careful and mind his business and never mention Leon Trotsky. Farrell was a hot rod; he picketed Ohrbach's; he got drunk in public to the chagrin of his new comrades, who kept trying to remind him that a revolutionary writer was a public figure with a responsibility for his dignity. It was Farrell who suggested that the 1935 session of the American Writers Congress be closed with the singing of "The International." Afterward, Alexander Trachtenberg, the Communist publisher,

came up and remonstrated that this was the kind of childish gesture sure to arouse the sprites of the capitalist press.

They were all very conventional young men and more than
anything else they feared the taint of bohemia. They were at
once devoid of education and the smallest desire for it. Edwin
Rolfe treated Farrell as an object of awe because he had read
Alfred North Whitehead and could thus move on a plateau of the
intellect beyond all the rest of them. But, as a group, they were
scornful of knowledge without direct revolutionary function; Sol
Funaroff, the Communist poet, complained that Pavlov had
wasted his time with those salivating dogs. Funaroff's hero was
the Soviet poet Mayakovsky who had turned his notable talents
to the composition of advertising slogans for the Government
Universal Store ("There is no place for doubt and thought/
GUM sells all a woman needs"), and was assumed to have attained universal truths sealed to Yeats and Eliot.

They read each other's books, and Gorki's and maybe Martin
Andersen Nexö's, and the literary section of the *New Masses,*
which, as Farrell said, was a pogrom, with every review reading,
"The crisis is sharpening, the proletariat is rising and this book
is no good." And they found that to be orthodox was the only
test, except for the established and the assured, who could be
forgiven aesthetic deviation so long as they kept a segment of the
political faith.*

---

* The *New Masses* reviewers scratched backs with a fervor that should
shame any commercial publisher. The November 24, 1936, issue contained
reviews that at once described Faulkner's *Absalom, Absalom* as "dull reading" and Westbrook Pegler as "an honest, courageous and observant journalist." Pegler earned his citation for sending greetings to that year's Communist Party convention. Steinbeck and William Saroyan were kindly treated
for a few weeks after they signed a call to a Western Writers Congress in
1937. But Steinbeck and Saroyan did not bother to show up, an antisocial
display which the *New Masses* proceeded to punish by declaring *Of Mice
and Men* a "mess of sentimentality and insidious innocence" and by deciding
that the only positive aspect of Saroyan's work was "the pathos of his intellectual predicament." Saroyan replied that he assumed that "inasmuch as
I have no use for Communists, Communists have no use for me." Farrell
threw dead cats at the Marxist critics throughout the early thirties; he was
forgiven for the sake of his prestige. Not until 1936 did Morris U. Schappes,
a Torquemada from City College, cry out in the pages of the *New Masses,*
"How long, oh Farrell, how long . . ."

By 1936, they had almost lost the power to believe in themselves. That was only five years after Edmund Wilson's voyage after hope, and already the dream of a revolutionary literature was lost. Many of the early converts were gone by now; those who remained had accepted the rule that the future belonged to the trustworthy; a writer's responsibility was celebration and not contemplation. They could not even argue the value of what they were doing; Robert Forsythe, the *New Masses* critic, faced up to the dead end of the proletarian novel by arguing blithely that the novel was an outdated form and that the revolution needed some other means of expression.

More and more of those who remained turned to simple malignity, making bad rhetoric of the quarrel with others because they were forbidden to make poetry of the quarrel with themselves. One *New Masses* critic expressed in print his wish that a rock would fall upon Farrell and kill him. After the Austrian Socialists were destroyed, Alfred Hayes composed a poem about Otto Bauer, their leader, who was even then hiding from the police: "All honor to them, Bauer! For you/ History prepares a shameful grave/ A nameless spot buried under weed and stone/ Where creeping jackals shall come to howl/ Stirred by ancient kinship with those bones!" To read that poem and to think that its author once gave his mother the pangs of birth is to understand why, if the Old Testament God and all his vengeance did not exist, man would have had to invent them.

Wilson and Anderson had articulated the mood with which the left began the thirties. It had been a mood of search and acceptance of submersion. In five years, they were gone and their places had been taken by young men whose search was over, whose instinct was survival and who had traded rebellion for conformity.

They had, of course, no one to lead them and no Mencken to defend them. Farrell did what he could; he kept telling them that a book was not a good book merely because it was on their side and about poor people, and that the proletarian novel was fatally weak because its characters had no souls. But, by 1936, Farrell could stand no more; they were even forbidden to read him; the lesser ones understood, as Cowley had of Yeats and

Joyce, that Farrell's was a lonely road. Ten years later, Albert Maltz, facing expulsion from the Communist Party, would declare that he did not wish to face Farrell's fate. Farrell's fate, the unspeakable, was to walk alone.

Dos Passos could have helped them, but he was so far away. He sent a message to the American Writers Congress of 1935 that warned them:

"No matter from how narrow a set of convictions you start, you will find yourself in your effort to probe deeper and deeper in men and events as you find them, less and less able to work with the minute prescriptions of doctrine; and you will find, more and more . . . that you are on the side, not with phrases and opinions, but really and truly, of liberty, fraternity and equality."

Dos Passos' message arrived too late to be read; they might not have listened to it anyway. A writer can blame, not party nor friend, but only himself.

They became one-novel men. Edward Dahlberg and Henry Roth, who for all their revulsion had held out the promise of a revived concern with a subterranean slum world, wrote nothing communicable after *Bottom Dogs* and *Call It Sleep*. The promise that they could assimilate their youth and then move on to the far more difficult task of assimilating their present died somewhere; the proletarian writer's present was not permissible matter for discussion; there was nothing between his past and his future.

By now, the prescriptions of doctrine had begun to shift. The proletarian novel had dried up and been replaced by something very different. In 1937, two years after *Marching-Marching*, Edward Newhouse defined the difference in his *This Is Your Day*, the last flurry of the proletarian manner. John Chamberlain described Newhouse as "the proletarian Hemingway," but *This Is Your Day* was almost purely a Party novel. Its locale was a farmers' strike in upstate New York, but its Communist hero's heart is always with the unit meeting he left behind in New York and he has no larger problem than the reconciliation of his wife, a casual young Communist in college, to the realities of the struggle.

With Newhouse, the proletarian novelist abandoned any effort to reach the workers and aimed at a public of young Communists torn between a career with the bourgeoisie or with the Party. *This Is Your Day* is choking with overtones of which *Marching-Marching* was totally unconscious: the hostility of Communists to workers, the perils of reflection and doubt, the necessity for deceit, and the sense of clinging to a sect—all those things which turned the Communist Party into a conspiracy, and were at work upon it long before the Nazi-Soviet pact which drove Newhouse out.

For, by 1937, the Party had laid aside the tocsins of revolution; anti-fascism was a cause demanding peace with all classes; in that cause, the movies were judged a medium more important to the future of man than the novel and the radio more important than the poem.

The bias of both these triumphant media was toward normality. *This Is Your Day's* Communist hero is designed to be just like the rest of us: he goes to taverns; he is an initiate in the Yankee dugout; he sleeps with other girls when his wife is out of town. From the same perspective, the proletarian poets turned to the composition of unrhymed and flatulent periods celebrating the promise of America; in no other time in our literary history were so many vast burlesques of Walt Whitman presented so seriously.

When the American Writers Congress met again in 1937, Waldo Frank, having protested the Moscow trials, had disappeared as chairman. He was replaced without ceremony by Donald Ogden Stewart, whose current literary reputation rested on his facility with light dialogue for actresses whose *haute couture* would have seemed the ultimate in fascist symbolism to the girls in *Marching-Marching*. There was between Frank and Stewart a terrible void in approach to the artist's responsibility; with Frank, almost the last of the serious and intense departed, and the trivial and the purchasable took its place. The poets were gone, and the journalists remained.*

* Ernest Hemingway and Archibald MacLeish were among those attending the 1937 Writers Congress; they could hardly be placed any lower in the scale than Frank and Dos Passos. But Hemingway and MacLeish represented an anti-fascist rather than a revolutionary approach; socialism was not central in their lives as it had been in those of Dos Passos and Frank.

The shift from rebellion to fashion was the only favor the Party could have done for some of its plebeians; with it, their flesh survived their spirit. Popular culture replaced proletarian culture; the *New Masses* offered unregarded pleasantries to Fannie Hurst; such of its contributors as Albert Maltz went to Hollywood; and others went into radio. The Henry Roths, the Edward Dahlbergs, and the Robert Cantwells, who left the Party's orbit, and the Jack Conroys, who remained, abandoned the craft of creation entirely; a whole literary movement had been born, cried up, and was now entombed after barely five years. We cannot say that its younger members would have been great novelists; but some of them might have been respectable ones, and now they had perished.

The fifties are a graveyard for young writers whose art was molded by the myth of the thirties. The author of one of the most admired proletarian novels of the period is now a magazine critic. Numbers of his contemporaries buried themselves in Hollywood to be disinterred and cast to the winds by the House Committee on Un-American Activities. Another once young proletarian novelist is a hopeless soak in Chicago; a former revolutionary poet writes empty novels of derivative passion.

There were 300 delegates to the first convention of the League of American Writers; of the younger ones, only Richard Wright, James Farrell, and Nelson Algren can be described as engaged any longer in the craft of the novel as against the pursuit of a living down its byways. No segment of a literary generation can be said to equal this one for self-destruction: just one per cent appears to have survived twenty years.

It was, for all its noise, a small and narrow world and with an impact remarkably superficial. Writers are a peculiarly vulnerable group. The college short story which dealt with the strike against war and fascism has been succeeded in our time by the college short story which deals with the search for God in some far-off country; the authors of each genre share an imminence of mortality, poetasting being an impulse common to every generation and changing only in form and fashion. It is very hard to find many of the young men who were inspired to write a novel by reading the *Communist Manifesto;* would it be any easier to trace the young men who were inspired to write a novel after reading *This Side of Paradise*?

And yet there is a difference: it could be argued that those writers who were young and touched by the myth of the thirties and still survive as functioning novelists were men whose real character and will to survive was formed by the twenties. Farrell can stand for all of them; in the twenties he went to church one day and refused to kneel. It was a youthful gesture, but of the twenties; the refusal to kneel was not characteristic of the committed of the thirties.

Man always hates his last blind alley; the more typical social realists of the thirties were sure that they were guillotining the candle-burners before the altar of art of the twenties. They did not realize that the revolution which they had rejected was both more fundamental than the one they were now accepting and better for the character. It could well be that for the committed at least, whether as artist or politician, the twenties were really the revolutionary era in America and that the thirties were a kind of folding of banners, a surrender to formation, the process by which a guerrilla army introduces the epaulet and starts calling the comrade commander the Comrade General.

Yeats said once that "Evil comes to us men of the imagination wearing as its mask all the virtues. I have certainly known more men destroyed by the desire to have wife and child and to keep them in comfort than I have seen destroyed by drink and harlots." The idea of the social revolution came to the writers we remember here dressed as the noblest of enterprises and wearing the mask of inspiration. It did not tempt them to dangerous or evil acts. After all, only Whittaker Chambers among them became a spy, and he escaped. It only destroyed them as writers, because it caused them to abandon the quarrel with self.

The storm which beat around Edmund Wilson's head in 1929 also tossed the proletarian writer to its surface. But it was an exterior storm; the tumult which beats inside every writer as long as he lives as a writer could not be abated by any cloak against the winds outside him. And so each of them, in his way, lost his cloak, and each of the best of them carried on in his way after his loss. Edmund Wilson was the first to lose his cloak, and he departed to quarrel with himself in his library.

John Dos Passos lost his cloak very soon thereafter. Still in December, 1936, he sent the *New Masses* a letter wishing that someone would return to "what we used to call the Movement, that upsurge of revolt" that had been a buried glory of American history. He cried out one more time for "the old, romantic, libertarian creed," and then he ceased to travel and went back to his library to quarrel with others. He thought that the Communists had destroyed his movement; Dos Passos hated the murderer so much that he forgot the victim. The romance of the Movement had, after all, been only one of its glories; the impulse against human suffering had been another.

Dos Passos was conditioned to dislike Roosevelt, because he thought of Roosevelt as the heir of Woodrow Wilson, the arch enemy of the radicals of the twenties, and as a temporizer and a confidence man. He disliked the Communists for making Roosevelt their temporary idol, and he disliked Roosevelt almost as much for becoming an idol. And, at the end, Dos Passos came to sum up the thirties as a conspiracy against the liberties of mankind, and to believe that the CIO had been organized by Communists, that the New Deal had been created by charlatans and cretins, and that honesty and devotion had somehow passed from the land. He could write about the Washington of the thirties only in the language of caricature; he had quarreled with the Communists so long that, by 1954, in *Most Likely to Succeed*, he could no longer describe them as people.

The thirties had been many things, some good and some bad, but it had been most of all a great economic revolution at whose end children no longer worked in factories and assembly hands spoke unafraid to their foremen. It had not changed the souls of men—no economic revolution could—but nothing entirely evil could have produced the healthiest generation of children that America had raised in a century.

In *A Handful of Blackberries*, Ignazio Silone, a social realist who also survived a Communist experience, makes Rocco, his ex-Communist hero, say to an Italian policeman:

"Leave the ignominies of distant countries out of it if you please. Look at this countryside, this landscape spread before your eyes, this land, this poverty that is so immemorial, so flagrant. The protagonists of the iniquity you see in the landscape are certainly not those unfortunate wretches of the party."

Communists and confidence men are not the entire landscape of the thirties. The party was never central for Dos Passos. He was not even quarreling with his old self when he quarreled with it. He had been wounded, and he could not walk his way any longer, and he was almost a ghost clanking chains he had never worn.

Still James T. Farrell carried on as he always had. He did not write easily and smoothly; he remained the plebeian writer painfully setting down the record of childhood and youth, his subjects buried people, his enemy time; and money and success meant to him only the stuff to go on. He had written twenty-seven books; some of the critics had given up on him long ago because his style did not please and his subjects seemed to them flat and literal. But those were questions of the limit of his capacity; they had nothing to do with Farrell's real triumph, which was in being true to himself and his calling.

Twenty-two years ago, he had argued it all with Whittaker Chambers and said at the end:

"Neither man nor God is going to tell me what to write."

In that narrow corner of self-surrender, those words had a wild, free ring; they have it still, even though time has not always been good to James Farrell, as it is seldom good to any of us. For he was the figure of an heroic idea; just to become a writer had been for him a fierce act of the will; just to continue as one, alone, meant the remorseless exercise of that will until it became a matter of wonder whether it had a bottom. He feared not defeat or disaster but only that time to come when he must cease to try.

All of this had nothing to do with Farrell's permanence. If he must pass, he would pass as a figure of tragedy and there would be a passion to his going that there had never been in the generation of his lost Communist friends who grew up with him and allowed themselves to smoke out so long before him. For he had felt no impulse to the warmth of an exterior flame; he almost alone could accept the prospect of oblivion and he almost alone would blame no one else for his fall.

So many of the other plebeians were gone, their graves unmarked; but he had remained a poet, awkward perhaps, doomed perhaps, but a poet still possessed by the passion which gave him birth.

5

DYING DREAMS sometimes last longest in hearts they have broken; hate, after all, can be the strongest of memories. That may be why so much of whatever pain and passion is left to the myth of the thirties is carried by its lost lovers, its apostates, and its armed disenchanted.

The most conspicuous, although not the most typical, ex-Communist of the fifties is a witness against the thirties, violent, vengeful, and insistent, as he was in the thirties, that he alone understands and that all save him are soft and apathetic. In this manifestation he remains, as he was then, the committed soldier in a society of noncombatants.

The roots of the apostate seem to me very complex ones and not to be described by words like renegade and turncoat, which are, after all, no more enlightening than words like Trotskyite and fascist were on his lips in that first phase of his commitment. For the thirties have bequeathed us a very mixed company of men still spiteful and cankered by their memories.

André Malraux once explained his departure from the revolutionary left by saying: "Communism changed; I didn't." It is difficult now, looking at the history of communism since the death of Lenin, to see where it has changed or been untrue to itself. But Malraux is right in his implication that men very seldom change; try though we will, beneath all the shifts of exterior doctrine, our hearts so often remain what they were.

And the committed apostates in their passion at least represent an almost intact image of those who burned with the myth of the thirties. To stand for them, I have chosen Dr. J. B. Matthews, who was never a Communist but a convinced revolutionary Marxist who describes himself as the most fervid fellow traveler of his time.

Matthews has become the grand archivist of the thirties and the guardian of their dead file. He is our leading collector of letterheads of the many deceased and few surviving Communist fronts, a former research director of the House Committee on Un-American Activities, and, very briefly, staff director of Senator Joseph R. McCarthy's Permanent Subcommittee on Investigations.

He makes his living now as a private consultant on the Communist problem, chiefly for the Hearst Corporation. He has become almost a rich man as a consequence of his commitment, his disillusion, and his long struggle against those who he says are still clinging to the lost vision of his youth. He lives well in the society of persons who are, like him, successful in the material sense. The rewards of apostasy as a profession are, I think, exaggerated; but, if anyone has been blessed with them, it must be J. B. Matthews.

J. B. Matthews came to consciousness first as a believer in the Methodist God. That belief carried him through successive stages of pacifism, commitment to the class struggle, and disenchantment. He is best known today for his public insistence that a significant number of Protestant ministers are under Communist influence. It has been the irony of his later years to be condemned to despoil the graveyard of his youth. However you judge the merit of that destiny, it has, I think, its quotient of tragedy.

In writing about J. B. Matthews and his circle, I have found his own *Odyssey of a Fellow Traveler* an especially valuable source. But most of all, I have to thank Matthews himself because he consented to talk for some hours last winter about his memories, a very generous act in a man who had no reason to expect generosity from me.

He has come so far from his commitments of only twenty years ago that he would like to believe that he has very few commitments today. He said again and again that he was simply a professional and that he enjoys his work and brings very little passion to it. But going through his life, I was struck over and over by how much the same J. B. Matthews has remained through what seems on the surface so wandering a history. Under that impulse, I have perhaps flawed my narrative through inability to resist anticipatory comparisons between the J. B. Matthews of 1934 and the J. B. Matthews of 1954. For it seemed to me that his passion was the same all along.

This is a book about believers and what the consequences of belief were for them. One of those consequences can be apostasy. I have chosen J. B. Matthews among so many other apostates because I think that he is and always has been a believer. He has come, after so much, to explain himself away as a pure professional, just as his enemies do. But money as an explanation for apostasy seems to me like lechery as an explanation for infidelity; it is a substitute for a lost, earlier passion and it is dross to the truly committed. It is what men take when the salt has lost its savor.

O'er Moor and Fen

J. B. Matthews and the Multiple Revelation

"Lead, kindly light, amid the encircling gloom,
Lead thou me on!
The night is dark, and I am far from home,
Lead thou me on!
Keep thou my feet! I do not ask to see
The distant scene; one step enough for me.
I was not ever thus, nor prayed that thou
Shouldst lead me on;
I loved to choose and see my path; but now
Lead thou me on!
I loved the garish day; and, spite of fears,
Pride ruled my will; remember not past years.
So long thy power hath blest me, sure it still
Will lead me on
O'er moor and fen, o'er crag and torrent till
The night is gone;
And with the morn those angel faces smile,
Which I have loved long since, and lost
awhile. Amen.

> JOSEPH HENRY NEWMAN, 1833; translated into
> the Malay by Joseph Brown Matthews in Java,
> 1916

"Ye are the salt of the earth; but if the salt have lost its
savor, wherewith shall it be salted? It is thenceforth good
for nothing, but to be cast out and to be trodden under
the foot of men"——Matthew, 5:13

J. B. MATTHEWS remembers his father as a big man with a
mustache stained by tobacco and other substances and with
a very worldly view of life. He served in the Kentucky legislature and was so practical a statesman that he was generally re-

garded as the lobbyist for the Louisville and Nashville Railroad.

J. B. Matthews' father put his son to work for a summer, when the boy was only six, carrying water to quarry laborers. He beat him severely for laughing in Sunday School at a Methodist circuit rider in white flannels. J. B. Matthews' father had founded the Sunday School; he was also a man who enjoyed his whisky, and J. B. describes him now as having had the look of an old pirate. He appears to have been a citizen typical of Hopkinsville, Kentucky, where his son, Joseph Brown, was born in 1894.

In Hopkinsville, God and Satan wrestled to a draw in almost every man; it was a town mixing public sin with public repentance; men shot at one another in feuds and shouted together in Methodist meeting halls. J. B. Matthews saw his first murder when he was six; he must have seen his first revival when he was much younger. There is every sign that, when he was young and reedy, the old Adam in his father appalled him. For the younger Matthews loved most the noise of the lower Protestants at their worship.

Hopkinsville, after its Saturday saturnalias, was the Sunday seat of shouting Methodists. On those Sundays, he remembered long afterward, "everything dark was as simple as sin, and men needed only to repent and be saved in order to set everything right."

He does not appear to have cherished Hopkinsville except in its interludes of prostration before the dark, vengeful Old Testament God. When he went to college in 1910, he remembered best those moments and he envisioned "the whole world's becoming something very much like a Kentucky Methodist meeting house, with its resounding hallelujahs." He does not appear to have remembered any other aspects of Hopkinsville, including his mixed and ambivalent father, with any such enchantment. For, when he finished college in Kentucky in 1914, he commenced the wanderings that lasted him a full generation and he never betrayed an inclination to come home until 1938.

The Kentucky meeting house must enchant the child it does not repel. The intoxication of its climaxes beat on little Joe Matthews then with a rhythm he would seek all his life, for it was his singular quality always to know in a flash without ever having learned, to burn with one absolute faith and to lose it for another, to catch the new revelation as though from the electric air, and always to believe with absolute assurance and to cry out for others to believe with him.

When he finished college, he went almost at once to Java to bring Jesus to the Malays. His hope then was for the evangelization of the world. The Bolsheviks swirled through St. Petersburg, Lenin proclaimed the seizure of power, the Soviets were enthroned, and J. B. Matthews was translating 102 Protestant hymns into the Malay language.

He came home in 1920 to teach at Scarritt College for Christian Workers in Tennessee. By now, he had been reborn to a faith less comfortable. He had become a pacifist and an advocate of equality for Negroes. In this new revelation, he was, as he later apologized, "terribly in earnest about the Christian social doctrine." No one in all Tennessee could claim such arduous labor for Robert M. La Follette's 1924 Presidential campaign. J. B. Matthews would speak anywhere without fee, for he had learned that the only thing more pleasant than attending a revival is speaking to one.

Scarritt was not an especially broad-gauged institution, and Matthews' tireless tongue quite soon began to afflict its trustees. After he had spoken for La Follete one Sunday night in Memphis, the local Methodist conference officially censured him, first for desecrating the Sabbath with a political utterance, then for sharing the platform with a Unitarian, and last for speaking in a theater.

But even after this public citation as hall boy to the Woman of Babylon, J. B. Matthews lingered on in Tennessee as an unending source of discomfort to the unenlightened. He delivered pacifist speeches to the American Federation of Labor; he appealed without success to the legislature to enact the child-labor amendment; he and the more earnest of his pupils defied the statutes enjoining the separation of the races.

Tennessee, along with much of the Middle South in the twenties, was a sort of social Sahara intermittently irrigated by oases of Christian social doctrine. Those oases knew the traveler Matthews and extravagantly admired him. A long time afterward, in disenchantment, he still held on to the flaking newsprint of the Southern church periodicals and was proud of adjectives like "classical in thought, powerful in delivery, tender in appeal" and of nouns like "deep spirituality, the exaltation of Jesus in his own life."

He carried on, a flickering candle in the night, until 1927, when, by mutual consent, Scarritt College suffered him to be snuffed out. His letter of resignation, the more welcome for being unforced, was a calm statement that he had only taken the Christian position in advocating freedom and justice for the Negro.

He was out of work, with a wife and two children to worry him, but he was proud of his choice and regretted nothing of it. Not until twenty-two years later did he wonder aloud why he was worshiped by so many people while he was breaking traditions and scourged by so many when he turned to upholding them. At the time, his consolations did not seem small. There was, for example, the round-robin letter from Scarritt graduate students all grateful for "that Christian ideal you so perfectly manifest." The Negroes, who do not forget even if they are not rich, provided some part-time teaching at two of their colleges. Matthews was still welcome as an unpaid speaker on his old platforms. But there was no permanent place for him in the South.

Most of all, there was no place for him in Hopkinsville, and if there had been, there was no impulse to return. And so, in 1929, he went to New York, like so many exiles before him, uprooted and displaced, a minister of the gospel without a church.

He had suffered as a pacifist; he was renowned for his touch with unformed youth; and the Fellowship of Reconciliation was very glad to acquire him as its executive secretary. The F.O.R. was the largest pacifist organization in America; even so, it had fewer than 8,000 members, and these represented a special kind of Christian conscience in the twenties. A majority of them had voted for Norman Thomas in 1928, a year of general social apathy. They were, of course, socialists of the ethic; J. B. Matthews was only following their temper when he joined the Socialist Party on November 6, 1929, having concluded that end of capitalism would mean the end of war.

The day after he accepted his commitment to the F.O.R., Matthews was invited to take the chair of Hebrew at an Eastern university. Afterward, with ashes in his mouth, he would wonder how different it might have been if he had taken that earlier chance to withdraw from the challenge of his time.

Chance is a force measureless in human affairs, but it seems hard to believe that the J. B. Matthews of 1929 could have been tempted by safe harbors. He was thirty-five years old, lean, ascetic, and believing in what he had done. The whole meaning of his life, since Java, pointed to this terminus as an ill-paid, itinerant apostle of universal peace; and, at thirty-five at least, men are jealous of the meaning of their lives.

For J. B. Matthews had a maw rapacious enough for any over-riding nostrum; first the vision of Methodism bestriding the world, then the vision of pacifism without borders or frontiers, and after a while the vision of Marxism universal. For him, each new dose of the truth beyond argument carried its own antidote to its displaced, competing truth. All his successive potations neither damaged the larynx nor affected the speech. The revelation which sat now upon his right shoulder may have but lately elbowed off some equal, previous revelation, but no sense that tenants were fleeting or leases short-termed ever showed upon Matthews' face.

The Fellowship of Reconciliation had never known as energetic an administrator. Matthews has always been appreciative of praise from any quarter, and he still preserves letters of gratification from his colleagues there, all full of awe that any man could be in so many places at once. He remained four years with the F.O.R. As at Scarritt, he was uncomfortable well before his departure. The gentle tones of pacifism already sounded a little thin in the pyrotechnics of New York. Matthews had discovered Karl Marx and the tossing foam of a Madison Square Garden meeting dedicated to his gospel.

It no longer seemed so clear to him that peace was to be cherished above all else. He had become a revolutionary Marxist. The F.O.R.'s inhibitions about means seemed less important to him than Marx's overmastering passion for ends.

The present director of the Fellowship of Reconciliation is A. J. Muste, an old radical who has returned to pacifism after a long journey in pursuit of strange gods. He knew Matthews well in the early thirties, when Matthews was a pacifist and Muste thought of himself as an independent Marxist-Leninist.

"Pacifism," Muste says, "is a matter both of resistance and reconciliation. Every pacifist is both reconciler and resister; and some are stronger in the one than the other. J. B. was always a little strong on the resistance side."

Few men like to confess that their emotions sit higher with them than their intellect, and J. B. Matthews has always asserted that reason and study changed him from pacifist to revolutionary Marxist in the early thirties. He aimed, he said, "at the complete mastery of Marx, and, for this mastery I *acquired* all the books." We may wonder whether he read them. He appears to have become a Marxist without reading more than the tiniest fragments of Marx, and we may surmise, without injustice, that he did not read Marx until he had become an anti-Marxist, which is a piece of intellectual history common to his period.

For, in the days of his commitment, there was hardly time to read anything. The good Lord, in any case, had blessed J. B. Matthews with more powers of speech than of reflection, just as He had stuffed him so full of faith and hope as to leave small room for charity. But these were times when he and his votaries felt more compulsion to be enchanted with his qualities than perturbed by his defects.

Matthews saw what he wished to see, and he had no need of books for knowledge. He visited the Soviet Union five times between 1927 and 1932. On his last trip, he took a group through the Ukraine. One of his sheep pointed to the existing famine, and he as her shepherd insisted that there was no such thing, and, anyway, look at India. He knew how to protect himself against shocks of recognition.

In 1935, Harry Lang, an old Socialist, wrote a detailed account of this same famine for the Hearst papers. Without reading Lang, Matthews faithfully denounced him for the *Daily Worker*. The state of mind he describes as "my Marxism" was an inoculation against scrutiny. Matthews says himself that, in all his years as a revolutionary, he very seldom read the *Daily Worker*.

The depth, the symmetry, the sense, and the syntax of J. B.

Matthews in those days may best be summarized in an excerpt from a speech he made to a Communist Party rally in Madison Square Garden on April 5, 1933:

"Essentially fascism is capitalism turned nudist. Bourgeois democracy is a fig leaf to hide the naked realities of the capitalist system. But just as soon as revolutionary action is threatened from the working class, the fig leaf is thrown aside."

Matthews remembers this flight of imagery as a piece of mad music to his audience.

"The band played its loudest. There were cheers, handclapping, singing of the 'International' and marching. It lasted almost ten minutes. I liked it. It was, in fact, thrilling."

Next day's *Daily Worker* described Matthews' debut at the Garden as "a trenchant attack upon the illusions of bourgeois democracy prevalent among the intelligentsia."

More people listened to J. B. Matthews that night than had ever heard him before in one place. It was the apogee of his life as a revolutionary. He has moved to other great stages since then, and all the passion which he brings to them is to the mutilation of that self of twenty-one years ago. And yet, the key idea summarized by the *Daily Worker* after that first night in Madison Square Garden remains today a core of Matthews' thought. He cannot speak or write without crying forth against "the illusions . . . prevailing among the intelligentsia."

He stirred the Garden in 1933, when he believed in the dictatorship of the proletariat, by denouncing those intellectuals who frittered and dallied while the guns of fascism beat outside their doors. In 1953, he declared that "if all the colleges in the United States had been closed during the last thirty-five years, our national situation could not be any worse so far as the understanding of Communism is concerned."

Hopkinsville, where he first saw the vision of the world as a meeting house, had been a focus of noise and action and faith beyond reason. J. B. Matthews would always be one who believed more than one who doubted; his view of the intellectual all along has always been the believer's revulsion from the doubter, and the recruiting sergeant's discontent with the immobilized. Only last year, he said, "I don't like the fellow who never got his feet wet." He has always preferred the enemy to the neutral.

In the Garden, that April of 1933, Matthews had taken his first sip of a heady brew. He appears to have no memories from the ensuing two years so electric as those nights at the Garden and its banks of ecstasy. On February 27, 1935, the *Daily Worker's* Simon Gerson discovered new dimensions of hyperbole to describe the effect of a Matthews speech. "It seemed," he throbbed, "that the very steel girders that arched across the roof would bend from the ear-splitting cheers that went up."

Those nights at Madison Square Garden, now outlawed by a timorous management, were not occasions for the contemplative. They did not require that the speaker be very deep or very penetrating; he was less orator than cheer leader. Once again, J. B. Matthews stood before his old vision of the world become Kentucky meeting house. No other stage seemed to mean quite so much to him. The pacifists around the F.O.R. office were pallid beside it. The salt had lost its savor.

Matthews began growing more secular. He took a drink every now and then; he would never qualify as a tosspot, but he would always talk like one, glorying in this smallest of sins like any man who discovers the pleasures of faint immorality late in life. He was moving with entire conviction and complete sincerity toward divorcing the wife who had been a missionary with him in Java and replacing her with a trimmer model along revolutionary socialist lines.

There appears to have been something in the air of those times which made it necessary for so many of the very few who felt their impact most to stride from home to home, always slamming the door behind them. Not eight years before, J. B. Matthews had departed Scarritt College with grace and dignity; now, in 1933, he had worn out his welcome with the Fellowship of Reconciliation, but he fought to stay with it. The attractions of salary did not hold him; the F.O.R. paid him just four thousand dollars a year. Between 1933 and 1935, his entire tangible reward for the torrent of words he poured forth after working hours at every drop of a handbill amounted to just three hundred dollars in traveling expenses and one ten-dollar honorarium. Money is the least of needs to a man sure he is bearing the light.

By 1933, Matthews no longer believed in the F.O.R.; pacifism had become one more piece of dead skin for him. He was frank to admit that the Fellowship was of interest to him only as a base from which to preach a harsher doctrine, for, whatever they say of him, J. B. Matthews was not born to be an underground man. But, as a revolutionary Marxist, he knew that he should not leave a strategic position without a principled, programmatic fight. The F.O.R. was a respectable organization; the slogans of combat had a special weight on the lips of a man who could speak as its executive secretary.

By now, the older F.O.R. leaders were almost as depressed as they were exhausted by the unremitting manifestations of their executive secretary's energy. The Fellowship's national chairman, who had formerly wondered with delighted surprise "how you have been able to get so much into twelve months," was commencing to wish Matthews would slow down.

In November, 1933, Matthews challenged the F.O.R. to disavow absolute pacifism enough to permit its members to scrimmage on the barricades. Violence in the class struggle is deplorable, conceded Matthews, who six months before at Madison Square Garden had seemed to find it delightful. But the class war was also inevitable, he declared, and a pacifist should be allowed to plunge into its violence to a degree impermissible in an international war.

Even in the thirties, there were not many Americans who held a basic faith and felt it challenged by Marxism at some fundamental point who did not choose the faith and reject the challenge. To Matthews' surprise, his suggested adulteration of the doctrine of nonviolence was overwhelmingly rejected by the Fellowship's members and he was asked to resign as executive secretary. The wisdom of total pacifism may be subject to dispute, but nowhere does it look more fair than in its low rate of producing backsliders. The few who accept its cloak do not lightly put it aside; they are trained to stand their ground, moved no more by the winds of passing passion than by the sound of trumpets.

So small a segment of the F.O.R.'s membership followed him out that Matthews soon abandoned his original notion of forming a sort of Fellowship-of-Reconciliation-With-All-Save-the-Class-Enemy. The beauty of a strong, lasting commitment is often best understood by a man incapable of it; and Matthews has always been generous in his assessment of the F.O.R.'s judgment in losing faith in him.

Early in 1934, Matthews was established at a new base—Consumers' Research, where he worked with his friend, Fred J. Schlink, co-author of *100,000,000 Guinea Pigs*, a splashy account of the depredations inflicted upon the consumer under free enterprise. Consumers' Research was an agency both to emancipate the consumer from the hypnosis of the advertiser and to advise him of the relative value of various products contesting for his dollar. Matthews became vice president of Consumers' Research and joined Schlink in writing *Partners In Plunder*, a sequel to *100,000,000 Guinea Pigs*. He helped edit its publications and made lecture tours in support of his new call.

But it remained a subsidiary call; the liberation of the consumer was never to be the panacea that universal Methodism, then pacifism, and now Marxism was for him. His heart was still with verbalization of the revolutionary impulse. For a few months in 1934, he was national chairman of the new American League against War and Fascism, which Communist Party chairman Earl Browder described as "led by our party quite openly." He remained a Socialist, although frequently under suspension for his on-again, off-again tendency to forgather with Communists. He left the American League in 1934, but for the next eighteen months, he could not resist the intoxicants of the Communists and kept sinking back toward their embrace.

"There was never anyone more confused than J. B. Matthews in those days," he says now. "Perhaps I'm still confused." But no sense of inner conflict appears ever to have caught his tongue.

There was an irresistible sense of immolation in the struggle of his time when the Communist Anti-Imperialist League invited him to address a dockside demonstration against an incoming Japanese diplomat, and the New York police knocked him from his chair.

In 1935, it was still exciting to be invited to Toronto to speak to a rally of the Canadian League against War and Fascism "built around your world-wide reputation" (the world was a meeting house, and its hallelujahs were all for him) and to be tendered the facetious pledge of "a polite deportation for you."

Try as Matthews would to swear off, the *Daily Worker* could report as late as May of 1935 that, at one Party-sponsored rally, "J. B. Matthews, a leading revolutionary socialist, was greeted with thunderous cheers." The *Worker's* correspondent reported him warping the girders of the Garden as late as February, 1935. He retained his special touch with the unformed; the National Student League, a Communist group, used him whenever it could; he cannot remember how many times he spoke to the NSL at City College of New York.

He wrote at various times for publications called *Revolutionary Age, Labor Action, Revolt, Fight,* and the *New Masses,* which shared a common rhetorical impulse and a rancorous dislike for each other. He preached wherever he could find a flock, and spread his favors with so fine an impartiality among such irreconcilables as Communists, Lovestoneite Communists, Musteite Leninists, Christian Socialists, and revolutionary Socialists that he seemed to many of his brothers in the struggle an odd fish, a visionary, a fool, or an untrustworthy fellow.

Our only surviving literary portrait of the J. B. Matthews of that period comes from Benjamin Gitlow, a particularly ravaged bit of wreckage from various Communist storms who met Matthews in 1934 and has traveled a long way with him since. By the time he met Matthews, Gitlow had been reduced by circumstance to an habitual tone of peevish lament.

He had been one of the first American Communists, and had gone to prison in 1919 for preparing a soggy translation of the new gospel of Lenin. It was his notion afterward that his comrades had turned him in to escape punishment themselves. He came out of prison a Bolshevik hero and was rewarded by being made secretary of the American Communist Party. In 1930, he was called to Moscow and expelled after a dispute with Stalin. He had left his other suit in a trunk in the New York office; he came home to find that his former admirers had stolen it. Ben

Gitlow's life was a history of peculiar experiences in degradation. After some vicissitudes, in 1934 he had sought shelter in
the Socialist Party and was distressed to find it drifting under
Communist influence. Matthews was at the time the Party's most
conspicuous advocate of collaboration with the Communists and
chairman of the Revolutionary Policy Committee, a Socialist faction highly susceptible to the Leninist, if not the Stalinist, pull.
That summer, Gitlow tried to reason with him.

Matthews, Gitlow reported later, showed a "surprising lack of
knowledge" and was "lackadaisical" about "matters in which he
should have been vitally interested." Still he gave Gitlow assurance that he would do his uttermost for the welfare of the workers. Gitlow wrote afterward, in his inevitable tone of grievance,
that Matthews' uttermost had little availed the common good.

"He seemed to me," he commented, "essentially a weak character, one who would not stand up in a crisis."

But Matthews ran his course for the next year, and no inner
doubt or weakness of purpose was audible in his ringing voice.
In February, 1935, the night he bent the girders of the Garden, he
shouted to a largely Communist audience: "We can build a party
of the working class and this party must include the Communist Party."

His last recorded appearance before an audience of Communist persuasion was on March 10, 1935, at a meeting in Detroit
called by the Friends of the Soviet Union "to protest the campaign of the Hearst press against Soviet Russia and the American
labor movement." "The best way to answer Hearst," said Matthews then, "is to elect Maurice Sugar," the Friends of the Soviet
Union's candidate for judge of the Detroit Recorders Court. He
was saying good-by to his past with a final insult to what was to
be his future.

Just a few months later, J. B. Matthews met what he and his
enemies agree was the crisis of his life. He had to make a choice
between his allies of the united front and his friend Fred Schlink.

As the founder and president of Consumers' Research, Schlink
was a man enormously exercised over a comparatively circum-
scribed area of injustice. His philosophy may be summarized as
indignation at what he conceived to be the common practice in

American industry of bottling up seven cents' worth of mud and chemicals, giving it an exotic name, and selling it for five dollars to ladies in search of a new and infinitely lovelier countenance. He was, in brief, that glory of American radicalism, the man who is cracked on a single subject.

But most of Schlink's associates at Consumers' Research were, like Matthews, persons of more extended vision; some of them at least were intimate Communist fellow travelers. Matthews was a link between them and Schlink. In August of 1935, the link was broken. Schlink's employees organized a union; and, upon presentation and rejection of its demands, there was a strike. Matthews, as vice president of Consumers' Research, sided with Schlink and denounced the uprising as "a Communist conspiracy."

There followed a vigorous demonstration of Matthews' view that violence was an inevitable and even commendable aspect of the class struggle. One day in September, he looked out of the window of his office to see a full-scale tear-gas riot between the police and his old friends on the picket line.

That summer's tumult was dreadfully destructive to Matthews as symbol of the united front of the revolutionary left. The strikers denounced him in the *New Masses*. They hired Town Hall for a public trial of Schlink and Matthews, with Vito Marcantonio as prosecutor and Matthews' old friend, Heywood Broun, as hanging judge. Matthews cried out all summer that the strike was the result of a Communist plot to destroy Matthews and Schlink. The strikers were certainly under Communist influence, but it was not a defense calculated to have much impact among Matthews' old associates.

There were efforts on the left to resolve the issue by appointing an impartial commission to investigate the strike. Matthews refused to accept any such suggestion. He himself had served on an impartial commission to investigate a furriers' strike, and he knew enough about the rules of evidence prevailing in those inquiries to refuse to subject himself to this one.

In the end, the strike petered out and the pickets, led by Arthur Kallet, one of Schlink's oldest collaborators, departed Consumers' Research to set up the rival Consumers' Union, which flourished so well since then that it sells its reports on such matters as the comparative merits of the Buick and the Chrysler to a largely middle-class audience in the hundreds of thousands. In 1952, Kallet proved that he too was no longer a leftist by subjecting himself to a lengthy strike by the CIO American Newspaper Guild.

But Kallet and others of the enraged committed made the fall of 1935 a season of slings and arrows for Matthews. He felt his revolutionary soul untouched by them. He sent his resignation to the American League against War and Fascism to spare it embarrassment, but he left with the fraternal hope that the League "may grow in effectiveness day by day."

He retained membership on the Board of Directors of the League for Industrial Democracy, a group oriented toward the Socialists. In the very depths of the Consumers' Research strike, he sat at an LID board meeting and voted for the merger of Socialist and Communist student groups which resulted in the American Student Union.

"Though he slay me," Norman Thomas remarked on that occasion, "yet will I trust him." Thomas had attacked Matthews during the Consumers' Research strike. Matthews accepted that observation as an oblique acknowledgment that even though the Communists were harassing him at Consumers' Research, he was clinging manfully to his illusions. He seems to have felt then that no temporary misunderstanding with a union could shake his devotion to the revolutionary mass.

We can suppose that he would have gone on speaking for the LID or even for the Communists at the Garden if either would have let him. But, for reasons that may now appear unjust, there was a certain resistance to a spokesman for united working-class action who was on the unfair list of a labor union.

Matthews was thereafter the victim of a general boycott, his final achievement at unifying the forces of the left, which shut him off from almost all the platforms he had adorned so tirelessly so long. He had become, as the tenants of *Red Channels* were to be later, a controversial figure, and there was no court of appeals for him. By January of 1936, in enforced farewell to all his banners, he had retreated to his Consumers' Research office at Washington, N. J.

Consumerism, pure and simple, could never have conjured up in J. B. Matthews' mind that key image of a room shaking with the shouts of men. Still he gave it his routine best. By mere process of competition with Consumers' Union, he and Schlink were beginning to find undetected virtues in free enterprise; presumably anything so distasteful to Kallet was good enough for them. But this was, after all, a private drama on a small stage. J. B. Matthews was not a man by nature happy to replace action with contemplation. His past religions had been more public than private. As a missionary, he was not mystic but song leader; as a Marxist, he was not so much student as shouter of rags and tags from the tail end of the *Communist Manifesto.* For him ideas were of no use except as weapons. He was conscientious but perfunctory in the assemblage of facts which was Consumers' Research's business. He was a poet condemned to a typewriter factory.

In the fall of 1936, he voted for Alfred M. Landon, the Republican candidate, for President. He does not appear during that interlude of peace to have performed any other conspicuous political act, and this one was out of character. For it was a gesture, by his standards, of normality; it put him in step with great numbers of the American people, and it is J. B. Matthews' usual compulsion to be alone and special. The Landon vote reflected the pastoral period of his life; in 1940, when he had returned to combat, he refused to vote for Wendell Willkie and later for Tom Dewey, because he considered them both concealed agents of the New Deal. He voted for President Eisenhower in 1952, under pressure from his friends, and there are signs now that he regrets that deviation exceedingly.

Then, in August of 1938, he emerged once more upon the great stage, this time as guest of the House Committee on Un-American Activities, with voice a little softer, with body not so lean, blinking at the spotlight but with confidence in self and assurance of rectitude once more restored.

Matthews testified before the House Committee on Un-American Activities for two full days. His old friend Heywood Broun, who was not in his most attractive phase then himself, described the scene this way:

"J. B. Matthews exorcised demons for a House committee. His voice became shrill and fervent as he attacked the Youth Congress. And then upon a note of almost sheer hysteria he thrust out a thin arm and screamed that Shirley Temple was a 'stooge' of the 'reds.' The chairman of the House committee leaned forward eagerly and said: 'Go on, professor.'"

Ever since then, his enemies have described him as an informer. But the material then was after all a matter of public record; and if an informer is a man offering facts otherwise buried in some secret cache, J. B. Matthews was unqualified to be one. He had never been a Communist; he had been simply an ornament on that illusory façade of broad mass influence which the Communist Party jerrybuilt in the early thirties. And so he came to Martin Dies and the Un-American Activities Committee, not as informer, but as bearer of the gospel that the façade was four-square granite; this had not been illusion but terrible, dangerous fact.

Matthews must have spent his seclusion going over the meaning of his life all the way back to Java. A man can look upon his life and accept it as good or evil; it is far, far harder for him to confess that it has been unimportant in the sum of things. All those long, turbid nights of shouts and mutterings that were the compound of his life as a radical had been a sequence of swindles in which he had been at once shill and dupe. The Communist fronts he had served had been structures of enormous pretension and pathetic foundation. He had dressed himself in a dozen costumes—the beloved and burning brand from the Anti-Imperialist League, the friend of the Friends of the Soviet Union, the ambassador extraordinary from the American League against War and Fascism—and all the while he had been thundering in the same little room to the same few people.

Matthews could not say that this had been a good work. But he dared not say that it had been an unimportant one. There may be some comfort in confessing yourself a sinner if you can confess yourself a substantial sinner. For J. B. Matthews had deceived himself for three years that he was talking to multitudes. That was the one illusion that he could not surrender.

In a certain sense, time was kind to J. B. Matthews. When he struck the trail of repentance in 1938, the thirties, at the heart of their myth at least, were already over. The literature of disillusion was already selling as well as the literature of illusion, although it would still be two years before *Darkness at Noon* would finally displace *The Coming Struggle for Power* in the libraries of the advanced. When a faith is dying, the best go first and lesser spirits trail behind. That qualitative apostasy which precedes any quantitative defection had set in before Matthews completed his final turn. The revolutionary spirit of 1932 had been devoted to the composition of the proletarian novel, a poor thing but its own; the survivors of that spirit in 1938 were reduced to collecting folk songs. In 1932, the revolutionary impulse had attracted such spirits as John Dos Passos and Edmund Wilson; by 1938, both were occupied with labors of disenchantment; and they had no successors. The creators of the myth had either defected or ceased to create.

And then J. B. Matthews emerged as the legatee of the thirties, the custodian of their archives, the patcher and pumper of all their deflated balloons. The historian of that time's surface could have no source so full as the files of J. B. Matthews, who was at once its great enemy and a soul dependent upon its preservation, the sleepless researcher into its dark corners, the one man whose life would be without meaning if he could not believe that it had all been terribly important, not as the tragedy of the few but the guilt of the many.

Looking back now, after twenty years, a detached observer might say that it had been a very little thing to which very few people came. But J. B. Matthews had to say, no, no, can't you see that everybody was there, that all America was listening to me in Madison Square Garden?

He could hardly say, of course, that many Americans had believed that fascism was capitalism gone nudist even in 1933. But most Americans had been against child labor. And it could only have been a compulsion to declare the guilt universal which impelled Matthews to apologize for his speeches against child labor with the public reflection that he had been water boy to a labor gang when he was six years old and that it hadn't hurt him.

He sat before the House Committee on Un-American Activities reading the long roll of his misdeeds, putting into the record the names of his old collaborators. He listed a total of twenty-eight Communist-directed enterprises, a modest count by later standards. He himself had held office in fifteen of them and had spoken for nineteen on a grand total of 106 occasions.

Matthews described a vast assemblage of "dupes, stooges, and decoys" lured into these fronts by the Communists. It seemed a little strange that he, as just one among so many gulls, should have been employed as protective coloration for more than half those deadfalls. With so many available suckers, the Communists appear to have inflicted abnormal exploitation upon just this one.

Among his cloud of sinners, Matthews included a number of old Socialist comrades, who had lost faith in co-operation with the Communists either before he had or during the period of his withdrawal. One of those targets was at the moment a highly vocal opponent of Communist influence in the National Labor Relations Board, and was a trifle surprised to be picked out by Matthews as the most dangerous man in the NLRB. His crime was not communism but collectivism, a sin more amorphous, which had revealed itself to Matthews while he was wrestling with the devil in Washington, N. J.

After his testimony, Matthews boarded a train with an old Socialist comrade, who refused to speak to him. Matthews was terribly shaken.

"Look," he said, "I know what you think. But, believe me, I have never exposed any Socialist who was not co-operating with me while I was co-operating with the Communists." That was a remark akin to the respect Matthews retained for the Fellowship of Reconciliation because it lost faith in him. The only unforgivable sin was to have trusted and followed J. B. Matthews up through 1935. He cried mercy for himself as shepherd and slaughter for the sheep.

In their revulsion, his old comrades and a great many people who had never been his comrades, preferred to say that Matthews was lying in detail, and to let the substance of his fantasy pass without comment. But, with a few exceptions, the details of Matthews' testimony were generally unassailable. Just one year later, almost all the organizations he cited as Communist fronts either disappeared or altered their policies beyond recognition in response to the Nazi-Soviet pact.

The fantasy which went unmentioned by Matthews' enemies and has now become the core of the myth of the fifties was in his description of the awesome power and influence of the Communists in the life of the thirties. As an instance, Matthews with perfect justice asserted that the American League for Peace and Democracy was a Communist front. The American League claimed to represent four million members, a species of inflation which Matthews passed on to Martin Dies and the House Committee on Un-American Activities as though it were fact. At the time of its dissolution in October, 1939, it had just twenty thousand members.

We might all have been better off today if the honest opponents of J. B. Matthews had conceded that the American League for Peace and Democracy was a Communist front and challenged the assumption that it had four million members. That way, we might have been rescued from the myth, shared equally by those who love and many who hate J. B. Matthews, that this was an era when "everyone" was influenced by the Communists.

The House Committee on Un-American Activities had produced a number of witnesses against communism; so far, there had been none like Matthews, an "insider" asserting himself still damp from the sewer and blessed with the obsession that he had left behind him countless hosts of the fallen. Committee Chairman Martin Dies had the reaction of stout Cortez upon the peak at the endless vista which Matthews spread before him. He hired this new prophet as soon as he was able and anointed him with the nickname "Doc," an honorary degree reflecting the semi-literate's awe of the scholar.

Doc Matthews was a new kind of apostate from communism. When Ben Gitlow was cast into the night in 1930, he regarded himself as a revolutionary socialist for the next six years, shambling from one splinter group to another, still hoping to find the true light somewhere in their weak phosphorescence. Ben Gitlow walked a long way to discover the world was round.

J. B. Matthews had made his homeward journey in half that

time. After him, in some special cases, the pace was to become as of Mercury. A young Southwesterner named Howard Rushmore had come to New York in the early thirties to join the staff of the Communist *Young Worker,* where his rangy frame and his gaunt, embattled head made him especially attractive as a photographic subject. Rushmore had grown up to the *Daily Worker,* where, as a junior reporter, he was assigned to film criticism. In the fall of 1938, he was dispatched to the assassination of *Gone With The Wind,* enjoyed it thoroughly, and, touched by ancestral aspirations toward the Articles of Secession, refused to accept the Marxist analysis of Vivien Leigh as Serpent of White Supremacy.

This was an extraordinary rock upon which to break a Bolshevik, but Rushmore crashed against it. Two days later, still dripping wet, he was describing the dark night of *his* soul to a Hearst editor. Within a week, he had become the Hearst papers' expert on communism and labor, touring his beat girt round with the Confederate Army belt of some departed ancestor, a premature anti-fascist become premature Dixiecrat.

Ben Gitlow's total repudiation of his thirties, his twenties, and his teens came a little later; in 1940, he went before the Dies Committee and repudiated collectivism too. Matthews, Rushmore, and even Gitlow had accepted Marx without reading much of him; and that may have been why they were conditioned for the ultimate acceptance of the anti-collectivism of other economic absolutists like Ludwig Von Mises almost without ever having heard of them.

The ultimate seemed Matthews' absolute necessity. In 1935, he had been telling Detroit how to defeat William Randolph Hearst. Three years later, he wrote of Hearst as the first among the captains against communism and the victim of a "classic" smear campaign. In 1940, a group of his old Revolutionary Policy Committee fellows entered into the Union for Democratic Action to support aid to Britain in direct dispute with the current Communist line. Matthews' response to this evidence of regeneration was to disinter the moldering associations of UDA's directors with long-gone Communists fronts and to denounce them as still collectivists. He was saying, as he had said in the Garden, that there was no middle way.

The early nineteen forties were not a period with much interest in the crimes of the thirties and they shunted the Un-American Activities Committee off on a sidetrack of the railroad of history. Martin Dies was sick and tired; J. B. Matthews was diverted to a languid hunt for native fascists, but his heart remained in the highlands hunting for the crypto-Bolsheviks about whom so few people were worried at the moment. Dies, scared of defeat, quit Congress without an election campaign.

And so he said his sad "So long, Doc," and went back to Texas. By now Matthews also had retreated into the shadows to await his time to come. By good chance, William Randolph Hearst still cared. J. B. Matthews transferred his files to the office of Hearst's International Corporation. And there he and they fattened and grew heavy with portent.

By 1948, history had come his way again. There were almost as many anti-Communist fronts abounding as there had been Communists fronts in the early thirties. The professional revolutionary had been replaced by the professional counterrevolutionary. J. B. Matthews was once again a dean.

His files had become by now a repository of truth as immutable as Marxism had been. They bulged with 500,000 names of persons who had been affiliated with left-wing groups, a separate card for each of 7,000 clergymen, carefully listing his pro-Communist affiliations, a separate card for each of 3,000 educators, likewise errant.

For Matthews was custodian of the tomb of the thirties. They lay embalmed in his cabinets, because no one cared about them any longer except as a sin requiring purgation; and J. B. Matthews held the roster of the fallen and the tempted. For compilations of this kind, largely from public documents of the Communist Party and its fringes, are essential to the extirpation of sin because the recollections of repentant Communists are themselves too limited to be totally satisfactory. In 1939, a year after he left the party, one professional ex-Communist found his stock of memories so depleted that he began canvassing more recent apostates for new material. He offered one such backslider a split in the profits from his reminiscence, explaining that his own cupboard was bare and needed new matter. J. B. Matthews' stature as an authority rests more on the 500,000 names in his great file than upon any special experience.

The possession of those jewels made Matthews the grand master of the new cadre of the disenchanted. He seemed to have mellowed a great deal by now, sybaritic, and wearing his glasses only to read, invoking his Maker only in moments of disturbance, as liberated from the shackles of John Wesley as from the fetters of Karl Marx.

He had new friends of every description; the ones he cherished most were, like himself, of the committed. The more fortunate among them could expect invitations to his penthouse apartment in Chelsea to eat shrimp prepared in the high Javanese fashion and indulge themselves in elephantine banter about King Charles's head. There is an organ in the apartment, and in his moments of peace Matthews' fingers from ancient habit may stray and his now thick voice may rise to "Lead, Kindly Light" as it was in Malaya so long ago.

But piety is not his pose, and he would be very happy to believe that, like his guests, he is a man successful in the worldly sense and that, unlike many of them, he is past his commitments.

"I have been misunderstood as a crusader," he said a year or so ago. "I don't consider myself a crusader. I am engaged in a very interesting field of investigation." His eye gleamed and his fingers met in the old gesture of the connoisseur. "To me the letterhead of a Communist front is a nugget. And I make a good living at it."

And yet, try though he would, he still believed; J. B. Matthews had to serve stranger gods than Mammon. The cards in his files were now his law and his prophets. When Anna Rosenberg was appointed assistant Secretary of Defense, Matthews fished out a card showing that an Anna Rosenberg had belonged to five Communist fronts in the thirties. This had to be the Anna Rosenberg, he insisted; there was no other Anna Rosenberg of her stature. The FBI was almost immediately to find another Anna Rosenberg, who freely affirmed that she had been the one listed by Matthews as a member of the John Reed Club.

The cards in the file were the records of the avenging Angel; and this angel, true to the God of Hopkinsville, had no time to judge the intentions of those who walked the road to hell. Innocence was not a word in his vocabulary. In 1938, after his regeneration, Matthews had been surprised to find that the *Daily*

Worker had listed him, in 1933, among five American representatives to the International Commission to Aid the Victims of German Fascism, a front of which he had never even heard.

He reflected then that "there is nothing extraordinary about a Communist using the names of persons without their permission." There was no room for that reflection in his files; the names of the ignorant and the innocent were impartially mixed there with the aware and the guilty.

Try though they will to be normal, J. B. Matthews and those of the armed disenchanted he serves as supply sergeant cannot escape a destiny of passions which affront or frighten ordinary men. In the spring of 1953, Matthews was appointed staff director for Senator Joseph R. McCarthy's Subcommittee on Investigations. Within a few weeks he was in trouble; the Senate was aroused over his charge that the Communists were nowhere stronger than in the Protestant churches. He clung to that position against all the clamor; and at length he was driven out by outraged Southern Democrats, who had been conservatives when he was a revolutionary but to whom any reflection on the purity of the Baptist and Methodist churches was a personal affront.

Joe McCarthy's picture still hangs on his wall, but J. B. Matthews is too controversial ever to serve McCarthy in any official sense. For the armed disenchanted, try though they will for normality, must always feel like an oppressed and dedicated minority. The totality of their disillusion is too much for the great majority who never knew even illusion. Ralph de Toledano, who is sometimes a guest at J. B. Matthews' evenings and who was a radical long ago, once asked me: "Can't you understand that the only place for an anarchist today is the Republican Party?"—a thesis that would certainly have pained Governor Fuller of Massachusetts as much as it could Bartolomeo Vanzetti.

And Matthews is unusual among the armed disenchanted because he is professionally successful where most of them exist on short rations. Their type is not Matthews but Ben Gitlow, for whom free enterprise has found very little comfort. Gitlow has wandered, an uneasy, hungry ghost before various committees and government boards, and he has written a book that did not sell. I last heard his voice in May of 1952, in lamentation before the New York Volunteers for Taft. He was especially exercised by the waste of our substance on loans to Europe. "We must," he declared, "act like ordinary businessmen; if we give a dollar's value, we ought to get a dollar back for it." The judge who sent Ben Gitlow to prison in the twenties expressed shock because he is "able-bodied, full of intellect [and] confesses he owns no property."

J. B. Matthews is fortunate, by contrast at least, in the material sense. But there are signs even for him that no man can be altogether happy when so much of his past lies buried with a lost civilization.

Last year, his old associate, A. J. Muste, now once more a pacifist and director of the Fellowship of Reconciliation, wrote Hearst columnist George Sokolsky to correct an imputation that the F.O.R. had been under Communist influence in the days Matthews was sojourning there. Sokolsky submitted Muste's letter to the guardian of the files. Matthews wrote back that the F.O.R. had indeed been free of Communist taint most of the time. But he regretted to inform Sokolsky that Muste had requested clemency for Julius and Ethel Rosenberg, the atom spies, and must thus be included among the 7,000 Communist-serving clergymen whom Matthews intended to cite to the House Committee on Un-American Activities. "In doing so," said Matthews, "I have no malice."

Sokolsky, as mediator with the foul fiend, sent Matthews' letter on to Muste, who responded with a long answer direct to Matthews. He enclosed in it the exact text of his appeal for clemency for the Rosenbergs; it had expressed the conviction that they had been fairly tried and had urged clemency only as proof of how much more humane democrats could be than totalitarians. Muste raised a mild question as to whether even the great file in J. B. Matthews' office was quite adequate to catalogue the heart of a man.

And, at the close, he said he would like to see Matthews again some time, because, after all, "I have never thought that the fact that people stand on different political platforms ought to mean the severance of human relationships." Matthews did not reply.

There were no eyes from all his past into which A. J. Muste was not glad to look. But there was at least one pair that was too much for J. B. Matthews.

But his was a life not without its moment of reward. The night before the feast of St. Valentine, 1953, his friends tendered J. B. Matthews a dinner in the Sert Room of the Hotel Waldorf-Astoria. They came in black ties and paid $12.50 a plate, men of all sorts and conditions, gathered in their twilight to honor the archivist of this last of so many of their faiths. There came Ben Mandel, former business manager of the *Daily Worker;* Max Eastman of the old *Masses;* George Sokolsky, flame of the anarchist segment of the Columbia University student body before World War I; Eugene Lyons, rapt biographer first of Sacco and Vanzetti and then of Herbert Hoover; Harvey Matusow, former social activities director at the Communist Camp Unity; Fred J. Schlink, co-author of *Partners in Plunder,* and a dozen others who had lost the way and found it again.

Howard Rushmore, who learned about entertainment at the *Daily Worker,* handled the arrangements; it is to be hoped that he found a free ticket for Ben Gitlow, who sat very far from the dais, in his shabby dinner jacket, somehow alone, aggrieved and trapped to the last. And there came too men who had never changed their faith: Harry Jung, former editor of the *American Gentile,* and Merwyn K. Hart and Joseph Kamp, foes since boyhood of all collectivisms except those of Benito Mussolini and Francisco Franco.

And there came, as chief among them, bearing the libations of his new and special salt, United States Senator Joseph R. McCarthy, a star brighter than Martin Dies had ever been; and J. B. Matthews was very glad to share their applause with him. They gave him and Mrs. Matthews a silver service and they unveiled a portrait of solid substance.

He arose, and so many rewards for his long watch beside the deathbed of the thirties were almost too much for him. He looked at George Sokolsky and said that, every time he heard that voice on the radio, he was reminded of the prophet Amos. There had been many faiths between Hopkinsville and the Waldorf; but always he had clutched at one, forsaking all others for the time being; and always there had been someone to remind him of the prophet Amos.

He stood there, no longer lean but still dedicated, with three chins now and white hair and a mustache and the weight fighting against his double-breasted dinner jacket. There was the sense that, in moments less scrubbed and polished, the mustache would droop and show stains of tobacco. He had about him the look of an old pirate, the look in short of the father he had fled and left behind in Hopkinsville forty years before.

6

OF ALL the prisoners of the myth of the thirties, none seemed more fortunate for a little while than the Hollywood Communists and none have suffered such extremes of punishment for their enchantment.

While they were Communists, the reality of their environment was Hollywood, which is a theater and very little of a reality at all. When the very rich are very foolish, literary convention is likely to treat them as comic figures. Eugene Lyons once described a film colony banquet in the thirties with its sated guests creaking up after the dessert to sing "Arise, ye prisoners of starvation," a satire dependent for its effect on the idea that starvation is a problem entirely of the flesh. But incongruity ceases to be comedy's essence when it becomes the incongruity which destroys men's lives.

The conflict between the Hollywood Communist's idea of self and the reality of his life was always incongruous and his punishment was even more so. His sins of commission were very small ones; they were punished as capital crimes. He became the protagonist of most of the post-war dramas of the House Committee on Un-American Activities. Except for the Hiss-Chambers interlude, the committee devoted the years 1947–51 almost entirely to subversion in Hollywood, and departed only when there were no actors left on the set.

When its ordeal was over, Hollywood remained almost as it had been, less some 300 inhabitants. They were people for whom most of Hollywood felt a certain sympathy, but whom it regarded as victims of one of those plagues which occasionally carry off one's friends and which in Hollywood are familiar misfortunes of nature.

Hollywood itself has always seemed to me more a conception than a reality. And when I had finished thinking about its lost Communists, I found myself unable to consider them and their character apart from the very nature of Hollywood itself. They seemed to me persons who had lived and died not so much true to Bolshevik notions of conduct as according to the customs of this institution which they had hoped to divert to the service of their ideas and which had ended up, as institutions will, by diverting them for itself.

The most conspicuous of the Hollywood Communists did not find the roots of their conversion there. They were men who had their start with the revolutionary theater movement in New York in the early thirties and who came to Hollywood with very mixed impulses. The medium which had given them impetus as playwrights had burned out very quickly. Hollywood was an escape from its ruins. It offered comfort and success; if they thought of it as an instrument for the propagation of their ideas, that notion did not survive their initiation. Their function thenceforth became that of fat cats and decorations. When the Un-American Activities Committee came to root them out, the one thing none of their worst enemies could say against them was that they had left any permanent impress upon the screen.

Their story is a failure of promise: first, of the promise in themselves, and last, of the promise of the Hollywood which was so kind to them until they became an embarrassment and then turned them out. The promise at the beginnings of most of them appears now to have been largely smoke and thunder; the promise which vanished at their end appears to have been tinsel, as Hollywood is tinsel. They were entombed, most of them, not for being true to themselves but for sitting up too long with their own press releases.

It seemed best to me to begin their story when they were young and hungry back in New York. I have concluded it in the endless records of Un-American Activities Committee hearings which are their tomb. The heart of this chapter is a piecing together of the stories told the committee by the repentant and the frightened among them, stories which, however valueless they seem to me for the salvation of the republic, are terrible documents of the effect upon the human spirit of living ten years between two fantasies.

I confess that Hollywood is not a piece of my direct experience and that, to a degree, I may have imagined it, which might be a dangerous practice even for a community which has after all so largely created itself from its own imagination. This is a study conditioned less by the convictions of the committed than by the customs of Hollywood. According to those customs, it is peopled by those who, after their first flush at least, did not believe very much and felt a professional compulsion to simulate belief and were burned as finally as if they had been believers.

The Day of the Locust

The Workers' Theater Goes to Hollywood

"[Hollywood] is such a slack, soft place . . . that withdrawal is practically a condition of safety . . . all gold
rushes are essentially negative. . . . Everywhere there is,
after a moment, either corruption or indifference."

> SCOTT FITZGERALD, letter to Gerald
> Murphy, September 1, 1940

"I forgot my working class mother. . . . Last week I
watched the May Day. I hid in the crowd. I watched how
the comrades marched with red flags and music. You see
where I bit my hand. I went down in the subway so I
couldn't hear the music."

> CLIFFORD ODETS, I Can't Sleep, a mono-
> logue written for performance at a benefit
> for the Marine Workers Industrial Union,
> some time in 1935

JOHN HOWARD LAWSON, displaced journeyman screen
writer, has so long ceased to interest anyone except grave
robbers and the House Committee on Un-American Activities
that it seems hard to believe that there were once persons of
taste who thought of him as an important American playwright.

That would have been more than thirty years ago when he
wrote *Processional*, the expressionist sort of thing the Germans
were doing in the twenties, with jerky speech rhythms, flat sets
and flat vaudeville characters and a band playing on stage much
of the time—"making the jazz today for the glory of the working
class." One of Lawson's stage directions explained: "They (the
bandsmen) do not keep time very well, but the effect is lively."

The effect was lively enough to be exciting—a mixture, as it was, of Henry Mencken with Bert Brecht and Marx with Minsky. John Howard Lawson won with it a reputation for freshness and experiment.

And having the reputation, he relaxed upon it, because Lawson appears to have been a rather conventional person at bottom. *Processional* retains some of its life force; his later plays were too pedestrian to inspire vivid recollection even as curiosities. John Howard Lawson's was always a consciously revolutionary voice; and *Processional* was a class-war piece. But, he did not become a Party man until rather late in the game when his promise in the theater was duller than it had been.

He always had a knack for the topical. Most of his close friends were Communists; and, late in the twenties, he wrote a play about foreign revolutionaries called *The International.* Perhaps, even then, the clatter and thunder of the Comintern myth provided those sound effects which can seem like a kinetic substitute for flagging resource. But John Howard Lawson did not join the Communist Party until 1934, during that brief period when it was giving America a workers' theater. The Party was highly flattered; he was still a young man; but, even so, he was the dean of revolutionary playwrights; and he assumed at once the aspect of an elder statesman.

Lawson wasn't producing very much at the moment. Still he was working on *the* proletarian play and *the* study of the playwright's art. In the meantime, he was very generous with his wisdom to his juniors in the left-wing New Theatre League.

His juniors were young men burning their own juice. One of them, Clifford Odets, said later that when he wrote his first play he was living on ten cents a day. The truth was harsh enough to require no such dramatic license. Odets' mother had worked in a stocking factory in Philadelphia when she was eleven and had died an old woman at forty-nine. When Clifford Odets' time came before the House Committee on Un-American Activities, he told its counsel: "I did not learn my hatred of poverty, sir, out of communism."

He was twenty-eight when his first play was produced, hungry and wild of hair, and he was famous before he was thirty. *Awake*

and Sing! and *Waiting for Lefty* were produced within a few
months of each other. *Till the Day I Die* took five days to write;
Odets offered it as his version of life in Nazi Germany; its source
was a letter to the *New Masses.*

Till the Day I Die was seriously produced and remains today
in print. What survives now are low comedy Nazis never seen
on land or sea, a Communist underground girl who reproaches
her Communist underground boy for male chauvinism, and a final
affirmation that this will pass and brothers will live in the Soviets
of the world. *Till the Day I Die* seemed to burn then, and it
gives off a faint glow still. A bad play celebrating a myth may
always seem better than a bad play regretting a myth.

Questions of Odets' limitations were not fashionable on the
left, or even in some sections of the middle, twenty years ago. It
seemed so probable that this was the first genius of the revolutionary theater. Odets has come closer to the earth since, and it
is easier to recognize that his talents were of the ear rather than
the vision and that he was more Chekhov than Gorki. Yet it was
for his message that he was worshiped by his candle-bearers in
those days. It was a message which they knew so well that they
were always two steps ahead of its delivery. They were not people
who would ask whether even Odets could accomplish the defini-
tive delineation of Nazi Germany in six days on no experience
deeper than a letter in the *New Masses.*

For the new social realism was concerned with more than
reality. The hunger was enough. *Waiting for Lefty* was Odets'
great triumph; he has always described it as "a light machine
gun." *Lefty* is an one-act play about the prelude to a taxi strike;
it is set in the framework of a union meeting and the audience
serves as a hesitant, increasingly aroused rank and file. At its
end, when the insurgents have beaten down the officials who had
betrayed them, Agate (for agitator), their Communist spokesman, shouts across the footlights:

"Hello, America, hello. We're stormbirds of the working class.
. . . And, when we die, they'll know what we did to make a new
world! Christ cut us up into little pieces! We'll die for what is
right! Put fruit trees where our ashes are!"

And back at him from the audience came the shout, unrehearsed but assured and inevitable:

"STRIKE, STRIKE, STRIKE ! ! !"

Odets wrote *Waiting for Lefty* without, he said, "having been near a strike in my life." Direct experience was not required. Elia Kazan, a young actor trying his hand at composition, wrote *Dimitrov* for the United Workers Organization; he had, of course, never seen the Reichstag or the Brown House. This seemed no handicap because these were not documentaries; they were the stuff of heroic myth.

They were all angry young apprentices. They began, most of them, during the Hoover administration, close to Union Square with the Workers Laboratory Theatre, whose offerings carried spare, didactic labels like *The Klein-Ohrbach Strike*. By 1934, many of them were with the Theatre Union, still downtown but apparently more substantial, and their productions conveyed an impression of foundation. George Sklar and Paul Peters wrote *Stevedore* (the waterfront); John Wexley contributed *Steel* and *They Shall Not Die* (the Scottsboro Boys); Albert Maltz, a little older than the others and the author of a commercial success, went to the West Virginia coal fields and came back with *Black Pit*, which had a depth and documentation and shadow of defeat uncommon to the new tradition.

By 1936, Odets at least was enough of a force to sustain the new Group Theatre in a move uptown; and Kazan and J. Edward Bromberg, the Agate of *Waiting for Lefty*, went with him. Archibald MacLeish, back from France, looked upon the works of the new playwrights and found that they "made everything else seem irrelevant" and that America now "had a workers theatre reflecting its time." By the mid-thirties, the revolutionary drama had moved from Union Square to the Theatre Guild itself. Sklar and Peters wrote *Parade*, a Bolshevik revue, and the Guild bought and produced it.

Odets and some of the others had been actors before they became playwrights; they wrote theater and not drama. Loyal as they were to the revolution, they were just as loyal to the traditions of the theater. When they had their pictures taken for their programs, they took off their glasses and combed their hair and had themselves photographed soft focus. That may have been a sign, undetected by subjects as by beholder, that they were really rather conventional young men.

Odets, who was the most famous of them, learned in 1935 just how conventional he was. That was the year Colonel Batista's *junta* captured control of Cuba with numerous reported infamies against the workers. As one of the ornaments of Communist culture, Odets was invited to be chairman of a Commission to Investigate Labor and Social Conditions in Cuba. In his own words, he accepted the invitation expecting "a beautiful trip across the water." The night before the commission arrived in Cuba, his idyllic anticipations were detonated when a more sophisticated traveler informed him that they could all expect arrest and immediate deportation upon landing.

The Cuban police did, in fact, toss Odets into jail and shoved him aboard the swiftest available return boat. As soon as he returned to New York, Odets rushed down to find the anti-fascist who had seduced him into this horrible excursion. Seventeen years later, the creator of *Till the Day I Die* told the House Committee on Un-American Activities:

"[I] was rather aroused by this idea that we had been manhandled because we were, and I was indignant because no one seemed to make a fight about that. During that time, I also said *it was very dangerous*, which it was, because there were dozens of secret police there with machine guns, some of them dressed as dock workers in overalls. *I said it was a very dangerous matter* and they said: 'Yes, it was so dangerous that we had originally intended to send Mother Bloor down as head of the delegation, but it was so dangerous we didn't send her.' She was an old lady."

It would appear, perhaps to his own surprise, to have been Clifford Odets' view that somebody else's ashes should fertilize those fruit trees. He wanted peace and comfort and safety of a sort foreign to the plays he wrote. And he does not appear to have been alone among the revolutionary dramatists in that withheld commitment.

For, just when its flower seemed most passionate, there was no more revolutionary school of the theater; everyone had been graduated. In 1934, when the tide was highest, the Communists organized the New Theatre League to propagate the workers' drama and to make available its plays without charge to little theatre groups of class-conscious timbre. By 1935 there were no revolutionary plays available. The League reported apologetically that its young comets had spurted off for the moment to other commitments; it was careful to avoid the word *commerce*.

But commerce had come to the workers' theater and destroyed it. The Theatre Guild had paid Sklar and Peters more for *Parade* than the Theatre Union had ever dreamt of. The conservative critics found Jimmy Savo its most memorable feature; the New Theatre League confessed that *Parade* had been adulterated to its detriment by "concessions to the Theatre Guild." By the mid-thirties Odets' company, the Group Theatre, was a commercial success; its members had no time for revolutionary drama. And there were no new voices. The New Theatre League announced a contest in 1935 for the best script about Angelo Herndon, a young Negro Communist condemned to a Georgia chain gang. There was no satisfactory entry.

At last, in 1937, a little behind the trend, John Howard Lawson came up with *Marching Song*, a play about a Michigan automobile strike. It was a flower on what was now the grave of the revolutionary drama. The flavor of *Marching Song* may be summarized at the moment in the second act when Bill, the organizer, sends a girl named Rose with a message to the union's underground printing plant:

"Rose: 'Don't worry about me.' "

"Bill: 'I'm not worried about you. What bothers me is the printing press. If they follow you an' find it, they'll bust it into a million pieces.' "

Even 1937 audiences were difficult to convince that the printed word meant quite so much more than life or even sex, and *Marching Song*, strenuous though the left critics were in their kindness, was a failure. Lawson had also completed his *Theory and Practice of Playwriting;* his votaries were a little surprised to find that the dean of the Bolshevik drama esteemed most of all among postwar plays the commercial successes of Robert

Emmet Sherwood, Maxwell Anderson, and Noel Coward. He was, by now, more of a politician than a playwright; his experiments were behind him.

But he could perform one more vanguard act. Early in 1936, he departed for Hollywood, to be followed by the heart of the revolutionary theater—Albert Maltz, John Wexley, and George Sklar plus such workers' theater actors as J. Edward Bromberg, Hester Sondegaard, Phoebe Brand, and John Garfield, the last, the aching, unrealized juvenile of Odets' *Awake and Sing*, living by the liberating myth without ever joining its Party.

Odets had been there before these prospectors; he went to Hollywood at intervals between 1935 and 1950, whenever, as he said, he needed money. His first trip was in 1935 when he wrote *The General Died at Dawn*, a script so typical of Hollywood melodrama that one of Odets' bourgeois admirers was moved to cry out: "Odets, where is thy sting?" The left critics, who still had a commitment to him, scoured the *General* for hidden class meanings with some of the same intensity and just about as much reason as the Un-American Activities Committee brought to its search for subversion in film scripts twelve years later.

When Odets came back in 1937 he found that his old friends were by now accepted Hollywood citizens unimperiled by deportation. The Workers Laboratory Theatre appeared to have moved, spiritually if not physically, over to the Warner Brothers lot. And, to a degree at least, Odets' old friends set the tone of the community, which was pro-Roosevelt and anti-fascist.

John Howard Lawson wrote a few scripts, none inflammatory, and made many more speeches. He occupied himself with a history of American freedom, a project subject to frequent new visions and revisions, as various Communist censors corrected his deviations on the Whisky Rebellion. Lawson, his kind, sheep-like face much less passionate than it had been, deferred to these custodians of truth with such grace that there was reason to doubt that he could ever finish his project. He had to go to prison twelve years later to be free to complete it.

But political men were rare enough in Hollywood when John Howard Lawson got there to make him seem almost a Plato.

There was a tide of fashion for liberalism there in the late thirties. Hollywood had an Anti-Nazi League and a Hollywood Democratic Committee and a Hollywood League for Democracy, and a number of auxiliary vehicles for anti-fascists who were not necessarily anti-totalitarian. But, even then, the Communists as Communists were not really fashionable.

For John Howard Lawson and his flock lived according to the special customs of Hollywood. Once, as an instance, Miss Ginger Rogers threw open her home to a tea for the Joint Anti-Fascist Refugee Committee, but she very firmly warned her guests to be careful of her new white rugs. In 1937, Joseph Freeman, then editor of the Communist *New Masses*, made the westward voyage in search of funds; he was told, when he arrived in Hollywood, that he must present himself as an anti-Nazi editor rather than as a Communist. On these terms, a reception was arranged for him at the home of a substantial Hollywood figure.

J. Edward Bromberg, an old friend from the workers' theater, drove Freeman to the scene and, when they arrived, said good-by.

"I haven't been invited," Bromberg explained, "I only make a thousand dollars a week. There won't be anyone there who makes less than fifteen hundred dollars. They'd resent it if I came in."

Freeman was then making thirty-five dollars a week. He thought this excuse so ridiculous that he fairly dragged poor Bromberg through the door. Once inside, he was shocked to see this twenty-five-dollar-an-hour pariah slink into the shadows, since none of the higher-bracket anti-fascists present dared to speak to him. Freeman's ancient notions of class and caste were so outraged by Bromberg's treatment that when he began his appeal he could not look his audience in the mascara. So he turned his back upon it and began speaking about the evils of fascism directly to his host's servants, two Negroes and two German refugees. In the middle of his speech, the refugees began to cry. The crowd was moved to contribute twenty thousand dollars on the spot; when he came home, Freeman's Hollywood comrades congratulated him on a brilliant stroke of stage business.

For Hollywood, and for its Communists too, life was a piece of stage business. To professionals like Freeman, whose stops there were a glittering interlude in an otherwise short-rationed existence, Hollywood seemed unreal and impossible to take seriously. There was a certain awe about so much gold; the *Daily Worker* once reported an eight-thousand-dollar-average return from Hollywood cocktail parties for Loyalist Spain: "Think of that, you provincials!"

But beneath this wonder there was a slight contempt. Earl Browder is supposed to have said that the Hollywood Communists were valuable for nothing but cash. The professionals always treated their film flock as children are treated. Special concessions to innocence and romance were required; and so the first outside organizer assigned to supervise the Hollywood Communists was introduced to them as a scarred veteran of the European underground. He was a breezy young man named Stanley Lawrence who had, in point of fact, been a Los Angeles taxi driver. He departed after a public *gaucherie* to the effect that his sheep were only "fat cows to be milked." He was succeeded by V. J. Jerome, a certified intellect from New York, who in turn gave way to John Howard Lawson, one of their own and their leader to the end.

Still there was one special group disposed to take the Hollywood Communists seriously. The Hollywood writer was a highly paid domestic, the butt of producers who seemed to him monstrous illiterates, the well-fed prisoner of a medium which he felt was beneath his capacities. He was that most unfortunate of craftsmen, the man of talent who once hoped to be a genius and is treated like a lackey.

In 1941, Leo C. Rosten polled a group of Hollywood professionals on their attitude toward the medium. He found that 133 out of 165 scriptwriters thought the movies were terrible. No other group registered so total a revulsion to the boss's product and no other group turned up so many persons susceptible to the Communist pull.

"I got a fifteen-hundred-dollar writer," said Monroe Stahr in Fitzgerald's *The Last Tycoon*, "that every time he walks through the commissary keeps saying 'Fink' behind other writers' chairs.

If he didn't scare hell out of them, it'd be funny." The sense of class is not just an economic sense.

In a society of caste, it was very warming to associate as an equal with your economic superiors, even privately, and to have John Howard Lawson, a real playwright and an A scriptwriter, help you with your craft. The pioneers began to conduct evening lectures at the vegetarian Hollywood Health Cafeteria. Their program mixed Marxism and movie techniques, the gospel of the Soviets with the formulae of success. Their audience was largely of the unrooted and the insecure—young screen writers longing for credits, young actors longing for parts, cutters longing to be directors. And, of that drifting throng, a few were held and enchained.

The words in the Health Cafeteria had, of course, very little to do with the language of their calling. It was the experience of many who thought themselves most committed in the thirties to spend their nights in direct conflict with their days. They moved from one watertight compartment which encased what they thought to another which encased what they did. Fantasy is a staple in Hollywood, and its Communists lived their fantasy at once more acutely and more comfortably than any group of their comrades anywhere else in America.

The crest of Communist influence in Hollywood is generally placed somewhere in the period between 1936 and 1939. There are two ways of measuring that influence. One is in terms of so many parties for Spain or so many dinners for V. J. Jerome. That is the backdrop. The other measure is what the Communists did in the industry which was their function. That is the heart of their lives.

There follows a *representative* list of films written by scriptwriters who appear to have been Communists in the thirties. (The intermittent critical comments are from contemporary reviews by the Daughters of the American Revolution):

John Howard Lawson wrote *They Shall Have Music* ("Delightful"——DAR) and *Algiers,* with Charles Boyer and Hedy Lamarr. Lawson thus coined Pepe Le Moko's line: "Come with me to the Casbah," which, next to Odets' "We could make beautiful music together" (*The General Died at Dawn*), may be considered the most permanent cultural contribution by a left-wing scriptwriter during the entire period.

Lester Cole had screen credits on *Winter Carnival, Secrets of a Nazi Spy,* and *I Stole a Million.*

John Wexley wrote *Confessions of a Nazi Spy* ("Excellent . . . no sentimentalized patriotism"——DAR) and *Angels with Dirty Faces* ("Good"——DAR).

Mortimer Offner wrote *Radio City Revels, Little Tough Guys in Society,* and *The Saint in New York.*

Samuel Ornitz was responsible for *Little Orphan Annie* and *Army Girl,* "Dedicated to the Men and Mounts of the United States Cavalry."

Dalton Trumbo had a hand in *The Kid from Kokomo* (prize fighting); *The Flying Irishman* (Wrong-Way Corrigan); *Sorority House* ("Wholesome"); *A Man to Remember* (tone unfriendly to the American Medical Association, but "Good"——DAR); and *Fugitive for a Night* (pro-labor).

Gordon Kahn listed seven screenplays, whose character is best indicated by their titles: *Mickey the Kid; S.O.S. Tidal Wave; I Stand Accused; Mama Runs Wild; The Tenth Avenue Kid; Newsboys' Home;* and *Ex-Champ.*

Jerome Chodorov wrote a Communist part for Lew Ayres in *Rich Girl, Poor Girl* ("Good"——DAR). The critics considered his treatment unsympathetic.

This was a period when Dorothy Parker contributed to the *New Masses.* "There is no longer 'I,' there is 'WE.' The day of the individual is dead." Scott Fitzgerald observed, "Dotty has embraced the church and reads her office faithfully every day, [but it] does not affect her indifference." Between offices Miss Parker wrote the scripts for: *Sweethearts,* with Jeannette Mac-Donald ("Excellent"——DAR), and *Trade Winds.*

Hollywood was not totally deaf to the movement of the thirties, and there were a few examples of social realism in the period. But, by himself, Dudley Nichols (*Grapes of Wrath*), who was never a Communist, contributed a larger number of socially conscious scripts than all John Howard Lawson's revolutionary cadre together.

The Communists, of course, appear to have engaged in some

talk, dutiful and half-hopeless, about exploiting their access to production to alert the great audience to the struggle against fascism. A director once told a left-wing actor to improvise some business to fill a dead spot in a scene where he was waiting for an elevator; he clutched at that free moment to whistle a few bars of the "International." Lester Cole produced a movie about life in a boys' school, and was proud that he could make the football coach tell the players that it is better to die on their feet than live on their knees, a slogan borrowed from La Pasionaria, the Spanish Communist.

John Howard Lawson had one great chance to subvert the screen. In 1936, after Ethiopia, Walter Wanger took the picture of Benito Mussolini off his wall and commissioned Lawson to write *Blockade*, a film about the Spanish Civil War.

Wanger was so proud of the result that he invited Lillian Hellman, a woman of the left, to a special screening. Miss Hellman told him that it was an exciting show but that she wasn't quite sure what side it was on. The Daughters of the American Revolution agreed with her. *Blockade*, said the DAR, "may *not* be labeled partisan propaganda." Fifteen years later, the Un-American Activities Committee treated Lawson's pale effort as though it had been *Ten Days That Shook the World*.

A few bars from the "International," a slogan of La Pasionaria: these, of course, are only the rags and tags of what these people are supposed to have believed. It is hard to understand why gestures so empty of meaning seemed important to men whose daily lives were spent consuming the comforts of commerce. To say that they were vagrant twinges of conscience does not seem quite adequate. They are more like gauges of culture. For most of the younger Hollywood Communists appear to have been persons whose knowledge of the Communist International was limited to a snatch of its anthem. Their vision of the Spanish War was confined to La Pasionaria's phrase about refusing to die on her knees, which does not sit uncomfortably on the lips of a football coach.

Life was a scenario to most of them: the Comintern was a musical and Spain the Rose Bowl. We are told now that this was a time when the Communists influenced Hollywood's most passionate creative minds; if that is true, we may wonder why so few of them felt any impulse to take time off and form independent companies to produce films of deeper social content and involvement than the stuff they were fabricating for the big studios. The answer must be that they did not really care and were not fundamentally ashamed of what they were doing.

Their cultural pattern was Hollywood's, and they fit easily into the demands of the B picture. Few of them indeed showed enough capacity at major film output to be crashing successes at it; of seventeen scriptwriters listed by Leo Rosten as Hollywood's highest paid in 1938, only one has since been identified as a Communist.

It is one of the myths of the fifties that communism in the thirties had a special attraction for the best talents. But whatever magnetism the Party had was transient for the first-rate and permanent only for some of the third-rate. In an essay on "Marxian Socialism in the United States," Daniel Bell offers this summary of Communist intellectual influence in the thirties:

"The earliest converts were the literary individuals concerned with problems of self-expression and integrity—Dos Passos, James Farrell, Richard Wright, Sherwood Anderson, and Edmund Wilson. As these became aware of the dishonesty of Communist tactics, a new group appeared, the slick writers, the actors, the stage people—in short 'Hollywood'—for whom causes brought excitement, purpose, and, equally important, answers to the world's problems."

The vanguard departed very soon, and the hinder-middle-guard took its place. In 1937, when the Communists made Hollywood's Donald Ogden Stewart chairman of the American Writers Congress, they were not so much recognizing his special merit as confessing that there were no more serious artisans available for the office. The Hollywood scriptwriter was not really a spoiled poet; in most cases, it did not take long for his complaints to become merely formal and for him to be happy and comfortable, almost proud of his medium, and seldom longing for any higher one.

The aesthetics of Hollywood were, after all, very much like

the aesthetics of Josef Stalin. Richard H. Rovere remembers those aesthetics in these terms:

"The American intellectuals who fell hardest for Communism were men, not of aristocratic tastes in art but of tastes at once conventional and execrable. Many of them, of course, had no literary tastes of any sort. The reading matter of Communists was the dreariest kind of journalism. If they read poetry at all, it was likely to be Whittier and Sandburg, not Rimbaud and Ezra Pound . . . the cultural tone they set in the thirties was . . . deplorable because it was metallic and strident. Communist culture was not aristocratic; it was cheap and vulgar and corny."*

The Hollywood Communists had not so much violated their essence as found their proper level. The slogans, the sweeping formulae, the superficial clangor of Communist culture had a certain fashion in Hollywood precisely because they were two-dimensional appeals to a two-dimensional community. To say that an idea is fashionable is to say, I think, that it has been adulterated to a point where it is hardly an idea at all. And the first element to depart is the sense of personal responsibility to the idea. The founders of the Hollywood Communist Party sounded passionate in their protest against Hitler or Franco or Tom Girdler and countless other distant devils. But they ceased very soon to be passionate in their protest against Hollywood.

Back in New York, in the beginning, they had been entirely conscious of the motion picture's debasement to the idols of the market place. Now Hollywood's improvement was far less spectacular than their own adjustment to life there. There is always a certain friction between the young and the middle-aged; and John Howard Lawson seems to have been least happy with his apprentices at those moments when they were bitterest about Hollywood. He was anxious for them to write serious social criticism; he encouraged them to write proletarian novels. But less and less did the Hollywood society which lay festering at their feet seem to him suitable material for the novel of protest.

Budd Wilson Schulberg, then a Communist, made that discovery when he wrote his Hollywood novel *What Makes Sammy*

* *Confluence,* December, 1952.

Run?. Lawson took an early avuncular interest in *Sammy*, but its sour, savage treatment of the industry's *mores* shocked him very soon. He and V. J. Jerome did so much to discourage Schulberg from this unfortunate experiment that they ended by chasing him from the Party. *Sammy* turned out to be a thundering success with almost everyone but the movie producers and the Communists. Schulberg had described Hollywood as a moral slum and most of its residents as nonsalvageable vultures. This treatment was greeted by the Communists as an affront to a great folk art and as a mass of "dirt and filth." Schulberg had sinned not by surrender to the status quo but by over-intense revulsion against it.

For the Party had a stake in Hollywood by now. A young man of proper tendencies and acquisitive talent could even make a career there. George Wilner, former host at a Catskills summer hotel, persuaded the *New Masses* in 1937 that a Hollywood office could be a mother lode. He came there, ran the *New Masses* for a year, and quit to become a successful literary agent. The Communists, having made every other adjustment to custom, now had their own ten-percenter.

Some of the bloom passed with the Nazi-Soviet pact. The antifascist fronts bumped and ground uneasily into antiwar fronts, with heavy losses in short-haul passengers. Hollywood never again became what it was as a financial resource for Communist causes. The House Un-American Activities Committee estimated in 1950 that the film industry had contributed $926,568.36 to eight Hollywood groups which the committee cited as Communist fronts. The most substantial of them deceased in 1939.*

---

* The figure is far less impressive than it sounds. Fund-raising is especially expensive for movie people, whose concept of a front is much more in Thorstein Veblen's terms than in Harold Velde's. And one of the most important of the Un-American-Activities-Committee-designated fronts was the Hollywood Democratic Committee, which spent most of its funds electing good Democrats to public office. Granted that much leakage, the Party would have been fortunate to net as much as half a million dollars out of its Hollywood fronts in fifteen years.

The dues of Party members were, of course, a resource harder to calculate. Robert Rossen, once one of the most successful Party members, estimates that he contributed forty thousand dollars to various Party enterprises in ten years. But Edward Dmytryk, another successful director, turned his earnings over to a business manager who limited him to a twenty-five-dollar-a-week

But there were minimal defections among the true believers; in accordance with Hollywood's tradition of cultural lag, the pact's shock had hardly penetrated when Germany invaded the Soviets in the summer of 1941, and things seemed once more as they had been. For the next three years, there was a false and fevered glow. John Howard Lawson was revising his history of freedom in America for the fourth time and making loud the night with speeches on the unity of all elements to win the war. Albert Maltz, who had come to Hollywood as a Communist in the mid-thirties and gone down a little since, underwent an almost Stakhanovite resurgence with such recruiting films as *Destination Tokyo, Pride of the Marines,* and *Cloak and Dagger.*

They seemed once again back in fashion. But the older ones among them were not by now what they had been; by 1945, they were ten years away from the revolutionary theater. As Scott Fitzgerald's Dick Diver once said, "The change came a long way back—but at first it didn't show. The manner remains intact for some time after the morale cracks."

The face they presented to Hollywood was very much as of old. Their devotion to the long night meetings remained intact. Their banners still carried the old wild cries. But inside they were different men; they did not feel for each other as they had; they lived according to Hollywood habit, and it was not unusual for them to step upon one another's faces.

By now, some of the founders had commenced to fade a little, and their juniors were more important to Hollywood than they were. Robert Rossen had grown to such substance as scriptwriter that by 1945 he was a producer. Edward Dmytryk and Adrian Scott were directors and producers. And Hollywood is a place where there is no definition of your worth earlier than your last picture.

John Wexley had been a jewel of the workers' theater; by 1945, he was nothing more than an unsatisfactory employee to Scott and Dmytryk. They hired him to write *Cornered,* an anti-

---

personal allowance and permitted no sizable contribution to the Party. Hollywood Party dues averaged five per cent of income. But this figure is deceptive too, if we accept the testimony of Leopold Atlas, a screen writer, who reported that members of his Communist unit habitually bleated for an amelioration of dues and that many "were constantly in arrears."

Nazi film. His script was so soggy that Dmytryk dropped him for another writer. Wexley went at once to Lawson to say that Scott and Dmytryk had produced a pro-Nazi film. They were subjected to a Party trial and severely censured. When they protested, Lawson observed with a cold smile that they had much to learn about discipline. Dmytryk left the Party and Scott became increasingly less active.

Leopold Atlas, another of the newcomers, rewrote *The Story of GI Joe* from a draft submitted by Philip Stevenson, a veteran of the Party and of the revolutionary theater. When Atlas was finished, there was barely a trace of Stevenson left in the script. Stevenson, desperate for a screen credit, appealed to Lawson to help him get equal billing with Atlas as author of *GI Joe*. Lawson managed to wangle a full credit for Stevenson from the Screen Writers Guild. He had rescued one of the old at the expense of one of the new. That crisis is a measure of the Hollywood Communists: one Bolshevik was fighting another for the empty merit badge of a commercial enterprise.

There were deeper crises, and one of them taught even Lawson that age and authority are no defense when your time comes. He had enjoyed the war very much, and no Hollywood Communist could claim to be closer to Earl Browder, that symbol of the Party's complete dedication to victory over the Nazis and lasting friendship between the United States and the Soviet Union. Then, in June of 1945, Browder was cast out as a counter-revolutionary. It looked then as if Lawson must go too; for a few hours he was deprived of all his Party honors. But, somehow, he scrambled back; and in the long watches of nights spent explaining the difficulties which certain comrades may have with the explanation of the new situation by the comrade chairman last night, John Howard Lawson's voice was heard, longer and longer and longer, reciting the crimes of his fallen friend.

If they felt the change in themselves and looked back and wondered what had happened to them, only Albert Maltz ever expressed any public hint of regret; and he was very soon sorry for it. In 1946, Maltz surveyed the impermanence of his screen work, his two novels, and his few short stories and wrote a sad little essay in the *New Masses* wondering whether he might not have been a better writer for being less of a Party man over the last decade.

It was not enough, said Maltz, to think of art as social weapon. The demands of orthodox communism upon the writer were, he had decided, "not a useful guide but a straitjacket." He had done his own best work when he was least conscious of the Party looking over his shoulder. A great writer did not have to be a Marxist. For a very little while, Maltz was a bit of a hero in Hollywood, and his younger comrades came around to squeeze his hand in congratulation.

And then the wolves fell upon him too. Samuel Sillen, editor of the *New Masses*, flew out to Hollywood and called a special Party meeting to flay Maltz for heresy. The Communists have always been tolerant of deviations in content and harsh with deviations in form. Their Hollywood comrades had written musical comedies, and jokes for Abbott and Costello, and empty banalities about the American system without ever hearing a word of censure from the *New Masses*. No one in the Hollywood Party had written as a Marxist for ten years. The Communists had never complained, for this was an acceptance of the Hollywood code. But now Maltz had implied that honesty was so important for a writer that Marxism must be sacrificed to it. And heresy is a crime of thought, not of action.

There was hardly a scriptwriter among the Communists who came to witness the trial of Albert Maltz who had not sold himself and betrayed the revolution with his typewriter to make a living every day he had worked in Hollywood. But he had kept his thoughts pure; and, as the Party's voice, Sillen was saying to him that there were no sins of the deed if the faith were held sacred. Leopold Atlas, who sat and watched it, remembered that, when Maltz rose to defend himself, all his friends shouted him down. He remembered Maltz's oldest comrades most of all as either silent or ravening for his destruction. Lawson for once sat quiet; but Atlas recalled Alvah Bessie's "bitter vituperation and venom," and Herbert Biberman, "his every accent dripping with hatred." Maltz, Biberman, and Bessie had been together as Communists since the thirties; three years later, the Un-American Activities Committee sent them to prison together.

George Beck, one of the younger ones, remembered that the burning of Albert Maltz had lasted through the night, and that, when he left, he stumbled over somebody who was asleep. A week later they were summoned to the assault again until Maltz, with the howls of triumph ringing about him, broke and recanted. The face of the Party had hardened and never again would the innocent and the uncommitted feel comfortable before it. The recollections of that period for repentant Hollywood Communists are of repetitive plunges into a cesspool. They have forgotten the abstractions of doctrine; they remember only Alvah Bessie "morosely clawing" at Lester Cole, Dalton Trumbo "ripping at" Cole, and Cole "tearing at" Lawson. They were walking toward a common grave, hating one another.

Rossen had gone by now; Dmytryk and Scott were inactive. Dozens of lesser people had stopped coming around. Perhaps a quarter of the Party's membership in Hollywood dropped away in the two years between Browder's fall and the onset of the House Committee on Un-American Activities.

The Un-American Activities Committee began spreading its subpoenas around Hollywood in September of 1947. For a little while the Communists were all together again, and their industry seemed to stand with them. Martin Dies had come to Los Angeles in 1940 and had been almost hooted out of town. The tide of fashion did not appear to run much stronger for Committee Chairman J. Parnell Thomas, and he had the additional social liability of carrying John Rankin of Mississippi in his stable.

The committee had summoned nineteen Hollywood personalities suspected of subversive affiliations. Their names were known very soon and they had the illusory status of popular heroes. Senator Claude Pepper was in Hollywood at the time; he was happy to meet all the subpoenees at Edward G. Robinson's house and advise them of their rights. The community tone was anything but hostile; the industry's leaders were uneasy, but affirmed their devotion to free thought.

On October 18, 1947, the night before the inquiry began, Bartley Crum and other attorneys for its nineteen individual targets met with Eric Johnston, president of the Motion Picture Association of America, at Washington's Shoreham Hotel. Crum reported an amiable, united session, in the course of which Johnston agreed that the House Committee was bent on censuring the movies and promised that there would never be a Hollywood blacklist against Communists.

The early scenes of J. Parnell Thomas' script were hardly calculated to shake Johnston. The most newsworthy witnesses were at once more personable than informative and true to that Hollywood tradition which dictates a maximum of language and a minimum of life force. Mrs. Leila Rogers, mother of Ginger, told of her daughter's refusal to accept a role tainted with one subversive speech: "Share and share alike—that's democracy!" Gary Cooper reported that he had "turned down quite a few scripts because they were tinged with Communistic ideas," but he could not recall the names of their authors. He had also heard statements at cocktail parties which struck him as "pinko mouthings."

But even these enemies of communism in Hollywood betrayed a sense that the Communists were after all members of the family. Adolph Menjou, who had wailed against collectivism for fifteen years, had no suggestion for controlling them beyond close supervision. "We have," he said, with obvious pride, "many Communist writers who are splendid writers." Jack L. Warner, of Warner Brothers, reported that some of his left-wing stable had been excessively pertinacious in slipping improper material into their scripts. But nothing serious had ever got by him, said Warner. He had found it necessary to get rid of a few habitual offenders, John Howard Lawson not among them.

But a general ban on Communists in Hollywood seemed to Warner almost unthinkable. "I can't for the life of me figure where men could get together . . . to deprive a man of his livelihood . . . because of his political beliefs." Dore Schary of R.K.O.-Radio, the most aggressive liberal among the producers, told the committee that he was not ready to purge his studio of Communists. "I would," he declared, "still maintain the right of any man to think as he pleases."

Even J. Parnell Thomas did not then appear to be committed to the proposition that Communists should be blacklisted without some proof of overt act. He began with an examination of various pictures for evidence of subversive ideas; the results were sparse. That was to be expected; whatever their ideas, the Hollywood Communists had written for Hollywood and not for Moscow.

By the time Thomas had wound up the case for the prosecution, those portions of the film industry which were not outraged at him were laughing at him. On the fifth day, John Howard Lawson was called as the first unfriendly witness. He faced the committee full of the illusion that he spoke for most of Hollywood and with entire faith in the promises of its princes.

Poor John Lawson had crawled a long time. He had used up or abused his talents, and he was almost a back number. Just this once he could enjoy a fling at freedom. "I am an American," said Lawson, "and I am not at all easy to intimidate, and don't think I am." He had forgotten in the splendor of this hour all those shabby nights in 1945, when he had allowed the bravoes from the Party headquarters to pummel him at their pleasure. Parnell Thomas asked him whether he was a Communist and he stood on the Bill of Rights. Thomas summoned the Capitol police to lift him off the stand, and announced that here was an obvious case of contempt of Congress.

Nine more of Lawson's hostile brotherhood went before Thomas over the next five days: Dalton Trumbo, Alvah Bessie, Albert Maltz, Samuel Ornitz, Herbert Biberman, Lester Cole, Ring Lardner, Jr., Edward Dmytryk, and Adrian Scott. Dmytryk was no longer a Communist; Scott was almost certainly not one; there may have been one or two other backsliders among the rest. But for the moment they were all together and defiant. They were not very attractive witnesses; their habits were Hollywood's, and long training had reduced their prose to the muddier depths of a Nash-Kelvinator ad. In all their contrived and mechanical outcries, there was only one glimpse of humanity. J. Parnell Thomas asked Ring Lardner, Jr., if he were a Communist, and Lardner replied:

"I could answer that question, but I would hate myself in the morning." He was rejected with all the rest.

They were not especially appetizing, of course, but very few people in Hollywood appeared at that point to think they deserved to go to prison on no greater proof of sin. In 1947, the myth of the fifties was not yet so powerful a weapon against the fringes of the thirties. The November 29, 1947, Gallup Poll found that 39 per cent of the public felt that the unfriendly ten witnesses should not be punished for their performance and that another 14 per cent were unconvinced that they should.

In Hollywood itself, the proportions of sympathy were much larger. A Hollywood defense committee sponsored a nationwide broadcast for the recalcitrant ten on November 2, 1947. The contributing artists included Judy Garland, Margaret Sullavan, Van Heflin, Myrna Loy, Robert Young, and Joseph Cotten, none of whom could be considered afflicted with left-wing associations.

After the program, Frank Sinatra said: "If this committee gets a green light from the American people, will it be possible to make a broadcast like this a year from today?" A year later, it was not possible, and no more because of J. Parnell Thomas than because of Hollywood. If there had been another such demonstration, Frank Sinatra would hardly have associated himself with it. For, just three weeks after this show of resistance, Hollywood collapsed before the Un-American Activities Committee.

Congress met on November 27th, and with near unanimity cited the hostile ten for contempt. They started the long trek which led them to federal prison. And they were almost alone when they began it. A committee of motion picture producers gathered at the Waldorf-Astoria. As they watched Congress, they felt more and more impelled to cleanse themselves of Lawson and his little band. Two days after the contempt citations, the producers announced that the Ten would be suspended until they had either been acquitted or had purged themselves of contempt.

The producers repeated their contention that "nothing subversive had ever appeared on the screen." But all the same they promised that they would never again knowingly employ a Communist in their industry. They had acquitted the defendants, and now they proceeded to punish their notions. It was a decision which surprised almost everyone, even J. Parnell Thomas. Robert Stripling, chief investigator of the Un-American Activities Com-

mittee, said later that the uproar against his Hollywood production had so befuddled Thomas that he might have called off his
troops if the industry had not rescued him by capitulation.

As a former screen writer, Dore Schary, now of M-G-M, was
deputized to explain the new, clean-sweep policy to a Screen
Writers Guild controlled by men whose anti-communism did not
prevent them from being highly distrustful of it. The choice of
Schary was a piece of symbolism; he himself had been a Hollywood liberal when the tide of fashion was highest; without ever
being a Communist, he had belonged to some of the organizations upon which Thomas' committee was now visiting its
disfavor. He very plainly did not enjoy his assignment. "We do
not ask you to condone this," he said very sadly; and then he
departed, pausing a moment, according to the testimony of an
unfriendly observer, to put his hand on Dalton Trumbo's shoulder and say a kind word. A little later Trumbo went to prison
and Dore Schary went to Metro-Goldwyn-Mayer as executive
producer.

The screen writers voted overwhelming displeasure at the new
policy. But there was very little they could do about it. Soft, slack
Hollywood had accepted the political purge which so few really
wanted. The protestants ceased their clamoring. Lawson and the
rest of the Hollywood Ten went to prison, and everywhere there
was indifference. The studios began the process of clearance for
the innocent and the clouded. The Un-American Activities Committee, whom weariness never afflicts and tedium never deters,
continued its search for the guilty, who by now seemed all to
have fled.

By 1948, the Hollywood Communists had almost ceased to
function as a group. George Beck, long since a backslider, was
writing at home one day when Mortimer Offner, an old comrade,
came around to ask him to rejoin the Party. "I said, 'No thanks.'
He didn't press me particularly. He did, however, rather sadly
comment, 'Gee, its getting tough, everybody is leaving.' "

They made pathetic efforts to cling to what had once been
theirs. Dalton Trumbo and Lester Cole appear to have slipped
through a script or so under pseudonyms. Then the House Committee called George Wilner, their literary agent, and asked him

about this underground traffic. Wilner stood on his privilege against self-incrimination on this and all other questions. There was no show of dangerous notions in anything Trumbo or Cole had submitted; there did not need to be.

By now, conscious of the results of brash speech to their pioneers, the Communists were standing on the Fifth Amendment. Each went before the committee, ran through his little formula, and disappeared. But now even the innocents were in too much danger to worry about the guilty. It was no longer enough to be able to swear that you were not a Communist. You had, in the delicate language of professionals in these matters, to get off the hook as a fellow traveler.

Edward G. Robinson, suddenly unassigned after lush years as an actor, told an unsympathetic committee that he had a clearance from William Randolph Hearst, Sr. There was no evidence that Robinson had been a Communist; he had simply given money to dubious causes. It took him two years to restore himself. John Garfield was unemployed too; he swore that, even during his days in the revolutionary theater, he had never been a Communist. But he remained displaced from Hollywood, wandering in New York, seeking the key to absolution, to die one night of a heart attack—with Clifford Odets weeping at his grave.

The day of the locust had its ironies. For Hollywood intended, if it could, to go on as it had. Human sacrifices were necessary, but they should, if possible, be limited. In this spirit, Dore Schary went through his sad duty of supervising the loyalty check at M-G-M.

One of those interviewed, according to legend, was a well-known comedian who searched a somewhat barren political past and finally remembered that he had once attended a meeting of the Hollywood Anti-Nazi League. His interrogator said that it was always a demonstration of good faith to give names, and would he please try to recall who had gone with him.

The comedian protested that it had all been so long ago. Then, under further prodding, a ray broke through and he said, "Gee, now I remember: Dore Schary went with me." There was a pause. "Okay," said the interrogator. "If you can't think of any names, you can't think of any names."

The names, the names, can't you give us the names, was the unchanging buzz of the wings of the locust. The House committee had by now lost its bite. It was very gentle with the recalcitrant and the repentant alike. The repentant were coming in streams, the duped, the floaters, the briefly committed, each with his sad little story of the dream and the gray dawn. The stories were very much the same; their testators all agreed that the Party had not done very much nor been very compelling. They all gave the same names now. The ritual of absolution was more important than any fresh revelation.

Edward Dmytryk, almost ruined, finished his prison term and, his duty done, told the committee about his life in the Party. Robert Rossen would say at first only that he had broken and would name no names, a piece of reticence which cost him one hundred thousand dollars in contracts. And then he too, now assured that no one could say he did it for money, came in and told his story.

And Clifford Odets, the release of his *Clash By Night* at stake, came down to say that it had all been so very long ago. The glow had passed from him; he had begun selling his Paul Klees. He told an old acquaintance from his days of glory that it was perhaps unfortunate to be considered a genius so young.

No one could say when it was all over what it had all meant. The House committee's long search through the ruins was hardly impressive by any rule of numbers. In December, 1952, the committee released a list of persons who had been identified to it as having been at one time or another members of the Hollywood Communist Party. The list totaled 222 employees or wives of employees of the film industry. It was presumably incomplete, although there have been few additions since. By no means all of them were Communists at the same time. Taken all together, they represented a little over one half of one per cent of the industry.

And there were signs that the committee had hardened them and given them, in their twilight, a brief, last fling at a moment like their dreams. The Communists themselves would seem to have been much more successful than the Un-American Activities

Committee in disillusioning Communists. Of the repentant Party members whose testimony before the committee was most thorough, Martin Berkley had broken in 1943; Budd Schulberg had left in 1939; Edward Dmytryk, Frank Tuttle, Leopold Atlas, and Robert Rossen were all out by 1946. Only Richard Collins appears to have been a Communist in September, 1947, when the committee began its investigation.

Almost every 1947 Party member would seem to have stood fast throughout the day of the locust. There is strong evidence that Dmytryk, Collins, Rossen, and Tuttle actually postponed a public breach with the Party out of loyalty to their friends in time of trouble.

As time went on, the Un-American Activities Committee's Hollywood investigation was less a search for the guilty than a confessional for the repentant. The committee was especially proud of its record of conversion and regeneration. But it was regeneration by force of arms. No one could say that the committee had not damaged the Communists. It had forced the industry to choose between its empty affirmations about freedom and the commercial code by which it lived. The choice was inevitable: it meant a blacklist of suspected Communists and a parade of unhappy sinners seeking clearance from the committee in order to return to the golden city from which they had been displaced. Persons who enjoy that sort of thing are welcome to their pleasures, but they should not ascribe to them the virtues of religious conversion.

William Faulkner, who is an old-fashioned man, sat by and watched the Hollywood jitters and found them a mystery. One of his friends wailed that he had been tapped by the Un-American Activities Committee, and that this could be his ruin. After the victim had departed, Faulkner observed, "—— don't have to worry none, so long as he writes good." It was an idea of art unfamiliar to Hollywood and its Communists, recalcitrant and repentant alike.

Dusty and almost forgotten, the Hollywood Ten came out of prison and wandered away. They had been of movies, the magic land of movies, and were fit for very little else. Maltz was in

Mexico, trying once more to be a writer, unhampered at last by compulsions about art as a weapon, unfettered in fact by anything but the loss of powers.

John Howard Lawson finished his history of American freedom and passed it for the last time through its political sieve. It had dried up on him; and when it was published it broke almost like dust in the hand.

He was free of commerce now and could be a political man. In 1951, he stood on a Union Square platform in New York and watched the comrades march on May Day. A young man was braying into a microphone over a straggly crowd that here come the youth, here come the anti-fascist forces of peace—over and over—sterile, mechanical noise past all meaning.

One of his elders leaned over and said that John Howard Lawson was on the platform and should be introduced. The voice paused a moment in its clangor. "And now," it rose again, "I want to introduce a great anti-fascist, a great fighter for peace, a man you all know." The young man stopped and turned to his mentor and, without bothering to put his hand over the microphone, asked for all to hear:

"What did you say his name was?"

7

THE LANGUAGE of love was seldom on the public lips of most of the persons in these studies. Their rhetoric held little room for its lights and shadows. They at least talked as though the passions of love and hate were not important to them. The passions are particular and their superficial concerns were for the general.

Theirs was a movement which offered a new place to woman. It was the place of partner and equal, and the surface of its image was sexless. The thirties promised a final triumph of feminism. And they buried—or thought they buried—forever the woman of the genteel tradition.

The tradition's image of woman had, of course, sickened and withered in the twenties. Ellen Glasgow, a detached if sympathetic observer at woman's bedside, once summed up her decay in the years after World War I:

"It is at least open to question whether women would ever have rebelled against their confining attitude had they not observed a diminishing humility in the novels written by men. At all events, after the War, male disillusionment with virtue, which had thickened like dust, invaded the whole flattened area of modern prose fiction. By some ironic reversal of the situation, woman, for so long the ideal of man, became, in a literary sense, the obstacle to all his higher activities. In a large majority of postwar novels, a woman or two women or even three women thrust themselves between almost every male character and some bright particular moon for which he is crying."

The new image of woman as impediment of which Miss Glasgow speaks was rather an old one in the American radical tradition. McCreary, the Wobbly in Dos Passos' *The 42nd Parallel*, was in Miss Glasgow's terms, a model of "man, the poet and dreamer, in perpetual flight from woman, the devourer of dreams and poets." McCreary's life is spent in intermixed flight from and entrapment by Maisie, the wife with whom he had nothing in common.

"When he was away from her he felt somehow sore at Maisie most of the time, but when he was with her he melted absolutely. He tried to get her to read pamphlets on socialism, but she laughed and looked at him with her big intimate blue eyes and said it was too deep for her. She liked to go to the theatre and eat in restaurants where the linen was starched and there were waiters in dress suits."

And yet, though they feared and fled woman in general, the Wobblies had their feminine ideal too. It was intensely feminine, almost indeed a banal replica of the tradition. The woman of their dreams was pure as Joan of Arc was pure; she traveled with the troops and was untouched by them. She did not aim to rule man but to inspire him. She was not a member of his General Executive Board, but the flame outside his prison cell. The ordinary woman was an enemy; she, the special woman, was the ideal.

The revolutionaries of the thirties widened that image and flattened it and made it general. They appeared to believe that every housewife could be a Joan of Arc. They gloried in the entombment of the ideal of the feminine as a special repository of love and inspiration. And they raised above the tomb the image of the Comrade Woman, the partner in the struggle.

The thirties appear in recollection to have swarmed with the Comrade Woman. She seemed constructed of whalebone, and often stronger than the male. Few of us who were not as strong as we should have been in those days can forget a moment's confrontation by some avenging female angel from the movement calling us back to our duties like a maiden elder sister calling us to supper.

They went to meetings and they marched in parades and they were incessant in that round of inanities which was so much of the routine of their commitment. They were the housekeepers of their movement. That may indicate that they were more conformist than they knew. Certainly they dressed with a care that was new among women of the left, and some of them were self-righteous to a degree hardly fitting their own image of themselves as rebels. There are incalculable risks in the ambition to be a member of the Central Committee. Not the least of those risks is the temptation to hold back part of oneself.

I think that in the end more of them found the movement empty than had been the experience of the rebel girls of the first two decades of this century. But that experience was never the same for all of them. Many found love in the movement, just as others found only the imitation of love as they had found only the imitation of rebellion. But in thinking about them all, I was more and more oppressed by those who spoiled their lives.

These were hardly typical of the women caught up in this lost time of our concern. But they were the most notorious, and their very notoriety seemed to me a clue to the difference between so many radical women of the thirties and the rebel girl of tradition. They were at least what the fifties chose to remember of the left woman of the thirties.

I thought of Elizabeth Bentley, who joined the Communist Party because she was lonely and who found love there, and became a spy because that was her lover's business. And I thought of Anne Moos, who, by her own account, married William Remington, not because she loved him but because she thought he held promise of leadership in the movement. Elizabeth Bentley's life was a dreadful, painful parody of marital fidelity; Anne Moos's was a caricature of the marriage of convenience.

Much of what I have written about Elizabeth Bentley comes from her own autobiographical *Out of Bondage*. My account of those strange young lovers, Anne and William Remington, comes in the main from their testimony before the various tribunals which ultimately found Remington guilty of perjury. And, against the three of them, I could not resist the memory of Mary Heaton Vorse, a surviving rebel girl at seventy-six, who has lived all her life in the same house.

They are none of them typical women of any time, but I am not sure that there are not some universals in their story. For Elizabeth Bentley and Anne Moos, at least, seem to me persons whose lives were warped and broken through a failure of love. The failures of the thirties were very often failures of that love which was so seldom a conscious concern to them; the punishment we receive in the end is so very often for the crime we committed with the least consideration.

The Rebel Girl

"Why should I blame her that she filled my days
With misery, that she would of late
Have taught to ignorant men most violent ways
Or hurled the little streets upon the great
Had they but courage equal to desire?"
WILLIAM BUTLER YEATS, No Second
Troy

"Women were thus endlessly absorbent, and to deal with
them was to walk on water."
HENRY JAMES, The Ambassadors

IN ALL her life, Mary Heaton Vorse has had no involvements which did not lie upon the outermost extremities of love.

She cannot leave behind her many monuments of substance. That is her own choice; even very late, she felt little disposition to write her autobiography or set her papers in order or perform any of the other rituals prescribed for persons with a sense of history.

For she brought to her old age no need for survival. She had been not *in* history but *of* history. The chronicles which cover her life span had small room for her name. But there was always an easy rule for locating her in time and space: whenever you read across forty years about an event in which men stood in that single, desperate moment which brings all past, all present, and all future to one sharp point for them, you could assume that Mary Vorse had been there.

In 1950, when she was seventy-six, she came to Morristown, Tennessee, to watch and write about a textile strike. She could not sit in its old hotel lobby without remembering that she had been there before, twenty years ago, on the same mission to coal miners. Then, as always, she set down the conversation of persons in trouble, because, then as always, Mary Vorse had no feeling for the abstract. Before she abandoned all sense of profit, she had written popular fiction for the magazines. At moments through her journey, she would stop and hole up in some hotel to dictate the easy flow of soft, popular language that paid her enough to return to the hard road of her choice.

She had known so many people so long ago, and she had buried most of them. Big Bill Haywood and the urban Wobblies were in and out of her Greenwich Village apartment forty years ago. She was married awhile to Robert Minor, then a distinguished cartoonist and afterward a Communist functionary. For a little while she was close to the Communists herself in the twenties, but never in any easy, comfortable, ceremonial sense. Her chief labor for them had been publicity for their Passaic, New Jersey, textile strike in 1926. But that had just been one of so many others, Wobbly strikes, independent uprisings, AFL and CIO strikes, the quiet ones and the noisy ones.

The coal and iron police rode her down at Braddock, Pennsylvania, in the 1919 steel strike. Eighteen years later, when she was in her sixties, she was clubbed by a policeman's billy in a Youngstown, Ohio, steel strike. And, in 1952, she was still in the game, talking to the longshoremen the other reporters neglected for a series on the New York waterfront.

There was very little about herself in all that she wrote about those battles ancient and modern; most of them were, in fact, records of the ordinary talk of strikers and their wives, spare and low-key language, all of it exactly as spoken, because Mary Vorse knew that the one thing most dangerous to falsify is the speech of men. And there will be nothing bitter in her so long as she lives. As Yeats said of another dedicated old lady, she needed upon her difficult road no spur of hate.

Mary Vorse, as early as the thirties, was a relict of a great tradition. But it was a tradition which, even for most of its children, was writ on water. The revolutionaries of the thirties were self-consciously in the line of an American history of social rebellion. They do not appear, however, to have known very much about that history. Their concern was not for the past. Their rhythms were not rhythms of memory. They seemed to feel they had sprung full-blown; if they had models, they were European. They sang a folk song about Joe Hill, the IWW poet; but very few of them could have told you who Joe Hill was or how he lived and died, except that the copper bosses got him.

Mary Vorse was a living figure from Joe Hill's tradition. The scorned and ragged rebels of the first three decades of the century might logically have considered the thirties a time of redemption in which their survivors would be treated as triumphant saints. It does not appear to have been that way for Mary Vorse, who in any case would hardly have asked so much. She traveled her road, and it is safe to assume that most of the girl comrades who might have been considered her daughters or at least her nieces had never even heard of her.

Her life certainly had very little meaning for Elizabeth Bentley and Anne Moos, who was to become Mrs. William Remington, even though both for a time accepted or thought they accepted a commitment very much like hers. Their lives, like Mary Vorse's, were controlled by love. For Elizabeth Bentley, love did not flow clear and constant as it had for Mary Vorse; it was absent more often than present, long withheld and briefly granted, and then taken away forever. Anne Moos's life was controlled by the absence of love; she built it upon a substitution of convenience for passion.

They died inside, these two women of the thirties, because their lovers came too late or not at all. Mary Vorse lived on because she found her love young and neither forsook nor was forsaken. For Mary Vorse had joined the avenging army in 1913, because men and women were suffering for its triumph. Elizabeth Bentley became a Communist twenty-two years later, because she was alone and suffering.

Elizabeth Bentley remembers very well the terrible evening in March of 1935 when she joined the Communist Party. She had been in New York less than a year, after Vassar and after some studies in Italy. Her family all were dead. In her whole life there was no one, and she had searched all day for a job. That afternoon, looking over Riverside Drive where the lovers walk, she thought of one woman friend, a purposeful friend, who could bear being alone, who was a Communist and held a harsh contempt for Elizabeth Bentley's New England inhibitions. And so she arose, in that first dreadful advance of the shadows of the end of the day, and went to the apartment of her friend and asked how she could become a Communist.

This woman of purpose was sitting by the stove, "curled up," in the image of Elizabeth Bentley's always domestic memory, with the *Daily Worker*. She melted when Elizabeth told of her decision. There were, she said, certain tests, but Elizabeth could be reasonably assured of acceptance. Somewhere at last she had been accepted.

Her new comrades had so intelligent a grasp of world affairs that poor Elizabeth wondered how *she* could ever develop such a keen brain. And they all had so much energy, sitting as they did in cafeterias long after the unit meeting, so animated, so intense, so absolutely exempt from the demands of slumber. But, even so, after barely a month's membership, these *epigoni* made her educational director of her party unit, and she felt more inadequate than ever.

There was now no more time to be lonely. She found a job with the New York City home-relief bureau and was naturally active with the union there. Along with her new intellectual responsibilities, there were the unit bureau meeting, the union meeting, and the meeting of the Communist fraction inside her union local.

All these consortia left, of course, very little time for the active liberation of mankind. Miss Bentley is able to recall one mass demonstration for the unemployed, during which she struck a policeman, presumably with her pocketbook, and found herself borne exhausted upon a tide of men hoarsely raising the first lines of the "International." Her novitiate seems otherwise to have been entirely concerned with housekeeping in narrow little rooms.

But these exercises so wore down Elizabeth Bentley that before long the doctor advised her to leave her home-relief job and find something easier. There were so few openings of that sort in those days that, for a while, she went on relief herself before finding a mixture of part-time typing, translating, and tutoring which barely sustained her.

By now her whole life was the Party—lunches at the Columbia cafeteria with three of the girls; evenings at sea with Marxism-Leninism at the Workers School (it was all too much for her, but the teachers were so friendly); and the meetings, always the meetings, the unit, the unit bureau, and the special section for agit-prop (agitation and propaganda) directors like herself, and, of course, the weekly parties for fund-raising and recruitment.

Eugene Lyons has left us one reminder of the unforced fraternity of those latter revels. In *The Red Decade,* Lyons fished up a Communist pamphlet titled: *Give a Party for the Party.* Its cover was a cartoon of dancing dice, a swing band, and the youth doing the Big Apple. Its text included these detailed directions: "Have a guest book to register names and addresses. This makes a mailing list afterwards. For entertainment, call the Party Entertainment Committee. . . . Add refreshments, dancing, mix well and dish out! . . . For beer parties, comrades, remember that pouring beer in the middle gives more foam and less liquid—stretches each barrel further."

Elizabeth Bentley was thus permitted to relax only at those intervals when she was not presiding over the guest roster and then drink what was not even an honest glass of beer. Otherwise she was one of those desperate women who are the soul of the Communist movement in New York City, flurrying through her round of idiocies, accomplishing nothing with the absolute assurance of accomplishment.

She was the sort of Communist who understood that it was her duty to report any lapses from purity. If Comrade X got drunk in public, she was expected to turn him in. When she heard of an opening in the Italian Library of Information, she trotted down to Thirteenth Street and asked the comrades if this wouldn't be a strategic underground position. When they said it would, she took the job and listened at keyholes and searched among scrap baskets like some old biddy. Elizabeth Bentley sounds like a rather nice little person, but she was unquestionably turning into an old maid.

The Comrade Woman of her incessant sort seems to follow a rather definite pattern. Miss Bentley recurs constantly in her autobiography to the lack of love in her life. She is frank to describe the whirl of Communist activity as a diversion from very real personal problems. She indicates that she maintained an unsullied ignorance about real affairs throughout the experience. And she appears unconscious of the total absence of social utility in all her efforts.*

Miss Bentley might have paddled in her shallow, turbulent pool without serious mischief had she not, in her own expression, "found the man I loved." Jacob Golos was introduced to her as a comrade from the Comintern interested in her reports on the Italian Library of Information, reports which, he patiently explained, were useless for being amateurish. Jacob Golos was no amateur. He had been a pioneer American Communist and was, even now, one of his Party's three chief disciplinarians. Miss Bentley is still almost proud to report that he attended all the more important Party meetings and sat behind a curtain so he would not be recognized.

He was also a representative of the Soviet secret police, a vocation somewhat at variance with Miss Bentley's description of his shy kindness and gentle ways and his mouth that was so much like her own dear, dead mother's. He was also a dog-tired man looking for a haven in his twilight. Elizabeth Bentley was Joan to his Darby.

She nagged at him to buy a new hat. Night after night, she held him in her arms trying to soothe him into relaxation. Nothing could have more enchanted a man borne down by experience than the innocence which might otherwise have seemed simple stupidity. One evening, while they were burning documents in domestic ecstasy, she came upon his old GPU card. The initials

* Elizabeth Bentley has no clinical psychiatric history; but, for some insight into her type, we might consider the findings of Dr. Herbert Krugman, who studied the case histories of a number of Communists under psychoanalysis. Krugman says that four out of five male Communists were described by their analysts as persons of real talent, while only two of five women subjects could be said to possess any talent at all. The average *neurotic* male Communist would thus appear to be a person who has talent without genius. The average *neurotic* female Communist would seem to be unafflicted with either. The women subjects of his study, said Krugman, had irrational life goals and were obsessed with the search for guilt-free outlets. The special frustrations of modern women, he concluded, made them altogether better haters than men.

seemed familiar, and she asked him what they meant. He told her the card was a Moscow streetcar pass.

He told her too how much he loved her and that he could even be very happy if it were not for the shadow that lay before them. Elizabeth Bentley was, of course, roughly as well equipped to understand this piece of total wisdom as Louisa May Alcott would have been in some similar involvement with Feodor Dostoevski. On her side, she was absolutely happy. She called him Yasha, and he called her *golubushka*, a Russian endearment derived from the word for "dove," which Elizabeth Bentley is apparently still unable to spell.

Life with Yasha meant divorcement from unit meetings and other pestilential aspects of open Party activity. But Elizabeth Bentley was glad to efface herself as Yasha's helpmeet in all his activities. He found a place for her with his United Shipping and Service Corporation, a holding company aimed at controlling all passenger and freight traffic to the Soviet Union. And after hours, she helped him gather documents from various underground contacts, chief among them a chemical engineer who stole blueprints, and Walter Lippmann's secretary, who sat with her on hot Saturday afternoons and filched documents from the boss's files.

In 1941, the FBI appears to have developed a certain interest in Yasha's business, and poor *golubushka* developed the art of dodging its agents. This was a fresh source of worry about Yasha. She knew that his heart was weak enough to kill him soon, and this new harassment terrified her as a burden possibly fatal to him.

Then the Nazis invaded Russia, and poor Yasha was so bemused by this new turn that he came home and forgot to kiss her. His new orders had made him absent-minded. The Soviet Union was fighting for its life and had to know all there was to know about the situation behind the scenes in Washington. Elizabeth must go there and assist in the development of a new information center. She said of course she would. Yasha kissed her very gently and said he had known he could depend on his *golubushka*.

And thenceforth, until Yasha died in her arms the night after

Thanksgiving, 1943, and for an empty ten months alone thereafter, Elizabeth Bentley was a courier between the Soviet secret
police and a group of Washington families who were feeding it
information. The friends she made then are almost all shadows
now. They do not seem to us persons of special interest, except
perhaps for William and Anne Moos Remington, who did not
know what they wanted and who were destroyed by the absence
of love.

The Remingtons, Miss Bentley testified later, had been brought
to the firm's attention by Joseph North, editor of the Communist
New Masses, and a friend of Anne's and her mother's in Croton,
New York. The Remingtons, according to Miss Bentley's version
of North's report, were young Communists who felt very isolated
in Washington and wished somebody would take an interest in
them. Remington had been assigned to a war agency in 1942;
there was reason to hope that he could pass on all sorts of delica-
cies sooner than the Soviets could get them through more conventional channels.

Yasha had described Remington as both reliable and brilliant,
but Miss Bentley found him almost useless as a source. Typical,
clean-cut American type, she decided, with her special feeling
for the trite. But nervous, elusive, generally a small boy trying to
avoid mowing the lawn. She complained to Yasha that the firm
would be better off without Remington entirely, but Yasha
couldn't bring himself to abandon promise so glittering.

William Remington told a tale so different that it brought him
to his death in Lewisburg Penitentiary. Anne Moos Remington
told several stories; her final one fitted Miss Bentley's version
more closely than that of the father of her children. But both Miss
Bentley and Remington agree on one thing: William Remington
thought her a nuisance and wished he had never committed himself to association with her.

But it was Bill Remington's undoing that he could never resist
the fascination of being something he was not constructed to be.
And Anne Moos, who is much less clear, seems always to have
searched for the thing that can be a substitute for feeling. It
was a search not uncommon in the thirties, and it was her disaster.

They had been brought together, these two young lovers, by the American Student Union at an anti-fascist meeting at Dartmouth College early in 1938, when he was a student there and she was at Bennington. That spring he drove her to Cambridge and a Harvard peace meeting; and, by her account, on the way home, he wooed her with tales of revolutionary conflict.

She remembers that he had leaned toward her in the car that night and said in the voice of Othello to Desdemona, "I am of course a member of the Young Communist League at Dartmouth, but the boys do not know that I am also a member of the Party." But when this Othello spoke in this wise of moving accidents by flood and field, there is no indication that his Desdemona loved him for the dangers he had passed, although he seems to have loved her under the illusion that she did pity them. For Anne Moos was a young lady who contained herself.

The core of the crime for which William Remington went to prison and death was fantasy—fantasy about himself and his world, but most of all fantasy about all the words he had said so long ago and had thought so fleeting and found so irrevocable. For just a little while before he met Anne he had tried to live according to the stuff of his conversation, and the experiment had not been a success.

For nine months in 1936, he had worked as a messenger boy for the Tennessee Valley Authority at Knoxville, Tennessee. During just that brief period, Remington acted like a boy playing truant. He had been a model pupil at Dartmouth, the holder of scholarships, the leader in student activities, altogether the "hard-driving kid" he described himself later in Washington.

But, at Knoxville, he ceased to cut his blond hair and ranged the Tennessee hills on an old motorcycle. His civil-service rating was unimpressive or worse. It described him as "bright but not adapted to minor routine work" and as "slow and . . . physically lazy, which was probably due to his activities after working hours." Those after hours seem to have been for Bill Remington a phantom of delight. He was very young and asked more of his days and nights than the transmission of pieces of government paper. He lived with Communists; he was serious about the local AFL federal workers union; he discoursed for its Workers Education Committee. Once he and his friends passed out leaflets for the CIO textile workers and were mildly pushed about by plant foremen. That last experience was the high point of his Knoxville experience. Upon his return to Dartmouth, Bill Remington seems to have described it in mounting crescendos of heroic meter until this puny jostling had become a beating by fifteen company thugs, who left him, as is their custom, for dead. *

There are at least two witnesses who claim to have attended Communist Party meetings with William Remington at Knoxville in 1937; we have no reason to consider them any less truthful than he is. But their own testimony indicates that the Knoxville Communists regarded Remington as something of a brat given to "demeanor and behavior uncommunistic."

Kenneth McConnell, then the Party's Knoxville organizer, had testified that he was especially disturbed by "the rough manner in which [Remington] dressed," Communists being no more bohemian, of course, than most other souls unfree. This quality of the juvenile and the unstable in William Remington is common to the recollections of all the ex-Communists who can summon up his memory. Elizabeth Bentley, who knew him last, declared that, "of the two, his wife was much the better Communist."

We may then surmise that the Communists allowed him to attend their meetings without ever considering him adult enough to be a trusted hand. That technicality may not alter the fact of his intentions, but it can explain the enthusiasm with which his purported comrades in Knoxville say they set about convincing him to go back to Dartmouth.

When he returned to Hanover, Bill Remington combed his hair and shaved and adopted toward Dartmouth's pin-feathered leftists an attitude of worldly experience which must have distressed them as much as similar manifestations among his Knoxville seniors had pained Remington himself. In 1938, an officer

---

* Remington was about nineteen at the time of this incident. At that age, I was equally addicted to exaggeration of my own revolutionary exploits, which, unadorned, were tepid stuff indeed. For that reason, I found these reports of Bill Remington's embroideries somewhat appealing if only as indication of a spirit of glory he does not appear to have demonstrated as an adult in peace or war.

of the American Student Union visited Dartmouth; one of his guides pointed out the distant, elegant figure of Bill Remington and identified it in cankered tones as that of a man who considered himself the embodiment of Marxist-Leninist theory on the campus. The tone implied that Remington did not often stoop to the petty concerns of Dartmouth's apprentice anti-fascists and was altogether condescending about them.

Besides Anne Moos, whose judgments drop like cold and rounded pebbles, we have one detailed witness on William Remington as a Dartmouth Senior. Robbins W. Barstow, who was then a Freshman, sought out Remington one night in January, 1938, talked about life, and carefully entered a summary of their talk in his journal. Barstow quoted Remington as saying that he was working for communism in the future "and for the CIO now for ultimate ends of workers' welfare." Communism, Remington explained, is a system of balanced consumption and production, "all one together."

He himself could say that he had known the barricades; one employer had hired fifteen thugs to kill him; and he had been "attacked and left for dead." "Russian communism a success," Remington was quoted in Barstow's summary. "Russia gone further in twenty years than any other country. New constitution, etc. The men executed were really very dangerous to the government and put there in a definite attempt to wreck the system." Barstow kept his record of that searching analysis for ten years and then submitted it to the Senate Internal Security Subcommittee as evidence against Remington.

William Remington could only answer that this summary of his lost words was "nonsense" and that Barstow had been a nuisance. But there is no reason to doubt their accuracy; a number of college Juniors talked about communism to Freshmen that way in 1937; it was not so much more unfashionable at the time as a vantage point for preachments of superior wisdom than T. S. Eliot is today. And the casual schoolboys' talk of William Remington became especially crucial to his fate because, even by Elizabeth Bentley's account, he could be said to have done very little about what he thought he believed.

The image of himself which William Remington offered to

Barstow was the image he is supposed to have offered to Anne Moos as a token of his love. There are no public witnesses of what Anne Moos was like in that spring of 1938 or since; Miss Bentley says only that Remington called Anne "Bing" and that she had the look of a solid, steady person, which by all indications she wasn't.

There is no way of knowing just what made Anne Moos a Communist. She managed to commit some human damage in the process; and, reading her own words, it is a little sad to see what meager passions we can sometimes bring to the destruction of souls. Elizabeth Moos, her mother, had been director of a progressive school near Croton, New York. Anne grew up in the liberated atmosphere of a time when her mother had complete faith in the triumph of the free intellect. Elizabeth Moos disagreed with her Communist friends in those days; her creed was the individual.

After Anne joined the Party, her mother trailed after her. "She used to imitate things I did," said Anne. "Her interest came after mine, I guess." The imitation of Anne survived long after Anne herself ceased to care. Elizabeth Moos has become an intense Communist, living for nothing else, her old age shadowed by public imbecility.

Anne Moos became involved with the Young Communist League at Bennington late in her stay there; she was a Senior when she met William Remington and she reports that her interest in these matters—Spain, unions, and the rest—was fairly new for her then. She could place upon the grave of her youth just a single rose: "We were pretty crazy in those days."

She liked him, of course, even though their courtship was a little odd for Hanover, where romance generally runs to puppy romps in the bright, white snowdrifts. She recalls that he took her to what he said was a meeting of the Dartmouth Young Communist League, the first such plenum she had ever attended. She did not love him, she would never love him, but he was a good match. They were married near the end of 1938; just before the ceremony she had an onset of doubt and she says she made him swear to well and truly try.

"It was in New York City. I asked him whether he was *sure*

that he would still be a member of the Communist Party and believe in the principles of communism and he assured me that he would. I need have no fear on that score. That was important to me then."

And so they were married. They asked her a long time later why she had married him if she did not love him, and she answered, "I often wondered. It was flattering to be pursued, and it seemed that he would amount to something. He was very smart." In all of this, there was nowhere the face of the father of her children.

He went back to Dartmouth and she to New York and a course at Columbia, where she joined the Party. In the intervals they were together, they "took some sort of course" at the Workers School, and went to Madison Square Garden, and tried to help the Browder campaign. In 1940 he got his job in Washington. It was a very lonely place, she says. They didn't know any Communists in government; everybody was too cagey. "We felt we were losing touch with the Party." She asked her mother's friend, Joseph North, if he could establish some contact for them. He found her Elizabeth Bentley, who called herself Helen Johnson.*

The first time Helen came, Anne Remington went down to Bill's office and together they drove up to Pennsylvania Avenue and Fourteenth Street to pick her up. Anne reached into her pocketbook, pulled out $20.10, and passed it to Bill, who gave it to Helen and said, "This is our dues."

"I asked her about literature. She didn't bring any literature. I was surprised." In the middle of December, 1942, Helen came back to their bleak, apart lives bearing two packages and saying either, "This is Merry Christmas" or "Christmas greetings from the Party." Her present for Bill was a wool knit tie and for Anne a brown wool scarf; ten years later, Anne laid these tokens as evidence before a federal grand jury.

Before long the Remingtons began to change, both toward each other and toward the Party and the Soviet Union. Anne said

* This, like the three paragraphs which follow, is Anne Moos's story. William Remington always insisted that he met "Helen" as a reporter and did not even suspect that she was a Communist until she began to talk so much like one that he dropped her.

that she commenced to lose interest after 1945, and "by and by, I ceased to consider myself a Communist." Her mother had grown harder and more fanatic with the years; Anne, who had set her on the road, after a while even stopped visiting her at Croton. She could no longer talk to Elizabeth Moos. They asked her in court whether she hated her mother, and she answered, "I wouldn't say that. I don't like her. When she couldn't boss me around, she lost interest." After 1947, William and Anne Remington separated and were divorced. She had long since ceased to call him to his wedding-eve pledge, and he was trying to forget it.

The Elizabeth Bentley they had known as Helen Johnson had been herself divorced from the Party long before. Yasha had died in her apartment on Thanksgiving night, 1943. The International Workers Order had carried him out in a canvas basket; she had sat at his chill Red Funeral and heard an American Communist leader whom Yasha had never liked preach the Party's farewell to him. The night of his death, she had "kissed his cold forehead" and pronounced her own farewell.

" 'Good-by, *golubchik*,' I said. 'Rest peacefully now that your labor is over. With you goes most of me, for without you I am nothing. My memorial to you will be to carry on your work the best I can in the spirit in which you yourself would have done it.' "

She spent the first ten loveless months of her widowhood attempting the fulfillment of that vow. The men who succeeded Yasha as representatives of the Soviet secret police bullied and drove her through "an endless procession of dreary days." She could not escape Yasha's memory.

"I would catch myself thinking I must go home and tell Yasha about this, and then the realization would come that he was gone forever." And so she went at last to the FBI she and Yasha had dodged so long before. She was a private information source for the government for two years. Then in 1948, Elizabeth Bentley became a public source and came to Washington again to set before the Congressional committees the names of her old associates, including truant William Remington.

But Bill Remington was no longer even what he and she had

once thought he was. Anne Moos was gone from him now; the memory of Helen Johnson was dim; he held an important position in the Department of Commerce. He talked to the committees as though he could barely recall those days when, as Anne said, "we were pretty crazy" and when he had believed in the Spanish Loyalists and the guilt of Leon Trotsky and all that mass of hopes, some of them false, some still true, all musty.

"I no longer believe," he swore, "in the type of government initiative on the scale that I believed it at that particular time." He had even left the President's Council of Economic Advisers because it was too New Dealish for his taste. But, Anne, gentlemen, Anne's was another case. Her mother had made her a Communist; and "I have to stand aside and see those children brought up in a creed that I hate more than anything else in the world."

The government sought out Anne Moos. Its agents were very solicitous in trying not to breach the ancient rule that a wife cannot testify against her husband. But couldn't Mrs. Remington think of anything that might have happened before they were married? She was very reluctant. She was sure that Bill was violently anti-Communist now. And, after all, she said once, Remington was still contributing to the children's support; and if he should be convicted, she would be left without support. But, the government answered, her children could hardly be proud of their father; this would give them a chance to be proud of their mother.

Her surrender came only with some gentle pressure. She complained later that the grand jury kept her in chambers through the lunch hour and she broke because she was tired and hungry. Then she told of her courtship and of Bill's giving Helen the information about making rubber, or was it explosives, out of garbage, and the Christmas presents and the dues. It had all been so inexpensive for Anne Remington; as a housewife, the Party had charged her just ten cents a month dues.

Presumably, when she became a Communist and William Remington said come with me and picket by the mill gates, there had been an image of total challenge to come. She might have thought that she would be tested with branding irons, if not for him, for something bigger than them both. That challenge had come down to a lunch skipped in a grand jury room, and even that had been too much for her.

Elizabeth Bentley served her time in the bright lights, pushing a pencil at her scraggly hair and saying, yes, that was the man. After awhile she found repose in religion; but part of her must still lie with Yasha in the cemetery of the International Workers Order. She does not yet seem able to tell herself that her time with him had not been the best years of her life.

William Remington went to prison for perjury and was murdered in a quarrel where he was only a bystander. Anne Moos Remington works for a Washington lawyer. Her mother, true to the worst to the last, flits between New York and Boston, bleating for the Communists.

A long time ago, the Communist Party ruled out all discussion of woman as woman; sex distinction was a crime it catalogued under the heading of male chauvinism. But, forty years ago, the Industrial Workers of the World had a special vision of the woman; Joe Hill put it down in a song called "The Rebel Girl."

She was, said Joe Hill, the only and the thoroughbred lady, with a heart in her bosom that was true to her class and her kind:

Oh, the rebel girl, the rebel girl
To the working class she's a precious pearl,
She brings courage, pride, and joy to her fighting rebel boy:
We've had girls before, but we need some more
In the Industrial Workers of the World,
For it's great to fight for freedom
With the fighting rebel girl.

It is by now a faintly comic song, because the Wobblies are by now a faintly comic organization. They have left very little behind them besides a few songs and the memory of great banks of roses at the funeral of the Lawrence strikers. They had a heroine in those days who delighted to call herself Boxcar Betty. There was another heroine named Elizabeth Gurley Flynn, who came in her middle age into the Communist Party and could be seen, while she awaited her time in prison, on the platforms of its ceremonials, the layers of flesh overcropping her shoetops, automatically intoning the grand, debased, old songs.

The rebel girl consumed herself and destroyed herself; she went down to the shadows of a racking old age, coughing alone, and she was glad to do it. But now Boxcar Betty is gone, if she ever lived; she would not have recognized Anne Moos Remington and Elizabeth Bentley. For the taunting core of the lives of those women of the thirties was how empty they were. Elizabeth Bentley, shuttling through the inconsequent round of meetings without purpose, the life of no person the better for anything she did, and ending in the cheap and terrible sort of treason which Boxcar Betty would have thought the evasion of cowards. And Anne Moos, pledging her husband to struggle without end, and then following him to Washington and a career where you were "a hard-driving kid," and you and everyone else were so cagey, and, "goodness," nobody would be caught reading the *Daily Worker*.

You can argue how to judge a life spent in search of a good thing that was never found. But there can be no argument about a life destroyed in a pursuit where the pursuer knew not what she sought and to which love never came or, if it came, left too soon.

Mary Vorse has gone on far past her time for going on. She will go on until she dies. We can leave her best at a CIO convention in 1949. It was during a coal strike; Mary Vorse could have walked into that convention with Bob Minor on her arm, and Philip Murray, the CIO's president, would have been glad to shake his hand.

For Mary Vorse is a woman who cannot look upon her past and find evil entire in any part of it. To have given the hostage of love once is to have surrendered a little part of it forever. She knew that to forgive is the first commandment of love, and she and Philip Murray knew that no price is too high for it. She bore up under all the attentions for three days. Then the things of state were too much for her, and she went back to the coal mines, saying as the last apology of the mother who knows her children are not worth all this care:

"There's an old fellow in Charleroi I knew long ago in the

Wobblies. He always tells me what's going on. I'll have to tell Phil; he'll remember him. One of the old fellows, one of the very old ones."

And she was gone to the bus station, her legs a little stiff, her eyes a little rheumy, because she was, after all, seventy-five years old. To have pledged yourself and to have forsaken all others for forty years, to have understood that to love is to abandon sleep and comfort and the ease of age, and to follow, always to follow, the desperate road love sets out for you, such was the limit of the rebel girl's commitment. Mary Vorse sat in her bus as upon a burnished throne.

8

MOST OF the persons in these studies came to their commitment by choice. They could never escape a certain envy for those they thought must reach the same commitment by automatic necessity. Their textbooks taught them, after all, that the purest revolutionaries are created by objective conditions of environment. By that standard, the Negro in America made the most perfect revolutionary material.

And yet the Communists, who may deserve a chapter in some histories of special corners of our society, can never be more than a footnote in any true history of the American Negro. He was a major object of their passion; they felt, or thought they felt, a special concern for his freedom. Still, the history of the relations of Negroes to the Communist Party is one of rejection. The mass of Negroes rejected the Communists and never joined the Party to any degree reflecting their own proportion to the population of the United States as a whole; no more than eight per cent of the Party's members at any time have been Negroes.

The few Negroes who came young to the Communists experienced a rejection of their own which drove the best of them from the Party. Ralph Ellison's *Invisible Man* and the autobiographical writings of Richard Wright, among the most notable products of Negro creation in the last two decades, contain recollections of experience as Communists that only complete the pattern of rejection and alienation from white institutions which Wright and Ellison reflect. Their life as Communists was only a renewed experience with exploitation. Both were as much outsiders there as they were everywhere else. The Communists were especially empty for Ellison. His association with them appears to have been the least creatively stimulating of his life; as an instance, *Invisible Man* indicates a combined immersion in Herman Melville, an acquisition from Western culture, and with Negro blues forms, an acquisition from his roots. The Communists were a part of Ellison's life between the blues and Melville; he took nothing from them except a fortified sense of rejection. If Ellison's experience is representative, the most important effect of Communist work among Negroes has been the most positive sort of negation.

So far I have been describing persons whose lives were conditioned by their affirmation of revolutionary fantasy. There seems to me little margin for myth in the life of the American Negro, and to discuss that life entirely in terms of the few Negroes who accepted the myth would be a serious distortion of an important piece of our history. We have seen in the past few years, I think, the beginning of a revolution in the position of the Negro in America. It has been carried out by Negroes whose first decisive act was their rejection of the revolutionary myth. The thirties talked much about the Negro and did comparatively little for him; their great revolutions were labor uprisings in whose course the Negro was swept along, on occasion against his own will. There is always a certain cultural lag for depressed ethnic groups in these matters; the Negro's own revolution did not manifest itself until the decades after the thirties. It is now, of course, only in its beginnings.

This is the revolution which concerns us here. Professed revolutionaries played only the smallest part in it, and Communists seem to have played almost no part at all. Its roots were, I believe, in the Negro's alienation from our own society and in his sense of his identification as a Negro, a sense forced upon him every day by the rest of us and the sense which has become his own best weapon. In the twenties, I think the Negro expressed his own identification best in the songs of Bessie Smith, which offered only resignation and endurance, and in Marcus Garvey's Back-to-Africa movement, which offered only Utopia. Beginning in the thirties and mounting to the present time, the Negro has asked something more than endurance, and has reached for it with his own hands. It was a grasp for reality, and has very little to do with the fantasies with which we have been here most largely involved.

To measure this reality, I have chosen, among many others, two men. One is Paul Robeson, who was a success and became a Communist; the other is Thomas Patterson, who could not be a success and became a Pullman porter, and who did not have time to be a Communist and became instead one of America's unconscious true revolutionaries.

George

"*I doan mind bein' in jail, but I got to stay there so long.*"
BESSIE SMITH, "The Jailhouse Blues"

"*I can see you're tired, son, and disappointed,*" said
*Guiditta to Rocco. "You have the sadness of one who set
out to go very far and ends up by finding himself where he
began. Didn't they teach you at school that the world is
round?*"
IGNAZIO SILONE, A Handful of Blackberries

"*Now, what are you going to get in this country? As I
see it, the colored brother is going to get what he can take.
You are not going to be able to take it unless you are going
to be able to pay the price to take it. Nobody else in this
country got anything unless they took it. They died and
suffered and sacrificed. They cut up the trees, lived and
suffered in the cold, and they took a country and built it
up. They brought us over here in chains, as some of our
speakers told us in this convention. We know that. We are
still in chains, to a large extent, light chains. The only way
those chains are going to be broken is we have to break
them. That is all. There isn't anybody else going to do it
for us.*"
MILTON WEBSTER, Speech to the Brotherhood of Sleeping Car Porters, Sept. 13,
1950

THE NEGRO has had his moments of patronage, but Bessie
Smith never knew many of them. Late in the twenties, there
was a rush of white tourists up to Harlem, where the Cotton Club
offered the music of Duke Ellington, the sight of a sleek yellow

chorus, and the assurance that no Negroes would be admitted except as entertainers.

Bessie Smith never sang at the Cotton Club. As she said herself, "I ain't no high yaller—just a deep, deep yaller brown." She was never fashionable. All her life, she could be found most often in the colored theaters and the colored dance halls—the Vendome in Chicago, the Apollo in New York, the Royal in Baltimore, or those other halls of fugitive joy in the Southern cities. Her first record began: "Thirty days in jail and my face turn' to the wall." Her last one, nearly twenty years later, ended: "I need a whole lot of lovin', 'cause I'm down in the dumps."

She hung her great body in white sequins. Her voice was contemptuous of microphones, rolling its layers of pain, loss, and longing laid upon pain, loss, and longing over the black faces to the farthest reaches of the great barns in which she sang. Over and over she told the story of the Negro transplanted to the great cities. Her devils were the landlord, the policeman, and the hoodoo; her ambiguous heroes were the easy riders going and coming back. The command of her ceremonies was to endure and straighten up at the very last, because every road had an end, every sin would be redeemed, every devil exorcised, every wanderer brought home.

Her records were packaged as "race" songs. She crossed the wall around the Negro only for the very few white inhabitants of the frontiers of jazz, most of them Europeans and not enough of them to grant her one of those Continental tours where the American Negro was treated like a potentate and allowed to forget what he was back home.

Even during the jazz revival of the thirties, Bessie Smith never sang in Carnegie Hall. There was one Sunday afternoon at the Famous Door on West Fifty-second Street where she stood in her furs and sang for a white audience goggling at her from camp chairs. After that, she went back to her race theaters and her tent shows. One afternoon in 1936, just outside Memphis, she was badly broken up in an automobile accident.

Memphis was her home. Its Negro hospital was on the other side of town. She could not get into the white hospital and the legend was that she bled to death on her way to a Negro doctor, dying as she had lived—on the race label. There was a song about Memphis' Ed Crump on Beale Street. "I don't care what Boss Crump don't 'low/ I'm goin' to beat my git-tar anyhow." But, in the end, if you were a Negro, Bessie Smith assumed that the Boss Crumps of Memphis would get you anyhow.

Still, Paul Robeson is a Negro, and the Boss Crumps seemed to have nothing to do with him. He appeared, with ease and grace, to have escaped them. Life was certainly never as easy for him as it appeared, but it was easy enough. His father was a New Jersey minister with a small parish, an old man when Paul was born; his mother died when her dress caught fire at the kitchen stove. They were not substantial Negroes, but they had a status superior to the average. Paul Robeson's father had been a slave and his life was a triumph of self-help. He drove and drilled his son to be perfect in all things.

Young Paul was close enough to perfection to be a wonder to his contemporaries. At Rutgers he attained Phi Beta Kappa without demonstrable effort and was its football team's main force. Walter Camp chose him as an All-American end; for Camp to select a Rutgers man was hardly less thinkable than for him to choose a Negro.

He was not, of course, entirely free of the knowledge that he was of a particular breed; and rival football players were accustomed to remind him that he was a Negro with concentrated violence. But his conduct on these occasions was a model for any sportsman. It was generally agreed that he knew his place. Only in 1950, so much later, would Paul Robeson remember his football days and report with dreadful satisfaction that there had been moments when he used his fist in the pile-ups.

In 1918, when Paul Robeson was graduated from Rutgers and entered Columbia Law School, there could exist the illusion that his place had no limit. Eugene O'Neill and the Provincetown Players were in their glory then. O'Neill wrote *The Emperor Jones* for Robeson, and he was wafted over the barriers of apprenticeship to become an established star of the theater.

O'Neill put him in *All God's Chillun Got Wings* and he had a firmer success. But outside the theater his margins were already narrowing. He finished law school with the distinction that was his custom and took his clerkship in a downtown firm. His admittance was not easy and his presence not always accepted. After a while he went away very courteously. There were, it appeared, more limits than he had thought.

But he remained a figure glowing with light in the Greenwich Village of the Edna Millays, the Heywood Brouns, and the Theodore Dreisers. Still there were only a few parts for Negro actors. Then nature laid upon him one more blessing; without training he became a singer and a fresh overnight triumph. He had been admired. Now he was worshiped. He himself used to complain that his was the miracle of the dog walking on his hind legs and that he had never been the football player they said he was, or the actor, or even the singer. Even so, the audience at his first concert collapsed into ecstasy when he began and into exhaustion when he finished, after imploring him through encore after encore into the morning.

Granting certain extraordinary attainments, it is not hard for a Negro to be worshiped by white persons. But there is always a measure of condescension in that worship, which may be why so many of Robeson's white friends from those first days weep for him now in the tones of those who remember how virtuous they were and how ungrateful God has been. O'Neill's *The Emperor Jones* presented a Negro who did no great violence to popular illusion. Robeson was especially appealing because he could act this Negro of theater tradition and appear thereafter at a Village party as a guest of intellectual distinction. He looked like a tribal deity, and he could swagger for his audience as an Ethiop clown and then talk after the show with engaging cultivation. He had some of the charm of a superbly tamed savage. There was a superior morality in bowing down before him as though to an African god with a Phi Beta Kappa key.

This moral elevation did not, of course, alter a situation in which the theater had no parts for Paul Robeson that were not Negro parts, and Negro parts tended to be either low or empty. The critics who adored him had no suggestion more daring than a production of *Othello;* it was hardly practical to observe that he would make a Macbeth of force and fire.

Even the O'Neill parts, try as O'Neill did, were either low or crude or ambiguous at best. Some sensitive Negroes thought *The Emperor Jones* was no service to them at all—Brutus Jones being a murderer, a thief, and, at his end, a reversion to the jungle of formless fears and voodoo drums. Brutus Jones was a Pullman porter who committed a murder over a crap game and then killed a white guard on the chain gang and escaped to a Caribbean Island and made himself its emperor, because he had learned one great lesson on the Pullman cars:

"For de little stealin' dey gits you in jail soon or late. For de big stealin' dey makes you Emperor and puts you in de Hall o' Fame when you croaks. If dey's one thing I learns on de Pullman ca's listenin' to de white quality talk, it's dat same fact. And when I gits a chance to use it I winds up Emperor . . ."

O'Neill was saying that Brutus Jones was the consequence of three hundred years of white mastery of the Negro. He aped the whites at their worst; he was contemptuous of the "bush nigger" and lived and died with his hand against every man. O'Neill's heroes were Negroes whose disaster was that they wanted to be white men. But they were not like ordinary Negroes and Brutus Jones was not an ordinary Pullman porter.

The Pullman porter rode his car, silent with all the chaff around him, always most agreeable when he was of the old school, accepting the generic designation of "George" as though it were a balm instead of an affront, a domestic apparently unaltered by the passage of time or the Emancipation Proclamation. A sensitive white man might look at him, at once deferential and removed, and wonder what he was really like. There was a certain thrill to the notion that he might be a Communist or a murderer or even an emperor—a doomed emperor of course—if his chance came and the constituency were inferior enough.

But he was, after all, only a man beneath his station, as every servant is a man beneath what should be his station. The resources of any of us being what they are, he might very well dream other dreams than those of the sort of man who sits up late drinking in a Pullman lounge. He might be less like Brutus Jones than, say, Thomas T. Patterson. Thomas Patterson was a functioning Pullman porter when Paul Robeson was acting the part of one. Patterson had ended up with the Pullman Company against his hopes and because he had tried all the other places. He had come to New York from the British West Indies and essayed first Wall Street, where they had made him an office porter, and then the subway system, where they had set him to cleaning their washrooms.

He had brought no special education with him from Jamaica. But he was bronzed and long-legged and courteous and altogether so obvious a piece of fine workmanship that everyone who employed him marked him as a person notably superior and was always apologetic when the time came to explain that there were no openings except for porters. The world which had seemed to open so wide for Paul Robeson was for Thomas Patterson just a long, narrow hall with a broom provided by the management and so much to be picked up.

Just after World War I, when he was working out of the old Weehawken Station of the New York Central, various passengers began sending in reports on his manner, character, and extraordinary attentions. A Pullman porter is by definition nonpromotable, and no commendation can serve him much. But after a while, Thomas Patterson's citations attained a tide where the superintendent of traffic called him to find out what it was that cut so deep into the consciousness of his passengers. Patterson could not help him very far toward an answer; he could only report that he did his best. They talked a long while, and then the superintendent said that Patterson ought to understand that he had no place as a Pullman porter. He was too good for the job. The company really did not want men of his special texture around. He should look for some place worthy of him. Thomas Patterson smiled and said that he had already looked everywhere. He was a Pullman porter because there was nothing else for him to be.

The pleasures of fantasy were not open to Thomas Patterson. He could not afford, as an instance, to nurse the hope that he of all Negroes might ever be treated as though he were white. Any white man who spoke to him spoke consciously to a Negro, which is a terrible barrier even for the best of men. Thomas Patterson's life was a process of enforcing recognition of his personality from a world which treated him as possessed of color without feature.

It was always mixing him up with the porter in the car ahead and asking him in simple bewilderment if he was its porter, because he was, after all, only a piece of furniture set out for the convenience of persons who saw no need to be connoisseurs of this sort of furniture.

The Pullman porter in those days had a certain stature among Negroes as a cosmopolite, because he lived so much of his life among white persons of substance, a fortunate auxiliary to a great world so far from the lives of most Negroes. The Pullman porter's presumed superiority was one compensation for the $27.50 a month wage at which Thomas Patterson began in the system. But it was the smallest of compensations. To respond automatically to the call for "George" was after all a confession that you had no identity as an individual.

Man of mark that he may have been among his own kind, Thomas Patterson had no white friends. At best he could have only white acquaintances, a conductor who enjoyed his company on the run, the superintendent who had recognized that he deserved something better, a passenger impressed by his demeanor.

To assert one's personality in this narrow world was a never-ceasing labor because, whatever his achievements, Thomas Patterson woke up every morning a Negro in a menial station and began all over again. Even the superintendent who was almost his admirer once dispatched him to pick up an assignment, charging him, as was normal, gawdam it, to be quick about it. Patterson moved to his Pullman car without answering, neither insolent nor accelerated. The superintendent came up and asked if he had heard all right. Patterson replied that he had heard perfectly well; the superintendent never again addressed him in those terms. His victories were no less cherished for being so small.

There had always been talk of a Pullman porters' union, wistful from its friends, scornful from its enemies. The established railway brotherhoods were not merely negative about the recruitment of Negroes; they were positive about eliminating them from any place on the railroads.

What small position the Negro held in industry had been achieved in many cases against the objections of the white labor unions; many Negroes got their first industrial jobs as strike-breakers. On the record, the Pullman Company seemed a better friend than the American Federation of Labor. The introduction of Negro porters into the Pullman system was considered an act of grace and a tender of opportunity. Robert Todd Lincoln, the Emancipator's son, was one of Pullman's directors and a symbol of its special tolerance of Negroes.

And so if the Pullman porters were to organize a union, they must expect to go it alone with little sympathy either from white labor or from large elements of their own community. They began with no special aspiration beyond raising their own wages. Circumstance forced them to make their fight as Negroes, because there was no one besides themselves to help them and because there was a revolutionary implication in the picture of a Negro sitting down to bargain with his white employer.

The porters made a few motions during World War I to the general inattention of the Railway Labor Board and the Pullman Company. Their leaders were untrained; theirs was not a course to make them popular with the corporation; before long many of them were encouraged to take their passions elsewhere. Milton Webster, the brashest and loudest of them, was fired and became a heeler for the Chicago Republicans. Thomas Patterson, who was a firm union man but very polite about it, clung to his berth and turned over a burdensome proportion of his wages to the union.

The world which was looking so delusively free for Paul Robeson could not offer even illusion to Negroes like Patterson and Webster. They were grown men without formal education, with no obvious talent, and with no access upward. Robeson could be the idol of a white cult, at once enraptured and a little condescending. Patterson and Webster were ordinary Negroes and the best they could expect was condescension.

In the year 1925, Patterson, Webster, and a few others began another effort to build a porters' union and Paul Robeson sailed for Europe to remain there, with only a few intervals of return, until the fall of 1939. Their roads were very different.

Ashley L. Totten, a founder of the Brotherhood of Sleeping Car Porters, was fired a few days after he announced its formation. No vocal union porter could thereafter hope to keep his job, and it was plain that outsiders must be drafted as organizers. Webster was out of the system, so it was safe for him to take over the union's Midwest office. Then the Brotherhood's leaders went to A. Philip Randolph, one of Harlem's throng of agitational voices, and asked him to become their president and public spokesman.

Randolph had never been a Pullman porter. He was a maverick and a street-corner orator, a Socialist who had been a pacifist in World War I and had once been called the most dangerous Negro in America. His father had been an itinerant Florida Methodist preacher; he himself had rejected God and the middle class. He had been an elevator operator, a janitor, and a ship's waiter. He was now the editor of a Negro magazine; his education had ended with a few courses at the City College of New York. But he had absorbed Shakespeare and the Bible and his bass voice rumbled in periods which mixed the cadences of the King James Version with the accent of massive cultivation.

The Negro was longing and moving and changing his magnetic impulse all through the twenties, and Randolph was by 1925 only one among a cluster of conflicting ideologues and not one of the more fashionable. At thirty-six, his time in fact appeared to have passed him by.

Eight years before, the Socialists had run him for Secretary of State of New York. An estimated one quarter of the Negroes of New York City had voted for him. But after the war they turned to wilder creeds. Marcus Garvey, a West Indian Messiah, had shaken Harlem as no one else had with his Back-to-Africa movement, a vision of an African Negro empire ruled by a pure and mighty race.

In 1920, Garvey turned fifty thousand of his congregation loose to parade through Harlem's streets behind their Black Nobility, their African Legion, and their Black Cross nurses, all purple and black and green and gold. For a while all the other salvationists paled beside Garvey's rich and ruddy glow; there was talk that he had ten million followers all over the world. Randolph went on saying that the Negroes were Americans and must solve their problems as Americans, but fewer and fewer people listened. It must have seemed to the Negro intellectual then that Garvey had driven an imperial chariot between him and his audience and left him isolated while his people strayed off to worship the crocodile in the sun beside the waters of the Congo.

Marcus Garvey went at last to Atlanta Penitentiary for mismanaging the affairs of his Court of Ethiopia, his Universal Negro Improvement Association and the other appurtenances of his glory. He passed thereafter into that special limbo tenanted by so many prior saviors of his people. The vision of Black Empire never again gripped Harlem as it had under Garvey's star. When the Back-to-Africa movement revived in the thirties, very few Negroes paid it any attention. The enabling act which would have shipped them back to the home they no longer felt was home was sponsored in the Senate by their ravening enemy, Theodore Bilbo of Mississippi.

But Marcus Garvey's mark never left his flock. He had made the ordinary Negro conscious of his color and he had articulated a knowledge of self that had been buried before. Always after Garvey, any white man who came to Harlem selling the elixir of freedom would be an alien. His barrier was the color line. Many white people, the Communists among them, came to the Negro thereafter, and offered him so very much. In his heart the Negro believed that, whatever its intentions, this was a tender of condescension and that, as Garvey had said, he himself was his own best friend.

The reasons why Garvey, disgraced and dead, would always deserve a chapter in the history of the American Negro were the reasons why the Communists could never be more than a footnote in that history. They labored very long to bring the Negro into the army of revolution; at no time have there been more than 5,000 American Negro Communists and they have always been strangers to their brothers. For the Communists, whatever their affirmations, were white men offering a potion, and most Negroes expected them after a while to exact a white man's fee.

Even Philip Randolph, with his faintly exotic associations, was held at arm's length by some leaders of the porters in the early days. He was their ambassador to foreign parts; but they were not sure in the beginning that he was really their man. He was removed and austere and of no common clay. The Pullman Company and those Negroes who held it in awe called him a Communist, which he had never been, and he had to make his obeisance to the community by joining the Negro Elks.

He was something between a high priest and an alien to the porters in the beginning. But he remained with them through the long years in the desert, when the very few who believed pawned their watches to pay the union's rent, and he himself met their highest test when he refused an offer from some friend of the established order to take ten thousand dollars and desert them and spend a year in Europe. The Garland Fund gave the porters ten thousand dollars to begin, and William Green tendered what assistance the American Federation of Labor permitted him to give. But they were really all by themselves.

There were only ten thousand porters to organize, but it took their Brotherhood almost ten years to win recognition from the Pullman Company and a little longer still to be admitted into the AFL as a union in good standing. They would always have a small union, but they managed their own affairs, and they quadrupled the wages of the porters. It is a measure of the Negro's circumstance that, in America, the smallest things usually take him so very long, and that, by the time he wins them, they are no longer little things: they are miracles.

Twelve years after the porters came to Randolph, Milton Webster, a cigar in his mouth and no rein on his tongue, was growling into the faces of lawyers for the railroads of the Middle West, and Thomas T. Patterson, grave and courtly but just as hard in his way, was standing up to the lawyers for the railroads of the East. The Pullman porters were a little army unafraid. Randolph had begun to rise at AFL conventions and suggest that it was time for the big unions to give the Negro equal treatment and to offer his futile motion for the expulsion of any affiliate which insisted on the color barrier. He was a nuisance of enormous presence, impelling one afflicted delegate from the carpenters to complain that it wasn't fair for this Harvard man to come in and outtalk them.

But Paul Robeson appeared to need no such small and terribly difficult victories. He was lionized in England and moved gracefully among its gentry. He lived awhile in the south of France and journeyed to the Soviet Union, where selected little children called him Pablo and he found a country where the Negro was not exploited, perhaps because the Negro did not exist.*

He came back to the United States at rare intervals, going to Hollywood for *Show Boat* in the late thirties, lounging and grinning about the screen as the shabby, shiny, lazy but truly loyal Cuffy of Southern tradition. This was the height of the decade when it has been seriously asserted that the Communist myth dominated the movies. But Hollywood's conception of the Negro offended no traditions except those of the Negro's dignity. Robeson was the Negro of the future, but they would not let him portray anyone but the Negro of the legendary past.

He took Hollywood's money and swore that he would never go back until they gave him a part worthy of a first-class citizen. He returned to England, and J. Arthur Rank put him in *Sanders of the River,* where he was the shiny, shabby, careless, but truly loyal, Number One boy of imperial tradition. In all these defeats there was the guilt of the white to the Negro, ancient beyond memory and always renewed. There was also the guilt to himself. There is no way of knowing even now which guilt made Paul Robeson a Communist.

When war broke out in Europe in 1939, Robeson came home, but not to Harlem. He bought himself a pre-Revolutionary house in Connecticut; his friends reported the break-through of a certain interior irony when he spoke of his new home as the old plantation. He toured to the old, enchanted audiences; his records sold in the hundreds of thousands; he remained a great, removed symbol of individual success.

He came to Harlem only upon special occasions, almost always for assemblages honoring the Negro's putative identification with the Soviet Union. He would arrive on the platform just before he was to sing; he would rumble his words about this land and our

* Even the British seem to have as hard a time as many white Americans believing that a Negro can drink tea without spilling it. Robeson's success in England's higher social quarters drove Evelyn Waugh to draw an envenomed portrait of him in *Decline and Fall*—a Robeson formal of dress, languorous and supercilious of manner, dripping Regency *patois* from thick purple lips. Waugh's American readers found this picture highly amusing, perhaps unconscious that its targets were, after all, not just the Negro but such revered national institutions as higher learning, the society of Phi Beta Kappa, the Bar Association, and the judgment of Walter Camp.

people, making his great entrance and his great exit, on stage only when the spotlight was upon him; and then he would go back to Connecticut.

But Philip Randolph was anchored to Harlem. By 1941, the Brotherhood which he and Patterson and the rest had built, had become a kind of cathedral. Randolph might have been nothing without it except a voice insistent and off the beat. But, as president of his union, he was a paladin of the Negro community. The Brotherhood had a reputation out of balance with its size; it was regarded as a pilot model of what the ordinary Negro could do if he tried. Randolph was the friend of Eleanor Roosevelt and Fiorello LaGuardia. He was the only Negro in America who was well known because he was a Negro radical and a labor leader.

Even so, by 1940 all the Brotherhood's notable history appeared to be behind it. There were few Pullman porters left to organize. The mass of Negroes were domestics or common laborers or WPA workers. They went into the Navy as messboys and into the Army as truckdrivers and into the Marines not at all. The Brotherhood was only a very small island.

As president of an AFL union, Randolph was a symbol and at times a source of pain to his white brethren. But his protests were after all matters doomed to interment in the record, because they were appeals to conscience where so faint a conscience existed. It appeared that he could not alter the state of things; with every Negro, he remained in prison.

His first move into the broad stream had brought Randolph nothing but regret. In 1937, he joined with the Communists to establish the National Negro Congress and became its president. In 1939, with the Nazi-Soviet pact, the Communists captured the Congress, and made it an amplifier for the proposition that no American Negro would fight against the Soviets. In April of 1940, Randolph resigned as president. His parting blast was that the Congress was not merely a Communist front but not even a true Negro organization. A third of the delegates to its last convention had been white and much of its funds had come from non-Negro sources.

That last was a new note for the Randolph who had stood up

all over Harlem against Marcus Garvey's call for Negro secession. But he was not the Randolph he had been. He had worked, after all, for fifteen years with Milton Webster, who was brusque where Randolph was gentle, cynical where Randolph was trusting, stripped of illusion where Randolph was a perambulatory dream. And, if Randolph had won Webster and changed him a little, Webster had seen Randolph change too. Together they had come to agree that the Negro's best hope was his own effort.

Webster, who thinks of himself as an ordinary Negro, never forgot the difference between them. He always remembered the time in those first terrible days when Randolph was invited to represent the Brotherhood at an interracial seminar in Cincinnati. Then word had gone about that he was a godless radical, and the Brotherhood was asked to provide another speaker. Randolph sent Webster.

"Of course," Webster says, "having heard Brother Randolph speak many times, I thought that, since I was representing him, I ought to prepare something pretty good. I spent a couple of weeks getting stuff together, including some of his poetry."

Webster arrived thus girt about with a reasonably accurate coloration of the master's manner and found a speakers' platform loaded with friends of the Pullman Company.

"A high-powered lawyer from Cincinnati, who is still down there, got up and made a speech about the Constitution, and then he read a written draft in which he said, 'Experience teaches us that the company form of organization is best for the Negro.' Then I took that speech I had prepared for two weeks and tore it up. I said this doesn't call for a speech. It calls for the same old rough stuff. So I have never attempted to prepare a speech since that time."

In January of 1941, these so different men were leaving Washington to tour the South. The defense boom had begun, but it appeared to hold no place for the Negro. The new war plants would not hire him. Just 240 of the 107,000 persons employed in the aircraft industry, the lustiest of the war babies, were Negroes. Vultee of Nashville had limited itself to the hope that it could take on a few porters when things got moving. North American

Aviation said frankly that no Negro, whatever his training, could expect employment as a mechanic; applications would be entertained only from janitors.

Randolph, as a representative Negro, had just been to see President Roosevelt to file one of the customary memorials against the immutable state of things. The President had been very gracious, but there was no indication that he felt capable of any particular performance.

Randolph and Webster sat on their southbound train and talked about this, the latest of so many feckless interviews. Randolph said that he did not think further conferences with the President could help much in placing Negroes in the defense industries. Webster agreed with him; there was a silence for fifteen minutes while Randolph observed the Virginia hills. At last he said in his soft and distant accents:

"I think we ought to do something about it. I think we ought to get ten thousand Negroes and march down Pennsylvania Avenue and protest against the discriminatory practices in this rapidly expanding defense economy."

"And where," asked Webster, "are you going to get the ten thousand Negroes?"

Randolph listened awhile to his inner voice and observed at last that he believed they could get them. So they continued south, offering the idea of a Negro March on Washington wherever they could find an audience.

"I think the first place we talked March on Washington was Savannah," says Milton Webster. "It scared everybody to death. The head colored man in Savannah opened up the meeting and introduced me, and ran off the platform to the last seat in the last row."

"So we talked March on Washington all through the South and then we came on back to the real God's country, and I went back to Chicago and he went on to New York, and, within the next thirty days, it had caught fire, particularly in the East, and everybody was talking March on Washington."

The National Association for the Advancement of Colored People, the Urban League, and a dozen other organizations representative of the Negro community joined the porters to announce that ten thousand Negroes would march on Washington on July 1st to shout their demand for defense jobs. The Negro is a buried segment of American life, and for two or three months Randolph's fire burned beneath its surface. In May, the Roosevelt administration began to get reports of the blaze: Negroes were hiring trains for the trip from Chicago, from Memphis, and from Cleveland. There was every sign that not just ten thousand but twenty-five thousand Negroes would pour into Washington crying for their rights, to the boundless embarrassment not merely of politicians but of the arsenal of democracy which had forgotten them.

President Roosevelt's first response to Randolph's threat was a June, 1941, letter to his defense subordinates urging industry to "take the initiative to open the door of employment to all loyal and qualified workers regardless of race, creed, and color." This appeal was offered to Randolph and his allies as proof of good faith. He answered that it was only a hope and a prayer and that he would launch his battalions against Washington on the appointed date.

Then he was called to New York's City Hall to be begged off by Mrs. Franklin D. Roosevelt and Mayor LaGuardia, two old friends of the Brotherhood whose intentions he could not question. "They, as all good white people, told us that the March on Washington was too drastic," Webster says now, "and you ought to depend on the people that are friendly to get the desired results."

Mrs. Roosevelt explained that the march was impractical: where would twenty-five thousand Negroes eat in Washington and where would they stay? Randolph answered, after due reflection, that they would go to the hotels and the restaurants and register and order dinner. Then his two good friends began to understand the dimensions of the challenge. Randolph was unchangeable in his dire intentions. And so at last President Roosevelt invited him and the other Negro leaders back to the White House.

Randolph told Mr. Roosevelt that his price for peace was an executive order barring discrimination for reasons of religion and color in the war industries. The President replied that he was reluctant to issue the order with a gun at his head. He looked at Randolph, and Randolph held the gun. On June 20, 1941, the President issued Executive Order 8803, banning discrimination on defense projects and setting up the Fair Employment Practices Committee.

Still Randolph would not take his gun away. He would only defer the March; and at every crisis in the FEPC's affairs, he was back with his hand on the trigger. His March on Washington touched the ordinary Negro as nothing had since Garvey. In March of 1942, he brought twenty-five thousand Negroes to Madison Square Garden; that evening Harlem's merchants cut off the lights in their stores for fifteen minutes to demonstrate their support. Milton Webster, the porters' representative on the FEPC, flew from the Garden to Birmingham, where the committee was holding its hearings on discrimination in the Deep South.

There were shouts and murmurs in Congress. Eugene Talmadge plastered Georgia with photographs of Webster sitting in judgment upon the white South. The administration backed and filled and doubted and fumbled. At every crisis in the FEPC there was the threat that Randolph would invade Washington; and the committee remained alive throughout the war.

The Negro did not come out of the war as a free worker in an open economy. But the FEPC had given him a place in the basic industries which he had never held before. In the future, whites and Negroes would work together in factories where the Negro had never existed as a skilled worker. There were many factors in this revolution, but none were more important than Philip Randolph and his Pullman Porters and their March on Washington.

The Communists, on the other hand, were hardly a factor at all. On the May afternoon of 1941, when Randolph and his friends visited President Roosevelt with their gun cocked, they had to cross a White House picket line of Communists agitating against the defense program and aid to Britain. During the Nazi-Soviet pact, the Communists were reluctant to press for the Negro's integration into the defense industries, for fear that his consequent prosperity would make the Negro pro-war.

After Germany's invasion of the Soviet Union, the Communists felt that Randolph's uproar against discrimination was inimical to their desire to bury all personal aspirations in order to aid the Soviets in their desperate hour. The Party's position was an absolute contradiction between one summer month of 1941 and the month which followed it, but in neither phase were the Communists enthusiastic for an uninhibited FEPC campaign. The ordinary Negro had little concern for the dialectical subtleties of the Communists' position; he tended to consider it in both cases an expression of the needs of white people.

The Communists neglected the FEPC for the same set of reasons which have always kept them from being any real factor in the Negro's progress and agitation in America. Their failure began with the Scottsboro case, which had for them the superficial clatter of triumph. The Scottsboro Boys were nine itinerant Negroes who were sentenced to death in April of 1931 for the supposed rape of two white women on a Chattanooga freight train. The Communists financed their early defense. Within two months after their case began, the International Labor Defense sent to Europe the mother of two of the prisoners; as "Mother" Wright she toured twenty-eight countries and heard shouts that "The Scottsboro boys shall not die" in a score of foreign tongues. She was so successful a missionary that there were indications that the ILD had at least eight Mother Wrights appearing at once in different parts of the world.

It has been estimated that the Communists collected nearly a million dollars for the Scottsboro Boys; the legitimate expenditures for their defense can hardly have exceeded sixty thousand dollars. During the course of their appeals, the Scottsboro Boys became the most famous Negroes in America; when their last appeal was lost, the ILD settled back and waited for injustice to triumph. The prisoners, after a long and painful effort, were finally rescued and set free by a committee of liberals led by the Rev. Allan Knight Chalmers, Morris Ernst, Walter White, and the late Grover Hall, of Montgomery, Alabama.

"I think," Chalmers has written, "that the Communists would have been content to lose the case if only they could publicize their part in it and point out the weakness of American legal practice."

There was something peculiarly hard about the Communists which especially showed itself to every Negro who fell into association with them. They offered only an initial kindness; in the end they were exploiters and without even that small, saving sense of sin which some other white men had.

But Negroes as a group have been so little subject to the Communist infection as to be very hard to excite against the few Negroes who *are* afflicted by it. It is difficult for a Negro to believe, so long as James Eastland sits in the United States Senate and Herman Talmadge is governor of Georgia, that the American Communist is the main author of his sufferings. Harlem sent Benjamin Davis, a Negro Communist, to the New York City Council during the war. It turned him out in 1949 for a number of reasons, by no means the least of these the fact that so many of his canvassers were whites that many Negroes began to wonder just what there was in his election for them. Randolph is a passionate Communist-baiter by Negro standards, but even he barred only *white* Communists from his March on Washington.

The typical Negro, through the thirties and today, has been bored by the Communist, whether he is presented as saint or devil. Those Negro Communists who were the most conspicuous and stayed the longest were, in an unusual number of cases, persons who thought they had escaped the Negro problem for a while and then had that sudden shock of recognition which is a daily experience for most Negroes.

Paul Robeson was such a person. Benjamin Davis was born in Atlanta; but, as the son of Georgia's Republican National Committeeman, he was able to attend Amherst and Harvard and do well as a lawyer in the North. In the thirties he made a fleeting return to Georgia to assist in the defense of Angelo Herndon, a Negro Communist organizer who had been indicted under that state's criminal syndicalism law. Davis was unsure about Georgia court procedure; as he arose, hesitant, the presiding judge said to him, "Well, nigger, go ahead and say what you have to say." Davis claims that this single, sudden moment of degradation made him a Communist.

Davis, an extraordinary Negro, remains a Communist leader; Herndon, an ordinary Negro, left the Communists quite soon after his release from prison. One element in his defection was the experience of meeting Anna Damon, the Communist lady in charge of his defense campaign, and having her look at him sadly and comment, "It's too bad you aren't blacker." The Communists were in the end no less unconscious than so many other white people of the Negro's existence as a human being.

But, then, perhaps Angelo Herndon was fortunate; it can be an advantage to discover, when you are young enough, that the world is round. The Pullman porter had made that discovery very early, and he had accepted it with resignation. When the war was over, no one had done more than the Pullman porter to achieve for the Negro a place in society which he himself had never known and was unlikely to know in his own lifetime.

His Brotherhood had contributed fifty thousand dollars to the March on Washington movement. As an individual he offered dollar upon dollar to campaigns which could bring him no personal profit, because he understood, from his own life, what Randolph meant when he said that "the Negro must supply the money and pay the price, make the sacrifices and endure the suffering to break down his barriers."

Thomas T. Patterson was only one Pullman porter. By day, as a union official, courteous and resolute, he argued with the railroads. After hours, as a Negro, just as politely he sued them. In 1945, Patterson was traveling to Atlanta with a reserved seat on a coach which the Southern Railroad had predestined for whites only. The conductor did his utmost to shoo him into the Negro coach all the way from Washington to Charlottesville, Virginia, and at last called the police of the native city of Thomas Jefferson. Patterson was taken off the train and put into jail as a disturber of the peace. The next morning, the police judge gave him the smallest fine possible and set him loose, almost with an apology, for it is the terrible strength of Thomas Patterson that it is so difficult for a white man to talk to him and not feel the shame of the Negro's 334 dark years of life in America.

Patterson sued the Southern Railroad for damages and collected three thousand dollars as an out-of-court settlement. He gave it to the March-on-Washington Committee. Three years later, he went to dinner in an Atlantic Coast Line dining car and refused to sit in its section reserved for Negroes. Once again, Thomas Patterson was ejected. He spent the next morning in friendly disputation with an Atlantic Coast Line lawyer over a subject of moment to the Brotherhood; that afternoon he sued the railroad for his "humiliation" in its diner. The Coast Line settled out of court; the partitions which screened Negroes from whites in its diner went down; and Patterson gave his profits to the Brotherhood of Sleeping Car Porters.

It is odd to think of a Pullman porter consciously practicing in the United States that doctrine of nonviolent resistance which is the root of the canonization of Mahatma Gandhi, but it is odder still that it works so well. By grace of litigation like Patterson's, American Negroes now ride through the South on nonsegregated trains and travel as guests on those Southern Pullmans on which they were once confined to acts of service; and no fires blaze and no shots whine.

Patterson is by now a proud tradition in the Brotherhood; and the Pullman porter, unobtrusive as always, often acts with the sense that he represents a long struggle for human freedom.

Just after the war, Ralph Bunche of the United Nations took a train to Atlanta and entered its diner to be escorted with ceremony behind the partition separating the white from the Negro. That was before Bunche won the Nobel Peace Prize, but we may assume that nothing could have altered his status at that table. He told the steward that he would prefer not to eat and went hungry back to his room.

Half an hour later, the buzzer rang at his door and he opened it to confront two Pullman porters and a dining-car waiter carrying a tray.

"They told me," said Bunche, who was a stranger to them, "that they had decided to bring me this food because no Negro, in their view, who refused to sit at that Jim Crow table should or would ever go hungry on a train on which they served. They didn't mention it, but I took it that the food was also at the compliments of the company. I got breakfast the next morning the same way."

In 1948, Philip Randolph went down to see Harry Truman, another President and one much harried at the flanks, to demand an end to segregation of Negroes in the armed forces. It was a polite conversation at first; but then Randolph said that, in his view, Negroes would before long refuse to join a peacetime army in which they could not hope for equal chance of advancement. Mr. Truman blew up and began talking about loyalty and patriotism. One of Randolph's companions expressed the hope that the President wanted facts and not compliments. And Harry Truman said, yes, he would prefer the facts. Randolph went away; and, before long, for this and other reasons, the armed services began the slow process of eliminating their color bars, and whites and Negroes fought together in Korea.

These things went on, very slow but very deep. It was as though Paul Robeson did not know that they were happening, because he was neither a white man nor a Negro and he did not see them. He had become by now almost an open Communist, no longer suitable for exploitation by patriotic concert managers, a subject of pain and blame to his lost friends from the great world, who knew that he had failed them but did not often think, as all men must, that somehow they had failed him too.

Paul Robeson, of course, did not know the Negro. He could not have been expected to; he had gone far away and he had taken a return road along which very few American Negroes traveled. He had, in fact, almost ceased to be an American Negro at all. In the winter of 1949, speaking from Paris, a measure of the distance between him and them, he promised that the fifteen million Negroes of the United States would never fight against the Soviet Union.

The mind of the Negro remains so subterranean to white eyes that the American newspapers suffered a tremor at Robeson's threat, because it is their custom to think of the Negro as unsatisfied, which he is, and as disaffected, which he is not.

Philip Randolph, who had articulated all the rumblings in all the Harlems of America, answered Robeson again and again:

"On every battlefield, from the war of 1776, Negroes have proudly and gallantly fought and died to defend and protect the flag and honor of our country. This is not a white man's country. It is the country of the people who helped to take it, worked to make it, and fought to save it. The United States is our home.

Our children are here. We have no other country. We have no other home.

"If there are wrongs in America, Negroes as Americans must help work and fight to correct them. If the problems of race and color are hard in the United States, so be it; let us not lose heart and run away from them, but gird to solve them."

Philip Randolph, for whom it has always been hard and who had begun disaffected and revolutionary, was opening his mouth for Thomas Patterson and all the other Pullman porters, who had never had room to invite an illusion inside and who had begun to take with their hands a portion of what had come so early and with such delusive ease to Paul Robeson. Robeson had traveled a long way to find that his world was surrounded by spikes and brick. The Pullman porters had known those spikes from the first. Their lives had been a process of beating at a succession of walls with their bare hands and, as each wall went down, of rallying their strength to assault the next one. The highest walls were still before them. But they had left too much of themselves in the wreckage behind them not to understand that the ground which you have taken yourself is your own particular ground and especially to be cherished and defended.

That lesson seemed to them so fundamental as to be an assumption. They did not think of what they had done as some alternative to the Communists, because for them the Communists did not really exist. If some of them wondered why Randolph felt compelled to reply to Robeson so often, it was only because Robeson seemed so far from where they lived.

There must be a great portion of every Negro which no one who is not a Negro can ever understand or reach. The white man of good will sits at night and argues with some passion that the Negro must be treated as an equal and arises the next morning to call a cleaning woman twenty years his senior by her first name and be called mister in return and never think that this pattern of the ages has anything to do with what he was saying the night before. He will talk on and on about what the white should do for the Negro and be all the time unaware of what the Negro has done for himself. He will use a word like tolerance and never reflect that tolerance might be at least as difficult for a Negro as for him.

But what is the hardest thing on earth for him to understand is that, for the Negro, he is at once omnipresent and nonexistent. His words, his advances, his tenders of friendship are only words thrown out to men who have been given very little in their lives and who have gained nothing which has not come hard to them.

And to them, the Communist was only another white man, less offensive than many, no more to be trusted than most. His failures with the Negro were not failures of tactics; they were failures of heart and love and trust, white men's failures. And so Paul Robeson wandered, an African god without votaries, an emperor without subjects. There was an absolute nothing between him and the people for whom he affected to speak. For they were not his children but Bessie Smith's, who had lived with them and died with them and sung to them of that long, lonesome road that they must walk all by themselves and who had promised: "You know, it's gotta en'." And yet they were children different from their mother; they endured on hope and not on resignation; they could not accept her lesson that to be born black meant to be scorned and cheated this side of the grave; their dreams of freedom were of this earth.

One summer evening in 1950, a Southern Railroad Pullman porter named William Mills was standing beside his sleeping car in the Atlanta station when a company of soldiers came trooping in. They were very young, most of them; they had their barracks bags on their shoulders; and they were moving loosely and casually, talking in accents that mingled the North and the South. They were a mixed company of whites and Negroes.

A stiff-backed regular army sergeant shepherded them aboard their cars and, once they were all inside, stood on the platform checking his roster. A white soldier leaned out the door and asked in Georgian accents how long, sergeant, are we gonna be travelin'. The sergeant returned the usual noncommittal noncom's answer and went on with his paper work.

Pullman Porter William Mills watched a while and then went over to him. The sergeant looked up. He did not wait for Mills to speak.

"I know what you're going to ask me," he said, "Yes, it's true. It's true."

It was true. The sergeant was a Negro and these were white

troops under his command. William Mills, Pullman porter and menial, had a sudden sense that out of all those years and all those meetings and all that money bet on a thin dream, a child had been born to him. He did not need to be told what America had done to him, or that it was not yet an easy place for a Negro to live in. But he did not need to be told either which was his country and whose monument stood before him.

9

The heart of the myth was not always interior storm. There were a very few to whom it was normal and in no way a creed of alienation, and who came to it by copying their fathers and not by defying them. They were the sons of old radicals. The thirties was a time of opportunity for them. Its storms were only exterior challenges, and they moved through it to the sort of stability which is the passion of normal young men.

They accepted the myth of the thirties at moments in their lives. But they were not fantasists by nature, and they carried the image of self with which they began almost intact through a time which broke so many other men. The best examples of their experience are Walter, Roy, and Victor Reuther, the sons of a German Socialist, who came to an untamed Detroit in the early thirties, were leaders of its revolution, and have become stewards of its tidy new order.

The story of the Reuthers is a strange one in our context. We have been here largely concerned with persons who would appear to have known very faintly what they wanted. The Reuthers seem always to have known exactly what they wanted. We have told stories largely of failure. Against these stories, the lives of the Reuthers—lives unconventional only at the surface—seem like an ordered progression along the road of that American legend which dictates the triumph of the young man who listens to his father, is exemplary of habit, and works harder than his companions.

At bottom the Reuthers are neither spectacular nor notorious and the excitement of their youth is largely an excitement of peculiar circumstance. It is as though history had played its final joke on the myth of the thirties by handing its garlands to these worthy, uncomplicated Reuthers, the very models of the kind of young man who was the appointed beneficiary of the earlier, simpler legend of the American dream.

The story of the Reuthers is the story of Detroit, the city to which they seemed such aliens, and the auto workers who appeared so unlike them. Two books by persons quite different from the Reuthers have seemed to me especially valuable as guides to that background. One is *Union Guy,* the autobiography of Clayton Fountain, who entered the auto industry as a rootless, drifting boy and who has ended as an international representative of the CIO Auto Workers Union. The other is *We Never Called Him Henry,* the autobiography of Harry Bennett, who ruled Detroit as Henry Ford's deputy with fist and gun when the Reuthers came there. For their memories of Detroit's 1937 storm, I have most to thank Roy Reuther, Emil Mazey, secretary-treasurer of the Auto Workers, and Myra Wolfgang, vice president of the AFL Hotel and Restaurant Workers, whose members conducted some of Detroit's most piquant sit-down strikes.

Almost everyone in these pages has experienced an end very different from his beginning. The Reuthers have not ended precisely as they began either. But their end has been with reality, as their lives have been with reality; the challenge they accepted in their youth was no less real for being peculiar. The myth of the thirties did not touch only persons afflicted with the need for fantasy. Its heritage is not only ruins; it left its monuments too.

Father and Sons

The Reuther Boys

*"I'll be back, you sons of bitches; I'll be back and or-
ganize this plant."*

> EMIL MAZEY, upon ejection from the
> Briggs Motor Corporation, December 1,
> 1936

*"The trouble with you, Reuther, is that you're still young
and full of piss and vinegar."*

> ARNOLD LENZ, plant manager, Flint
> Chevrolet, to Roy Reuther, March,
> 1937

*"Mr. Ford, in his new benign mood, said, 'Oh, well,
Harry, live and let live.'*

*"Still so angry I spoke without thinking, I snapped back,
'It's kind of late to say that, isn't it?'*

*"The minute it was out I could have bitten my tongue.
'I'm sorry I said that, Mr. Ford,' I apologized, 'I was sore
and I just wasn't thinking.'*

*"'Oh,' Mr. Ford said, 'that's all right. I WAS JUST
THINKING OF PEOPLE IN GENERAL.'"*

> HARRY BENNETT, We Never Called Him
> Henry

VALENTINE REUTHER'S father brought him from Imperial Germany when he was nine years old out of that
variety of impulses which were at the bottom of the historic quarrel of one Germany with the other—distaste for the army, distaste for the empire, distaste for Bismarck.

They settled in Wheeling, West Virginia, late in the eighties. Almost before Valentine had grown up, he went to work in the breweries, almost as determined an occupational terminus for the immigrant German as the dress shop for the immigrant Jew, the trolley car for the Irish, the open ditch for the Italian.

In the beginning, he earned $1.50 a day driving a brewery wagon. He spent some of it on courses from the International Correspondence Schools. After awhile this devotion to self-help qualified Valentine Reuther to be secretary of his AFL brewery workers' local. He earned a wage large enough for marriage for a man of moderate appetites. Valentine Reuther's four sons came close together—first Ted, then Walter in 1907, then Roy in 1909, and last of all Victor. At the time Roy was born, Valentine Reuther had climbed off his brewery wagon to become an organizer for his union and the rest of the AFL in the Ohio Valley. But this elevation brought no marked change in social status; his was a routine of close rations and prolonged trips from home.

When Roy was a little boy, he used to cry in the night because of his father's long absences; and Valentine Reuther was then quietly and easily reconciled to abandoning the road and confining his efforts for the world he wanted to Wheeling. But it was an entirely geographical compromise. Valentine Reuther never had to struggle with his natural impulses. He was a German working man; and so he had at once a sense of family and helped his union and voted Socialist and was happy and uncomplicated in all these processes.

He ran for Congress as a Socialist; he was president of the Ohio Valley AFL and he hoped for greater things from his sons. But Valentine Reuther inhabited a quiet pond of the American dream. He distrusted glittering success and glaring failure alike; vagabondage was as distasteful to him as any other kind of conspicuous consumption. And so he wanted his sons to be more successful than he had been, but in a fashion in no wise pretentious. The Germany of the last century had conditioned even its rebels to order and social stratification and to the idea that there are levels of achievement and that the good artisan should have pride of place.

Valentine Reuther taught his boys that each must have a trade.

Walter would be a machinist, and Roy an electrician, and Victor seemed to hold promise as a plumber. Ted alone among them could expect to wear a white collar; he went into an office after he left high school. There was in their adolescence no rebellion, no slamming of doors, no apparent alienation. Their mother felt very deep the impress of German Protestantism; they were so faithful at Sunday School that each of their chests was heavy with the attendance pin and its ladder of bars certifying seven years without a Sunday missed.

In high school, the Reuther boys accepted with no sign of dissatisfaction the course in self-improvement their father prescribed for them. He would send them to the town library after school. On Sunday afternoons in winter, they would go to their bedroom and split into two-man teams to debate pacifism, capital punishment, or women in industry—what Valentine Reuther called "social questions"—while their father sat in a corner and graded them on how well they had organized and presented their material.

On Sunday afternoons in summer, this uncomplained-of regimen eased, and the Reuther boys would polish the family car and drive their parents to the public picnic grounds. They were adolescents of the twenties, a decade when by popular recollection the family was turning upon itself; it was a civil war which passed them by. Improvement of oneself and one's world was a basic goal in the home where the Reuthers grew up, but they appear to have shown little sense that their parents were old-fashioned or that there was an outside world with newer, easier standards than those by which Valentine Reuther ordered his life.

Roy is the only one of them who can recollect any temptation to live by the dictates of simple enjoyment. He was talented enough at track and basketball to consider a career as an athletic instructor; but his father told him that this was "rah-rah" stuff and brought him easily back to the family pattern. Roy and Victor finished high school in Wheeling. Walter had dropped out when he was sixteen to become an apprentice toolmaker. After three years he was a master mechanic and unemployed, having lost his last job for agitating against Sunday work.

And so he went, as all good unattached toolmakers seemed to go, to Detroit. For Detroit was the golden city of the twenties, a haven of promise for factory workers dreaming of a hundred-dollar-a-week pay check. It was a city of native immigrants, wandering prospectors, floaters, all drawn by Henry Ford's five-dollar-a-day base rate, which the imagination of ordinary men could so easily multiply through repetition to ten dollars or even fifteen dollars a day. The workers came there like pretty girls to Hollywood, clustering outside the works gates on rumors that so-and-so was hiring, husbanding themselves with odd jobs, and always waiting for the great chance that would open to them when they were taken on the assembly line. The old toolmakers had come early; the tide of migrants into Detroit in the twenties was of the untrained, drawn by Ford's promise to pay five dollars a day for skills that were minimal if they could be called skills at all.

Walter Reuther was not like most of these men, who had come to Detroit as though to Canaan and found it very much like the homes they had left behind, only noisier and less open and so much more cruel. The world is especially round to the unskilled. The dollar came only a little faster and a lot more painfully in Detroit than in most other places. But its workers did not study their failure and their loss and draw any large social judgments from them. They would sum up this latest piece of deception with some bit of pith about life in the harsher plants ("If poison fails, try Briggs") and wash it down with a boilermaker and go home to sleep off their exhaustion. Detroit was after all the last Klondike; no other delusive promise seemed to shimmer with a sheen making it worthwhile to move along.

They were all sorts of men, but to find their archetype we should look less to Walter Reuther than to Clayton Fountain, who grew up to become an international representative of the CIO Auto Workers Union. Fountain had been born in a Great Lakes fishing village and had drifted into Detroit with only two dollars left in his pocket. He was just eighteen when he was hired on at Packard in 1927; that night he went to sleep to dreams "full of new suits and Saturday nights with a pocketful of dough to spend in speakeasies."

At Packard, Clayton Fountain worked a twelve-hour shift and learned to sleep in ten-minute snatches in the washroom; he never made more than forty-five dollars a week and turned to fresh dreams of commercial aviation. Then he was fired and caught on at Briggs, which gave him a stake to get married. "We celebrated the event with two quarts of prohibition gin in a little wooden house owned by her father." Three months later Clayton Fountain decided that Detroit was a blind alley and went bumming about the country in search of new scenery.

He was broke when he got to Kansas City, so he took a job running a punch press and counted himself lucky because the machine clipped off a finger joint and his employer gave him one hundred and fifty dollars accident compensation. Some of that profit he spent on a hotel suite and much on apricot brandy. He split what was left with his friends and took the southbound freight to Texas, where he had hopes of shipping out to sea. That prospect, like so many others before it, evaporated, and then he tried New Orleans and lived on bananas snitched off its docks until he decided to catch the Illinois Central boxcars back to Michigan.

But something impelled him to drop off in Memphis and hobble over to the Salvation Army for breakfast. He found a job as a trucker's helper and stayed there until the police picked him up drunk in January, 1930, and sent him to Shelby County workhouse for ten days. When he came out, he went back to the Salvation Army to pick up his clothes and fell into a place as a tractor driver on a Tennessee plantation. He was there all winter and spring and then came back to Detroit in the summer of 1930 by bus.

Clayton Fountain came home, if you could call it that, to find the depression, an act of nature unsuspected in the Tennessee back country, where booms and crashes alike sounded faint and where their tremors came late. His father-in-law found him a job digging ditches for the city—the auto plants were already moribund—and it lasted him until February, 1931. After that, "two and a half years were to pass before I got my hands on a regular pay check."

No man is typical of a quarter million others, and Clayton

Fountain was a little more casual and a little less fettered than most of his shopmates. But he was like them, lifted by boom, brought to earth by bust, with no fundamental sense of what was happening to him. Detroit, for all the substance of its majesty, was raw as gold-rush cities are raw. There were aspects of the frontier in the rootless, now fat, now lean, existence of its ordinary tenants and in the rough justice of its landlords.

Detroit's patron was Henry Ford, a man of strange terrors with a little boy's awe and affection for the tough and the violent. He did not want his hands to smoke or drink or skip church, but he hired gangsters to supervise them and keep them docile and pure of heart. He was the Don Quixote of an heraldic legend of self-interest; his Sancho Panza was an old navy saloon fighter named Harry Bennett, hired by Ford with the simple, direct question: "Can you shoot?" and master of his plant police and the police of Detroit and the state of Michigan as well.

Ford believed, in all matters except faith and morals, that if a man did not take care of himself, no one else should take care of him. All over America men read of his banner wage and trooped to Detroit. Once there, the fortunate among them worked the twelve-hour shift in his River Rouge plant eight months a year and were laid off four months for the model changeover, year after year, in the best of times. But that was their problem and not his.

Henry Ford delighted in visiting Bennett's office at the Rouge to take target practice; together they inhabited a swarm-haunted fortress from the Middle Ages where the show of violence was never hidden and where Bennett used his fists freely on his fellow executives and where they passed the compliment on to their inferiors. They ruled by whim and iron. In the spring of 1927, Ford discontinued the Model T and closed his works to retool for the Model A. For most of that year, 60,000 unemployed Detroit auto workers awaited the reopening of the golden door. They came back to be rehired according to custom as new employees, the young and the old each taking his place again at five dollars a day.

The executives had gotten rich too fast, and the production

hands were broke too often. There was no ease and peace and quiet in Detroit; the classes hated one another, but in a way they were quite alike. They were at once careless and uncertain of the morrow; they were alike violent, brawling, and unconscious of any meaning in their lives. Communication in the city of the puritan Henry Ford was habitually conducted in language barely printable. Its typical citizens drank too much and wasted their substance and lost their jobs and went hungry and got them back and ate fairly well up on the hog and wondered all the while why it was so different from what they had expected.

If they were executives at Ford, they did things they were ashamed to do; but, as Bennett says, "they knew what side their bread was buttered on and did as they were told." Since they could not consciously hate themselves, they hated Henry Ford and one another. If they were only production hands at Ford, they spent their blood on the lines and too much of their wages in gin mills and made up bitter saws and longed for home. When the depression came and the jobs were gone, nearly a third of them went back to Mississippi or Missouri or Pennsylvania or took to the road that might lead them to some new, though no more promising, home.

Walter Reuther does not appear to have wondered; he was like neither the executives nor the men with whom he worked. From the very beginning, his life in Detroit was unusual for its stability and for what was even a moderate success. He began on the night shift at Briggs. Before very long, his skill told, and he was able to transfer to Ford with a higher rating, and after a while he was a foreman. He went to Dearborn High School, and thereafter to Wayne University, where, instead of engineering, he studied the social sciences.

The difference between him and the others is framed best in one of Reuther's own favorite memories of those days. Every afternoon when he came on, his predecessor on shift would ask him how the ball game was going. Reuther never knew and always forgot to find out. At last his shopmate suspended his inquiries with the final judgment: "Reuther, you're the dumbest bastard I ever knew." Reuther replied by asking, "Do you know the name of your Congressman?" His mate answered that of course he didn't, and Reuther returned a triumphant "Then you're the dumbest bastard I've ever known."

Walter Reuther has a special affection for making a point, and his zeal in this pursuit occasionally takes him into areas of platform reminiscence which sound suspiciously like apocrypha. He has of late been accustomed to cap this anecdote with a sequel. Fourteen years after their last argument, he says he was inspecting a CIO picket line and encountered his old detractor on gloomy parade.

"How're you doing?" Reuther chirped. "Not so good, Reuther," the picket replied and took off his cap to display a lump the size of an egg, the consequence of conflict with the police. Reuther observed it without comment. At last his old shopmate asked, "Aren't you going to say you're sorry for me?" And Reuther says he answered, "No, I'm not sorry for you. If you'd known who your Congressman was back then, you wouldn't have a lump on your head now." Reuther and the ordinary auto worker have happily reconciled their differences. But, even so, when Reuther tells that story, his audience must have a hard time escaping a faint chill at the back and a sense that to accept Walter Reuther is to expect a comfort sometimes frigid.

Back in the twenties, when so few men were reputed to be like their fathers, Walter Reuther had no ideals of which his father could not entirely approve. Henry Ford's ban on smoking in or about Highland Park was no deprivation to him. He saved his money; he was a model workman; and he was a Socialist accepting his father's assurance that Detroit's chills and fevers were the ordained results of private enterprise. If the union had never come, no one can be sure that this revolutionary would not today be a foreman at River Rouge, living as he does now and earning not too much less than he makes as president of the United Auto Workers and Congress of Industrial Organizations. Even his tireless talking about the union did not cost him his job at Ford until very late in 1932; unlike so many of the others, he was able to work right into the trough of the depression and even save money. The Reuther boys were very normal except for their socialist bug. And there is something excessively normal about sons who acquire the parental bug.

Victor Reuther had taken Walter's path to Detroit late in the twenties. They went to Wayne together and worked in the auto plants and tried to build a fire there. But their efforts made little early mark. For Detroit was as quiet inside as it was noisy on the surface. Its residents managed at once to seem heavy with social portent and to make few social motions. There was a general assumption that if the revolution came at all, it would come to Detroit first. Yet, rough, disinherited, and ready for violence though Detroit's workers seemed, there had not been a union in its factories since they were carriage works before World War I.

In this context, Walter Reuther seemed clearly out of step in all he said and did. He was a Socialist when many of his shop-mates voted for Herbert Hoover. He was talking about a union through the boom and into the bust, when few of them would listen. He was working in the depression, when few of them could find jobs. In 1932, he campaigned for Norman Thomas and Detroit's auto workers voted for Franklin D. Roosevelt.

His passion for the 1932 Socialist campaign cost him his job at Ford. The politics which was one of his differences from ordinary men had thus put an end to the job security which was another difference and left Walter Reuther for once like so many of the rest—out of work in a crash town.

Ford's 1927 shift to the Model A had given Detroit a taste of depression. The 1929 bust laid it lower than any city of comparable size in the United States. It was beggared by the collapse of the auto industry which had made it rich. In 1929, there were nearly half a million persons employed in Michigan car factories; two years later there were barely 250,000. By 1932 Ford was producing almost alone among Detroit's giants, and the bulk of its orders were coming from the Soviet Union. The machine was coughing everywhere else; in Detroit, it was almost silent.

There were whole city blocks without light or artificial heat. Families missed their rent or mortgage payments. But no bank or landlord dared evict them; to leave a house vacant was to risk its being stripped of its wires, its plumbing, and even its woodwork for fuel. At the onset of spring in 1932, Detroit's Welfare Department was the entire support of an estimated 250,000 persons. So many families had their water turned off that the schools instituted compulsory weekly showers for their pupils; in some neighborhoods, there were no graduation exercises because the graduates had no proper clothes for them.

The old values were melting and property laws breaking up. At one moment that spring, the city administration was so sunk in debt that grocers refused to accept nine million dollars of its welfare scrip. Mayor Frank Murphy called their representatives in to report that five stores had been entered and stripped the night before. The police had kept that fact out of the papers; but, once it became known, he could not guarantee an unrifled stock of groceries in Detroit. The storekeepers capitulated, and some time later Frank Murphy found the bank credit to honor his scrip.

Clayton Fountain and his friends rode past the comfortable residences of Rosedale Park snitching milk off their doorsteps. Emil Mazey, a Hungarian violinist, came out of high school in 1932, when he was nineteen. For want of a job he attached himself to the Citizens' Unemployed League, an alliance of Detroit's non-Communist radicals. One day a week, Emil Mazey found work in a bakery; he was paid off in bread and took it back to the League's food pool.

"We had a squad of men who were experts on the light meters. We'd go around to the houses of people who'd had their lights turned off and we'd jump the meter and turn them on again. People used to keep the shades down all day, in case the light might show outside and some stoolie tell the company. We could do it with the gas too, but that was a little harder, and after a while the company fixed us by pulling the pipes out. We didn't think we were breaking any law."

Detroit had always been flexible about theories of legality; now it appeared ready to dispense with law entirely. The city was a stewpot of conflicting economic yeasayers—Father Charles E. Coughlin's funny-money Social Justice movement; the Technocrats; the Proletarian Party, a pro-Soviet, anti-official-Communist revolutionary movement with which Emil Mazey briefly flirted; the orthodox Communists; the traditional Socialists; even the Ku Klux Klan. Each offered its personal and drastic purgative. To be drastic seemed normal in a city where a Knight of Columbus was secretary of the Citizens' Unemployed League with its program which mixed co-operation with expropriation.

But the revolution did not come and there was only one damp run of it. One February day in 1932, ten thousand persons, led by Communists, marched on River Rouge and were beaten back by the Dearborn police, first with fire hoses and then with bullets. When they had gone, Harry Bennett was stretched unconscious from a shower of rocks, and four demonstrators were dead. It was the disparity in casualties to be expected on the barricades in Detroit, and there were no further trials of physical strength.

Herbert Hoover came to Detroit that fall struggling for re-election. A hundred thousand people came out to see him. He drove past them through block after block of total, ghastly silence. The Secret Service speeded up his cortege; Detroit was as usual assumed to be the rim of violence, and no one was sure that even the President of the United States was immune from its buried passions.

Walter Reuther had his father's answer to all these terrors. Roy Reuther remembers Walter coming back to Wheeling in the summer of 1932 in a car covered with Thomas stickers and organizing a Socialist campaign meeting. A purpose was, as always, Walter Reuther's greatest pleasure. The Thomas campaign was as much his concept of a proper vacation pursuit as the family debate had been his idea of the best of possible Sunday afternoons.

He was not yet, of course, in step with history; in Wheeling, he had no trouble persuading Roy to vote for Thomas. All his arts could not persuade even Roy, then and there, to join the Socialist Party. But Roy came back to Detroit with his brothers; and before very long he had joined the Party too. Except for Ted, who was now in business in Wheeling, the Reuthers had all followed their father.

The year 1932 was one when the Socialists could believe that they were conducting their last campaign as a minority party.

They had no illusions about Thomas winning the 1932 election. But they assumed his defeat was only the first battle with Roosevelt. It seemed to them impossible, especially from Detroit, that the old system could be put in order again, and they took it for granted that, within four years, the Democrats would be no less discredited than the Republicans and that 1936 would be the Socialist Party's time.

And this assumption of quick Socialist conquest seemed hardly less plausible than any idea that organized labor could assume a place in Detroit's industries at any early time—organized labor being then constituted as the American Federation of Labor with only two million members, none of them in the auto plants, and with leaders undisposed to fill any breach with their own bodies.

The Reuther boys had an hereditary faith in unions as instruments for social revolt. But the icons of their father's home were not labor leaders like Samuel Gompers and William Green but political figures like Eugene V. Debs and Robert M. La Follette. Debs might have known ease as president of one of those steam-driven, low-pressure railroad unions; he had chosen instead a course which made him a Socialist and destroyed him at last in prison for opposing World War I. Valentine Reuther approved every step along this, his personal saint's, path. Even as an AFL organizer, he had believed, with Debs, that Samuel Gompers was dissipating the large to grasp at the small.

The AFL national leadership had seemed to him narrow and petty and unconscious of its historic function, and Debs had seemed a knight with no dross on his shield and no dust on his plumes and no less glorious because his reward was of the future. Valentine Reuther was a German trade unionist of the nineties; to a German trade unionist, no little victory of his union was as anything set next to the vision of ultimate victory for all the workers. If the Reuther boys took from his house any vision of themselves grown up, it was an image of Debs renewed, not of Gompers repeated.

In November of 1932, Detroit inflicted impartial neglect upon Herbert Hoover and Norman Thomas alike. The auto workers, in bad times as in good, had shown no disposition to indulge the revolutionary politics which so many men hoped or feared was their potential. But very soon there were fresh alarms: the auto workers went on strike at Briggs, the place they had described so often in their bars as at once more certain and less comfortable than poison. Reporters came in from all around the country to watch what could be the onset of revolution.

But Detroit did not blow up. The Briggs strikers discovered in mid-passage that their leaders were Communists and threw them out. Briggs, of course, rewarded this demonstration of loyalty to American institutions by freezing and finally breaking their strike. But Walter and Victor were not around for the death of the Briggs strike. They had become infected with the auto worker's old impulse to wander.

Walter Reuther could not find a new job. He and Victor were so certain that this was no Paris Commune upon which they were trembling that they decided to go to Europe. Walter had a bank account large enough to pay their passage and, with his customary knack for the act of good fortune, withdrew it the day before the beginning of the runs which were to make Detroit the cradle of the 1933 banking crisis.

He and Victor were still asleep on their departure day when Roy arose for his duties at the Briggs strike kitchen. He shook hands with them both and said good-by; he would not see them again for almost three years. They were already at sea when the police broke up the Briggs picket line, pushed Roy into an iron fence, and gave him the scar he still carries on his ankle.

With Roosevelt and the National Recovery Act, the auto factories lifted up their heads again, but there were no Reuthers in their industry. Roy Reuther was the last one left; when the Briggs strike reached its ordained disaster, he went off to the University of Wisconsin and thereafter to Brookwood Labor College on the Hudson River, where the Rev. A. J. Muste was patiently training radical missionaries to a labor movement which appeared to have no use for them. Roy Reuther went to Massachusetts in 1934 to teach a workers' education project for the AFL; he moved from there to Flint, Michigan, a General Motors city. There he was city supervisor of adult education, a term which to him meant classes in unionism.

Walter and Victor Reuther went wandering through Europe.

They had started in England on their bicycles. Once Walter fell and broke his arm; he completed the British tour wearing a sling; every morning he and Victor would walk to the top of a hill and Victor would help him on his bicycle and push him to give him the start which was all Walter Reuther ever needed.

They tarried longest in Western Europe to visit their German cousins. The Nazis were absorbing the Germany of Valentine Reuther; the Reuther boys walked the streets of their mother's home town and watched the storm troopers pulling in persons so like their parents. After that, they moved across Europe to the Soviet Union and a new kind of Ford plant, the Ford *autostroy* at Gorki. There Walter Reuther was a Stakhanovite leading a shock brigade, winning medals as a Hero of Production, and sharpening his didactic style with letters to the *Moscow Daily News* on the improvement of industrial techniques.

He and Victor lived with other American workers, and they had very little off-hours association with Russians. Henry Ford was Josef Stalin's image of what was right with America, and the Ford works at Gorki were thus a model by Russian standards. Gorki itself was Nizhni Novgorod made over; it was a purposeful city, whose managers believed themselves pioneers and lived at a reasonable distance from the noisome quarrels that were festering in Moscow and would soon infect the entire Soviet state. Walter and Victor Reuther spent sixteen months seeing the Soviet Union at its deceptive best.

Given these conditions, it might seem odd that the Reuthers did not there and then become Communists. They had left Detroit prostrate; they had passed through a Germany sinking under blood and steel; and they had settled in a Soviet Union which seemed to them busy, peaceful, rational, and altogether a fair prospect between the terror of their ancestral and the chaos of their adopted home. But the enthusiasm of the Reuther boys for socialist construction in the Soviet Union was the enthusiasm of the conscious outsider, and there was detachment in their sympathy. Walter appears to have felt that the Russians had a lot to learn; his medals for skill might have been worth more to him if he had not suspected that any American artisan would be a prodigy to the Soviets.

That was a major difference between Walter and Victor Reuther and most American pilgrims to Russia in the thirties. The others came as acolytes seeking light from the highest of priests; the leaders of the Soviets were master workmen at revolution and all foreign radicals were apprentices to them. But at Gorki, Walter Reuther was a master workman, and his Russian colleagues were apprentices beside him. He could hardly believe that a people with so much to learn about toolmaking had quite so much to teach him about social tactics.

Many of us find it difficult to recognize that a man can pass through a consequential social event without any special change of mind, and the Reuthers and their enemies have alike tended to exaggerate the effect of their Soviet experience upon them. A few years ago, Walter Reuther asserted in a broadcast for the Voice of America that he had been shocked by the terror and repression he saw at first hand in the Soviet Union. In contradistinction to this recollection, his detractors have made incessant use of a letter sent by Victor from Gorki, signed with both their names and studded with juvenile enthusiasm for the Soviet experiment.

The real impression left by their Soviet experience would seem to lie somewhere between enthrallment and revulsion. Gorki touched neither of them to the soul. The Communist Party of Detroit probably did more to turn the Reuthers against the Soviets than anything they saw in Russia. Any deceptive glimpse of communism's constructive future they brought home from Gorki would hardly survive the ceaseless manifestations of communism's destructive present they found in the Detroit Party.

It is hard to believe that there is anything so very remarkable about the final capacity of the Reuthers to resist the enticements of the Communists, who do not after all offer such an irresistible brew to man in a state of reason. Reuther says, as an instance, that Louis Budenz took him on a mountaintop in 1938 and offered him "the moon" if he would go along with the Communists. In a man of Reuther's abilities it seems no special achievement to recognize that, if there are men wandering the earth with pieces of the moon in their pockets, Louis Budenz is hardly one of them.

But, from their haven in Gorki in 1934, Walter and Victor sent back reports of moderate glow to Detroit, and those who read them might be forgiven the onset of envy. For the Reuthers were in the bosom of a revolution which, whatever its failures, looked at least hopeful and partly successful. In Detroit hope and success seemed farther and farther away.

The NRA came and passed. At its outset, the AFL had recruited 100,000 auto workers, all assuming, in John L. Lewis' phrase, that Franklin D. Roosevelt wanted them to join a union. By 1936, the AFL lost 90 per cent of these newcomers. There had been a successful strike in 1934 at the Autolite Company in Toledo, Ohio; there was another, less successful, at Chevrolet in Cleveland in 1935; but these were at the industry's fringe; its major bastions remained untroubled.

In Roosevelt's third year, Detroit appeared, if anything, less vulnerable to the unions than it had on the day of his inauguration. The industry was functioning again, and its fearsome, lowering army of unemployed had begun to diminish. Emil Mazey, a volunteer union organizer, was enduring the life the Reuthers might have known if they had been in Detroit.

"I couldn't exist with the violin," Mazey says now, "so I went to Gulf Refining in nineteen thirty-four. They had a strike in Cleveland. I watched it. We were making eighty-one dollars a month; after the strike, we made a few motions at the company and they gave us twenty to forty-five dollars a month more.

"I thought after that I could get the men to go AFL, but they sort of let me down and I got fired. After that I hung around the Y awhile and read on the bulletin board that Rotary Steel wanted people, so a bunch of us from the Y went up there and hired on. After a little while I got the boys from the Y to form an independent union and we went up to the AFL office to see if they'd take us in. The AFL didn't care much, and nothing happened, and after a while, I got fired there too.

"That didn't leave much but Briggs, so I ended up there in April of nineteen thirty-six. We did a little organizing and in the month of November, we had fifty-one sit-down strikes. They must have figured it was me giving them the trouble, because on

December the first, nineteen thirty-six, a couple of plant guards took me off the line and threw me out in the street.

"They roughed me up pretty good and I got up and said: 'All right, you sons of bitches, I'll be back; I'll be back and organize this plant.'

"The next day, they fired my father and my brother for being related to me; they even tried to fire another fellow whose name was spelt like mine until he convinced them he wasn't a relative. But, after that, my brother and the old man joined the union, so I at least organized my own family."

Emil Mazey's was the course of the unpaid labor agitator in Detroit in the early thirties, first let down by his own, then thrown down by the AFL, then thrown out by the company. Walter and Victor Reuther returned to that life from the Soviet Union by way of India, Japan, and a Pacific freighter, late in 1935.

Walter caught on at General Motors Ternstedt on Detroit's West Side. By now he was blacklisted and had to assume a new name to get his job. Even under this disguise, he made enough of a nuisance of himself to be fired before long, and thereafter settled down in the cold to supervise the six AFL auto locals on the West Side. When he showed up for the auto union convention in South Bend, Indiana, all six aggregated fewer than eighty members.

Even that close to solitude he was impressive enough to win election to his union's first national executive board. In those days any Detroit delegate to an auto workers' convention was a candle in the night. The capital city of the industry was otherwise so sunk in darkness that the convention voted unanimously against holding its 1937 session in Detroit because a thirsty visitor could not find a union bar there, or an unshaven one a union barber.

At South Bend, in 1936, the United Auto Workers, AFL for the moment, elected Homer Martin, a St. Louis minister, as their president; George Addes, a Toledo Autolite strike leader, as their secretary treasurer; and a Milwaukee production hand named Ed Hall and an old Pennsylvania coal miner named Wyndham

Mortimer as vice presidents. Detroit offered no representative with enough followers to qualify him for national office; only a thousand workers in the industry's center belonged to the union. Walter Reuther, a delegate who had trouble even being seated, was elected to the national board for want of anyone else from Detroit. Today he alone, among those early leaders, still survives as a UAW official.

Almost at once, the auto union moved over into John L. Lewis' Committee for Industrial Organization and was expelled from the AFL, which made little immediate difference in its fortunes. It had no treasury; John Lewis sent in one hundred thousand dollars, just twenty-five cents for every potential member in Detroit alone. It seemed a massive sum to delegates who had hitchhiked to South Bend and slept six in a hotel room.

There was room in Lewis' donation to put one Reuther on the UAW payroll. Roy Reuther had been a teacher in Flint, which was the heart of General Motors, so he was hired as an organizer there. He was the only member of the family earning a regular salary from the union. Walter and Victor continued their search for water in the dry sands of the West Side. The summer of 1936 was not encouraging; no sensible prophet suggested that Detroit was any longer on the edge of revolution. The union might pick off a few stragglers, but the enemy seemed safe in its castle with the invaders doomed to bed down outside the moat.

Roosevelt was campaigning for re-election. There were few arguments in the auto plants. He could expect to sweep Detroit, even though the Reuther boys and a few out-of-step persons argued that the New Deal had given the auto worker nothing and did what they could to get votes for Norman Thomas. But even their focus was shifting; they were too busy with the union to give as much time to Thomas as they had in 1932.

On the surface at least, the worst recollections of the depression had been buried. There was little talk of boom, but there appeared to be a growing sense that before long things might be as they were when people thought they had been so much happier than they really had been. Yet all that summer things were happening to foreshadow the flame which burst upon Detroit in the summer of 1937. First of all, the UAW was beginning to win recruits. There were not many of them, but they were the ordinary auto workers from whom the Reuthers had until then seemed so different.

The most important new arrival was the Chrysler independent union, which came into the UAW led by Richard Frankensteen, a raucous, fleshy giant who had been a tackle for the University of Dayton and had come to Chrysler to start at the bottom and had been anchored there by the depression. Frankensteen and the other Chrysler leaders had no ideological eccentricities and no spiritual ties except with Father Coughlin, the witch doctor from the Shrine of the Little Flower. Frankensteen was glad to use Coughlin; Frankensteen would have used Mephistopheles if the imps would pay union dues.

The qualities of sin and virtue were mixed in Richard Frankensteen as they are in most men, and far more evenly than they are ever likely to be in Walter Reuther. Labor spying was one of Detroit's staple industries in those days; General Motors alone was spending for private detectives a sum more than twice as large as its president's salary. The way a Chrysler spy once deceived Richard Frankensteen was a gauge of his difference from Walter Reuther.

The Chrysler local was always shorthanded, and in 1936 Frankensteen was rejoiced by the tireless assistance of a young man named John Andrews. Andrews was valuable for more than his devotion to the union. He was a delightful companion with a millionaire uncle of abiding benevolence; and Andrews and Frankensteen were accustomed to relax together on week ends in the company of Andrews' uncle, never stinting a desire and never paying a check. Then, in 1937, Frankensteen learned from a Senate committee that John Andrews and his rich uncle had both been private detectives for Chrysler. The company had been buying the drinks, and his companions had been taking down his unguarded observations on union business for transmittal to Chrysler.

Dick Frankensteen had been hooked, but he had been hooked in the auto worker's fashion—with a few drinks and the image of a rich uncle, one of those successful men he wanted so much to be like. And so his followers could not blame him for being taken that way; they had but to assess the lure and their own incapacity to resist it, Calvinism being a minor element in the auto worker's philosophy.

Walter Reuther could hardly have been captured, even temporarily, with a tender of good fellowship from a private detective posing as a capitalist. The only feasible distraction for him would have been the loan of a home power lathe, a subtlety beyond the imagination of the corporations. They were different men. But Dick Frankensteen had his uses, for he was like the men in the plants, capable of violent activity between long periods of sloth, roaring in the short and slumbrous in the long, never mad at anyone for more than a little while.

Frankensteen brought along enough followers to make him the UAW's Detroit organizer. His time came very soon and blazed fleetingly, and after that he was hammering a cold anvil until, bored and empty, he left for good a life that seemed routine thereafter. For, unlike Walter Reuther, he was a man only for the sudden shock and the reeling crisis; but, together, for a little while they made the Detroit revolution.

The revolution began in the fall of 1936 in little, undisciplined strikes, which annoyed the industry more than they scared it. Briggs was the worst; but its wave of sit-down strikes ebbed, and on December 1st, Emil Mazey was out in the street and the season of peace, if not good will, was presumed to be at hand.

And then suddenly Walter Reuther won a big plant. His West Side local struck the Kelsey-Hayes Wheel Company in December. The strikers did a thing Detroit labor had never done before: they seized the administration offices, fortified the plant, and sat there, an army of occupation, for nine days, until the company gave in and accepted the union. Detroit's now quiet, now fitful quarrel had passed to a military phase. The Kelsey-Hayes strikers were captained by a young man named George Edwards, lately out of the Harvard Business School, and he fought like a line officer. The reports on the capture of Kelsey-Hayes were in the language of war:

"That morning we barricaded the Kelsey gates. The main gates were blocked by a solid, three-foot-high wall of steel, formed from a dozen carefully placed steel containers. We loaded each container with a couple of tons of hub-castings, and behind the barricade we set a dolly-load of eighteen-inch T irons."

They sat thus impregnable while Walter Reuther haggled with their company's displaced officers. Victor Reuther made hideous the noon outside with his sound truck; and one of the union delegates observed that this was the voice of Walter's brother. Someone brought in a Detroit paper with its picture of Roy Reuther stirring up Flint.

"Jesus Christ," said a Kelsey-Hayes official, the first of his breed to feel the sense of encirclement, "how many of you bastards are there?" The Reuther boys, in whom profanity does not spring naturally and who husband it for great occasions, are a bottomless inspiration for it in others.

But Kelsey-Hayes was not a major salient. The auto union's fate rested with Roy Reuther and the others who sat on the main line at Flint, the capital of General Motors and the company town of 150,000 persons where Chevrolets were made. There the union's organizers moved delicately among a very few who could be trusted, a few more who belonged to the enemy, and a great many who only stood and watched.

Every social war is a battle between the very few on both sides who care and who fire their shots across a crowd of spectators. The ordinary Flint auto worker might well have voted for the union, granted the chance for the peaceful proceedings of a National Labor Relations Board election, but he would not risk his job for it. Peaceful proceedings were very far from Flint. The men who worked in Chevrolet were completely conscious of the dangers of public affirmation. In the beginning most of them stayed outside the union.

Wyndham Mortimer, the first UAW organizer in Flint, found a union local there with twenty-four dollars in its treasury and a heavy proportion of its active members employees of the Pinkerton Agency with a professional interest in keeping the union alive but not kicking. Flint's General Motors delegate to the 1936 UAW convention was a Pinkerton agent. And, for most of their stay there, Roy Reuther and his associates had no reason to assume that, whenever two or three were gathered to-

gether in the union's name, the Pinkertons would not be represented.

A combat officer on such a field must depend not on the mass
but on a small, mobile, and itself dubious force of the dedicated.
He must live by crisis and choose the moments when he is bold
and his enemies indecisive and the army of neutrals can be moved
his way by tidal shock. The sit-down strike was a military action,
and Roy Reuther was a battalion commander.

The ground upon which he fought was clustered all about
Flint—the two Fisher Body plants, the ramparts of Chevrolet
where 14,000 people worked, the Buick and Cadillac enclaves.
Chevrolet held the key to the citadel, but at first it seemed be-
yond assault. Whatever strength the union had was in Fisher
Number One, where the bodies were made for Cadillacs, Buicks,
and Oldsmobiles. The first battle was there. Late in December,
Cleveland Fisher, the Chevrolet center, went on strike. If the
UAW could stop Flint Fisher One, it could tie up 80 per cent of
GM's production.

The war for Flint began on December 30, 1936, when 3,000
men sat down in Fisher Number One. They started in a carnival
mood. On New Year's Eve, a foreman brought in liquor; two
prostitutes came across the lines; the casual and the neutral began drifting out; by dawn fewer than a hundred men remained.
The dedicated thereafter threw out their guests, sent for rein-
forcements, banned all whisky, and settled down to the sit-down
strike's unaccustomed discipline for the next six weeks.

They slept in unfinished bodies or made their beds of car-
cushion wadding and labeled them "Hotel Astor" or "Hotel
Sloan," the latter for the chairman of the board of General
Motors. A group of them took a vow not to shave until the strike
was over; but they were required to take a shower every day.
Each afternoon they swept up their garbage and saw it carried
away by GM's disposal crew. They ran a daily inspection of
quarters for cleanliness. Hour after hour, in groups, they practiced throwing car hinges at a piece of beaverboard to train
themselves to repel invaders. But when they walked out, they
left the company's property otherwise intact, except for the
gougings of someone's file on a few car bodies, an act which Bud

Simons, a Communist activist inside the plant, described in terms of the outraged morality of these incendiaries: "Only a stoolie would have done such a disgusting thing."

Every night they braced for a counterattack that never came. GM was trying the courts and the governor and the state police and every device but an invasion in force. None of their rulers could quite muster the decision to challenge the auto workers with the heavy battalions which might have broken them. But they were under siege. Outside their gates Flint was angry and restive; four-fifths of its workers were jobless, a majority not by choice. Late in January, GM announced a back-to-work movement. Governor Murphy was a bending reed; an unfavorable court decision could be deferred no longer; its certain consequence would be an injunction ordering Fisher Number One purged of its trespassers. The strike was not going well; it could be saved only by some stroke of strength and passion. The only worthwhile target was Chevrolet.

But Flint was quiet when GM reopened its unstruck plants on January 24, 1937. The company had redoubled its guards in and about the Chevrolet works. This ground, unhealthy in December, seemed deadly in January.

The union's leaders huddled in their headquarters the night of January 27th and surveyed their unpromising situation. Chevrolet Plant Number Four, where the engines were made, was the only operation worth stopping; the UAW's resources there were terribly small; there were, in fact, only fifty trustworthy men in all Flint Chevrolet. Roy Reuther had a fresh shirt sitting on his desk. He reached over and drew out its cardboard backing and, with a blue pencil, commenced to sketch a diagram of their objective: Chevvy Number Four, the main target, and Chevrolet Number Nine to its right, and Chevrolets Six and Eight, where the few sure believers were, just above that.

It was a diagram of battle undreamed of at the University of Wisconsin, unthought of even at Brookwood Labor College. Their only chance, said Roy Reuther, was in a diversion. The union would call in its noncoms and announce a plan to capture Chevrolet Number Nine, just across the way from Number Four. The Pinkertons could be expected to inform the company of this

schedule and GM would strip its other plants of guards to protect the threatened point. And, while the battle was on and the
UAW's partisans were diverting the enemy in Number Nine,
twenty-five of the union's most trusted bravoes would attempt the
seizure of Chevrolet Number Four.

On January 29th, Chevrolet Works Manager Arnold Lenz,
alerted as expected, showed up with all his guards to meet the
decoy invasion as it came. They fought in clouds of gas, the
guards with blackjacks, the strikers with oil pumps, for the forty
minutes which Roy Reuther thought his auxiliaries would need
to raid and subdue Chevrolet Four.

Roy Reuther had sent a call for fireworks outside Chevrolet
Nine. Victor was on the street with his sound truck and Walter
with his Kelsey-Hayes shock troops to lend color to Roy's diversion. The windows of Number Nine were clouded; the crowd
outside could see only the shadows of struggling men. Once
someone broke a window and they could see the tear-gas smoke
seeping out and they knew the battle was going badly. A few
members of Walter Reuther's legion set up a clamor to charge
the gates. He grabbed the loudest of them and knocked him out
to quiet him. Walter Reuther knew, in the hot moments as in
the cold, the sacrifices required of men assigned to serve as a
diversion.

But, by now, a skeleton crew of foremen was all that was left
to fight for General Motors inside Chevrolet Four. There was no
one else there except neutrals and UAW partisans. Roy Reuther's
squad subdued it quickly, marching through with their wrenches,
calling out their friends, cowing the undecided. As the battle for
Chevrolet Nine swirled toward its predestined end, there was a
sudden silence from Chevrolet Four; and the pickets outside
understood that GM's main engine plant had been halted.

The battalion in Chevrolet Nine executed an orderly withdrawal. The new garrison in Number Four was throwing up its
barricade—gondolas loaded with 8,000 pounds of stock and piled
one on top of the other against the great doors. Joe Sayen, a
Chevrolet Four worker thereafter unheard upon any great stage
again, climbed the spiked fence outside Chevrolet and told the
pickets that the bastions had fallen:

"We want the whole world to know what we are fighting for. We are fighting for freedom and life and liberty. This is our great opportunity. What if we should be defeated? What if we should be killed? We have only one life. That is all we can lose and we might as well die like heroes than like slaves."

For his little while, the auto worker was speaking a language beyond the dreams of the Reuther boys, his words like those Shakespeare put into the mouth of the tailor called to the wars: "By my troth I care not; a man can die but once; we owe God a death; . . . and let it go which way it will, he that dies this year is quit for the next."

The seizure of Chevrolet Four meant the end of the GM strike; the company recognized that it had lost the ascendancy; John Lewis came in to invest the men in its plants with his own heroic effrontery, to strut and fret and wangle a settlement. The union had won very little on paper. Outsiders wondered if it had won anything at all. But the men in the plants knew that this was a victory; it was summed up for them in the words of a striker who announced that he would slug the first foreman who looked cock-eyed at him.

On February 11, 1937, they marched out in the twilight, down Chevrolet Avenue, the beards still on so many of their faces, the cigars in their mouths, the confetti sifting down from the gates of Chevrole Four, on into the center of Flint, and no one who watched them could doubt who the winners were.

The fire they had set would blaze through Detroit for two more months. Briggs had its sit-down in February. Emil Mazey settled it in the early hours of the morning. "I came out of the personnel office at four A.M. and climbed on a barrel and made a soapbox speech and told the boys we'd won."

The Bureau of Labor Statistics reported that 192,000 Americans sat down on strike in the month of March and they all seemed to be sitting in Detroit. The sit-down strike was a civic epidemic there. Myra Wolfgang, just out of Carnegie Tech and the fifteen-dollar-a-week business agent of the AFL Hotel and Restaurant Employees, had been fretting for months over the low temperature of her flock; now, of a sudden, it was swept by high fever.

"You'd be sitting in the office any March day of 1937," she says now, "and the phone would ring and the voice at the other end would say, 'My name is Mary Jones; I'm a soda clerk at Liggett's; we've thrown the manager out and we've got the keys. What do we do now?' And you'd hurry over to the company to negotiate and over there they'd say, 'I think it's the height of irresponsibility to call a strike before you've even asked us for a contract,' and all you could answer was 'You're so right.' "

Myra Wolfgang tried to act like a lady. One afternoon she walked into the Crowley-Milner Department Store with her intentions limited to striking its coffee shop at the least inconvenient moment for business. She gave the signal and the entire store sat down.

"You think that was simple? What do you do to protect property in cases like that? There was eleven million dollars' worth of merchandise in that store. Suppose somebody walked out with a mink coat. We had to guard those doors twenty-four hours a day."

Their banners bore the strangest devices: waitresses in Stouffer's sat down because their employer lined them up just before duty to inspect their fingernails for the prescribed shade and brand of polish; Negro wet-nurses in Chicago, who did not even have a union, sat down for a higher rate per ounce of milk. Myra Wolfgang herself was on the twenty-third floor of the Book-Cadillac negotiating a contract when she heard the voice outside calling, "All chambermaids down to the eighteenth floor; all bell-boys up to the twenty-fourth floor," and could only wail, "I've been caught too."

Lily Pons, in Detroit for a concert, sat in the lobby of the Book-Cadillac and wept because she had come all this distance in pursuit of her art and was trapped in a "seet-on." When the hotel workers struck the Statler, Dick Frankensteen swarmed in with 5,000 Chrysler pickets. The Statler's manager, William Klare, a backslid member of the Intercollegiate Socialist Society at Ann Arbor, looked out at them, remembered his forsworn vision of the advancing proletariat on the day of justice, and clutched at an old comrade from the hotel union: "Tell me, Al, tell me, is this *it*?"

But this was, of course, not *it*. The sit-down strikes defied all the laws of property. Still theirs was only a fundamental and unconscious challenge. In all matters of the conscious and the superficial, they were fully aware of what was theirs and what was the company's. Detroit's Woolworth strikers sang: "Barbara Hutton's got the dough, *parlez-vous/* Where she gets it, sure we know, *parlez-vous.*" But they faithfully fed the canaries at Miss Hutton's birdseed counter; and, whenever they needed an item from the stock, they were careful to leave a dime in exchange.

The sit-down strike was the most orderly of armed insurrections. Its general use as a technique explains better than any other factor why Detroit's great change was so free of blood. Once a union seized a plant, the risk of property damage from evicting the strikers so inhibited the employer and the authorities that their tenure was apt to be peaceful. By this challenge to total war, the unions seem to have avoided the risks of limited conflict; the bloodiest labor struggle of 1937 was the CIO Little Steel strike, where the union abstained from the sit-down and relied on the traditional walkout.

Industry deserves some credit for all this order in disorder, if only because it never thought of any general technique for meeting the challenge of the sit-downs. The solitary contribution of American productive genius to defense against the sit-down strike was the invention of Howard Keele, a vice president of the Fansteel Corporation. Keele devised a platform upon which Chicago police could be wheeled into action and from which they could pour tear-gas bombs into the second barricade of Fansteel's sit-downers. Keele had begun as an instructor in English at the University of Illinois, a fact which may serve as some counter to the theory that in the thirties all scholars in the humanities chose the improper side of the barricades.

During the March fires of 1937, Dick Frankensteen, age 32, roared through Detroit like a great bellows; Walter Reuther, 30, hurled his implacable voice at employers bruised in pride and helpless to avenge themselves. Victor Reuther, 26, moved his sound truck from command post to command post. Emil Mazey, 23, was president of a local union with 22,000 members. Roy

Reuther, 28, could never go to sleep in his Flint Hotel without expecting to awake to a telephone ringing its summons to go to some GM plant at once; the line had been struck again.

GM's Arnold Lenz spoke for all the Detroit that was passing when he growled at Roy Reuther one afternoon, "The trouble with you, Reuther, and all you fellows, is that you are young and full of piss and vinegar." Arnold Lenz had a dim sense that he was fighting youth and the future. Even to him it must have seemed, as it did to the Reuthers then, a future without the limits of compromise.

General Motors fought with the same desperate sense even after the Flint strike was settled, as though every inch given was so much more surrendered from the last ditch. It was hard to believe that men who would seize your property and fight you like soldiers dug in on the high ground had any intention but your total destruction.

The most articulate citizens of Detroit thought then that the United Auto Workers was something more than a union, that it was in fact a revolutionary army whose final destination was the conquest of all power for labor. Through the next thirteen years, every action of the union and every counteraction of its industry reflected the illusion of fundamental revolution which had infected Detroit in March of 1937. Until 1950, every strike had its mood of basic crisis; the union and the company alike talked as though very life hung on its decision.

But there was only one March of 1937. When it had passed, the passion lifted from Detroit as suddenly as it had come. The city would never be exactly as it had been; but it would be settled and normal in its fashion. The men who had barricaded themselves in the fortresses of their proprietors had wanted something badly enough to face death for it. But they had not wanted to be masters. They had asked only to be equals.

The striker who had affirmed his resolve to slug any foreman who looked cross-eyed at him in the future had not been offended by the fact of the foreman's existence as an institution. He had accepted the system and was demanding only a measure of amenity in its confines.

Through the spring of 1937 there was a cooling and a settling in Detroit and the limits of its great insurrection began to appear. They were limits detectable mostly to the vision of hindsight. Walter Reuther was only the most articulate of a number of UAW leaders who remained certain for a while longer that the politics, the economics, the culture, the whole future of Detroit and ultimately of this country belonged to these emancipated auto workers, whose vision had no bounds, and whose passions would not slack.

That summer of 1937, the UAW entered its own candidate for mayor of Detroit; Walter Reuther, Dick Frankensteen, and four others ran for the City Council under the unashamed label of a labor slate. The politicians beat them with unexpected ease. And that same summer, Henry Ford braced to resistance. He alone remained unbeaten and almost undamaged among the rulers of Detroit. He fought the union as he always had, with spies and blackjacks and blacklists, and he stopped its revolution cold.

One day near early summer, Walter Reuther, Dick Frankensteen, and a group of other UAW organizers walked near the overpass at Ford's River Rouge works to distribute union leaflets. Harry Bennett met them in force; Frankensteen later testified that fully fifty Ford service men assaulted him and Reuther. Frankensteen, with the ill-considered vanity of an old football player, made an effort to defend himself. Reuther only covered his face with his hands and let them take him; false pride was not one of Walter Reuther's problems. Afterward he described it all to the National Labor Relations Board in cold, sparse, exact terms:

"Seven times they raised me off the concrete and threw me down on it. They pinned my arms and shot short jabs to my face. I was punched and dragged by my feet to the stairway. I grabbed the railing and they wrenched me loose. I was thrown down the first flight of iron steps. Then they kicked me down the other flight of steps until I found myself on the ground where I was beaten and kicked. . . . At that time girls and women who came from Detroit with circulars tried to get off the streetcars, and so the men seemed to lose interest in me."

It all sounded so terribly matter of fact, as though circumstance were a minor condition beside Walter Reuther's need to function. He had worked fifteen months in a Soviet factory; Rouge was only the hottest of the plant gates at which he was pummeled; in 1948, when he seemed to have reached a stable plane, he was shot by some still unknown fugitive from Detroit's days of wrath. All that has happened has made no more change in him than if it had never happened. The Soviet experience did not exalt him beyond reason; the Rouge beating did not reduce him to the rhetoric of self-pity; even the shotgun did not alter his will to function.

The 1948 shooting almost tore his right arm off; it was only saved by an intricate operation on the radial nerves. A little while after he left the hospital bed, a visitor found him pacing the floor, talking as always, but with pain in the set of his mouth and sweat on his forehead. It was a sight so discomforting that his visitor begged Reuther to sit down and be quiet.

"Don't you see," said Walter Reuther, "that I've got to live with this thing?"

Every new circumstance was a thing that he would live with, and that must not damage, divert, or alter him. Edward Levinson, then publicity director of the UAW, drove him from Detroit to New York for a union board meeting on December 7, 1941. Reuther was then chairman of the UAW's housing committee, and a report on its work was his chief assignment at the meeting. There was no radio in the car; they arrived at their hotel to find the newsboys holding up the extras reporting Japan's attack on Pearl Harbor.

It was a moment in history. Levinson's first instinct was to rush from the car up to Times Square and see how New York was taking it. The flat voice of Walter Reuther came up from the back seat:

"Well, Eddie, this means we'll have to rewrite the report. We'd better go and wash up and I'll see you in the room in twenty minutes."

For Walter Reuther never felt the impulse to lose himself in any tide of history; every exterior crash seemed to break upon the rock of his will to independent function. Yet this was a will detached from circumstance but not blind to it. If his world changed, he would live with the change.

And back in that summer of 1937, he recognized that circumstances were not what they had seemed only last March, and that he must live with a new state of things. The men for whom he had bled at the Rouge looked at his scars without interest; the politicians had beaten him for the City Council. March had been only a flash fire. The revolution would move no longer at the double-quick. He and Roy and Victor could not again be captains in a war of movement; what stretched ahead was a stewardship that would seem routine more often than it seemed electric.

Once, not very long ago, Walter Reuther had wanted much more; he had thought of the union as an instrument to reshape America sharp and fast. Now the surge of that promise was over, and he was left with the ebb. For the auto worker had now won most of what had seemed to him worth the chance of disaster: security on his job, higher wages, shorter hours, and the sense that he was no less human than his foreman. The union was important in his life, but it was not the only thing. All the diversions which turn men away from further assault upon the heights were at work now. There was nothing on the heights which seemed to the auto worker worth an immediate, desperate, dangerous grasp.

His institution would not change for Walter Reuther, and so Walter Reuther changed for it. He began by leaving the Socialist Party in the late thirties, quietly and without pain; he was on his way to becoming a rock of stability. It was a change not easy for many of the UAW's founding field commanders, and they lost their offices or wandered away for want of the will or the capacity to deal with the new condition.

Homer Martin, a preacher and a flame in time of war, became just a man who talked too much in time of truce and lost his union presidency in 1940 for dealings with Henry Ford and Harry Bennett that may have been devious or may have been guileless but were fatal to him in either case. Ford's caprices could be marked on occasion by kindness as by brutality, and he eased Martin's exile by buying him a farm.

Dick Frankensteen had been a great captain of light cavalry, but he was a poor and neglectful administrator of a conquered province. He hung on until 1946 and then departed for private business, in one case representing a company in negotiations with his old union. George Addes, the UAW's first secretary-treasurer, lost his office in 1947. He had begun as leader of the Toledo local whose strike at Autolite had been the UAW's first real victory; after his ouster, he became a West Coast distributor for the same company he had rocked just thirteen years before.

Martin, Frankensteen, and Addes will always be described by their old associates, with diminishing passion, as renegades. But each, in his way, was doing what the average auto worker would have done. For each was expressing that dream of conventional success which, in the twenties, had brought so many of the men to Detroit who had been turned, once cheated, to the great uprisings of the middle thirties. Walter Reuther was, after all, a toolmaker; in defeat, he could have gone back to the shop. But these others were production hands; and not many men would choose to work on an assembly line if anything else offered.

The change in Walter Reuther, if it can be called a change, must have begun very soon after the sit-downs, but it did not show itself to the clouded eye. Detroit had been very briefly a pillar of flame, but its vision would not soon leave the minds of those who had so long believed the labor movement could be the cleansing agent of the social revolution and who had clutched that belief through numberless discouragements from the manners, the barnacled social vision, and the soggy prose of the leaders of the American Federation of Labor.

They had watched the flames of Detroit for the emergence of a new sort of labor leader—a walking sword conscious of the mission of which his profession had been by tradition but semiconscious and ready to thrust through to an America whose old rulers would be overthrown and whose old oppressed would be finally triumphant. With the cooling of the fires of 1937, every UAW figure except those of the Reuthers appeared to their anxious eyes disappointingly like the old-fashioned labor professional.

The Reuthers alone in Detroit seemed to speak with a confident voice of labor's wider destiny. They spoke of co-operatives and labor parties and labor control of industry and the revolutionary aspirations of the workers of Asia. And they were figures of history with a growing army behind them. If figures of history could speak with the tongue of the scorned and lonely left of Valentine Reuther, there was cause to hope that history might be going Valentine Reuther's way.

In the very late thirties, none of the Reuthers was a national officer of the auto workers' union, which was itself just a fragment of the labor movement. Yet even then, except for John Lewis, Philip Murray, and Harry Bridges, Walter Reuther was better known to the public at large than anyone in the CIO. All over America, there were people who thought of him, young, purposeful, and sure of his destiny, as a symbol of a unionism that promised everything.

To them Walter Reuther appeared like some Archangel Michael; but there were others of his acquaintance to whom he appeared, as Michael had to Lucifer, as an abhorrent shape and who wished he would be hence. The burning of incense and the singing of hosannas around Walter Reuther was a natural source of discomfort to his colleagues in the UAW who ranked him in office but trailed so far behind him in public excitement.

And the old rulers of Detroit, dislocated and sore in bones and pride, heard the rattle of the tumbrels in his speeches and thought they detected a young man after the jugular. There must be men of property who fairly long for the knife at their throats; there are certainly men without security who seek always for someone to thrust the knife for them; and it took both groups a long while to be disappointed in Walter Reuther.

They watched with fear and fascination his rise in the auto union, feeling each beat of its conventions—turning now for him and now against him—as though the balance of all life hung on those delegates hoarsely shouting their votes and their locals' numbers. And yet, when Walter Reuther had become president of the auto workers, none of his upward steps seemed as periled and as faltering as they had at the time he took them. With hindsight his progress seemed assured from the beginning, as though nature had intended him to succeed Henry Ford as the first citizen of a Detroit which, however unchecked its own passions, must always have a household god who neither smokes nor drinks.

And all of it had been so little the result of the primary qualities which the public assigned to Walter Reuther. It had been so little a progress of rhetoric; Reuther remained, as always, available for discourse to the laity on elevating social subjects as other men are available for poker or drinks around the corner. But rhetoric was only his pleasure. Reality of function was his pursuit and his true passion.

Those made timid and those exalted by his image could wake together in the fifties to find that Walter Reuther was not a barn-burner after all. Valentine Reuther did not bring his boys up to burn barns. Walter Reuther was, in fact, rather conservative and unexpectedly normal in his lack of the impulse to destruction. The auto workers, for all their flash of fundamental challenge, were with time more conservative and more normal than anyone could have believed seventeen years ago. For even in Detroit, men do not march long under wild flags. And if Walter Reuther had summoned his troops to any wild flag, they would have been his troops no longer.

There had been a few desperate hours after 1937. Ford had hung on until 1941, and had surrendered only to the last of the sit-down strikes. When it was over, he gave the union a little more than it asked with the expectation that these incursors would commence to fight among themselves for the spoils and after a while go away. But it was Henry Ford who went away at last. After his death, the service men departed and were replaced, to a degree at least, by college boys who put away the Anglo-Saxon diction of the middle thirties and fought their skirmishes with Walter Reuther through the soft fog which is the uniform of the labor relations man's language. And Harry Bennett, an obsolete model, retired to his residence near Lake Michigan.

General Motors cherished the hope that the new order would pass and carried that hope through a one-hundred-and-seven-day strike in 1946, a quiet affair but no less passionate for its lack of violence. That strike ended with the assumption that Detroit's two great powers would glare at one another for the predictable future through an armed truce broken biennially by a marathon strike.

But then Charles E. Wilson, president of General Motors, and

Walter Reuther suddenly shook hands across Detroit's wall. In 1950, GM agreed to give the auto union a five-year contract, keying its wages to the cost of living, guaranteeing its members a yearly increase reflecting their company's technological progress. The other companies trooped to follow; there has not been a major auto strike in Detroit since that spring.

When Walter Reuther came to Detroit, he entered an industrial dictatorship. Each auto worker was alone and fragmented; his future did not extend beyond the spring layoff, and the foreman was his master in fact. In 1937, the Reuther boys were commanders at war with the whole order of society in Detroit; it did not seem possible that their war could end with quarter. But today Detroit is quiet; it moves not, nor shakes, nor seems pregnant with violence as it once did. There has come upon it the peace of understanding. An auto worker earns a minimum of $84 a week; he has a pension and a paid vacation and the automatic assurance that his wages will move up and up; he is in short the unexpected inhabitant of an industrial democracy.

This miracle accomplished by the rabble captained by Roy, exhorted by Victor, and maneuvered by Walter Reuther is no less a miracle for being not quite the sort expected of them. Walter Reuther and the auto makers of Detroit, who seemed so irreconcilable, have ended by sharing a common response to the moments of passion in their lives. They alike understand the necessity of living with things as they are.

The auto union is very rich; a few years ago it sold its old headquarters to General Motors and built a new office building on the lake front estate that once belonged to Edsel Ford. Last fall, Emil Mazey, now secretary-treasurer of the auto workers, left the picture window and the rich dark wood of his office and went over to the Briggs Motor Corporation to talk to a vice president. On his way in, Mazey met the superintendent of plant guards, who looked at him a moment and said, "Christ, now I remember you; I threw you out of the plant maybe twenty years ago." They both decided that it seemed a long way back.

Walter Reuther is forty-six. He remains brash and undiplomatic and apt on all occasions to return to the tireless periods of the schoolboy debater whom Valentine Reuther trained on those

Sunday afternoons in Wheeling. The office of sexton in a cathedral does not sit on the Reuther boys with entire comfort; Detroit's horizons have already become a little narrow for Roy Reuther, who devotes his time to the UAW's national political campaigns, and for Victor Reuther, who is the CIO's expert on international affairs.

And there are signs that Walter Reuther sometimes feels that he has done almost too well and that his once restless, alienated throng is now too satisfied with the present to fight hard for the future. Those are times when he prods them to walk a little faster. But he will go at their pace, because he recognizes that it is not his function to walk alone.

So much has happened to the Reuther boys—some of it heroic, some of it almost tragic, all of it rather fantastic—that it is surprising how little it has done to them. They have had adventures, but they were not raised to be adventurers. They were raised to follow a trade and be a credit to their home. Of all the heritage their father passed on to them from the Eugene Debs who was his hero, he passed on most the notion that it is better to rise with your class than from it.

There are limitations to that portion of Valentine Reuther's estate. A man ingrained with its vision is not apt to be exalted, to dare everything for great and distant passions, or to enjoy tumult for its own sake, for the class from which Walter Reuther came is not long committed to any of these diversions. But those are also its virtues; in spite of Deb's own tragedy, his heritage encompasses the normal and the unalienated.

The Reuther boys saw life in the ideal image of their father's house and their father's aspirations; they did not seek their revolution on their father's grave. And so, through all the tombstones of the thirties, they have walked unchanged and unafflicted, because they were very normal young men caught in a wild circumstance and glad to pass through it to normality again.

10

The Shadow Line

"*Is there still any shadow there, on the rainwet window of
the coffeepot,
Between the haberdasher's and the pinball arcade
There, where we stood one night in the warm, fine rain,
and smoked and laughed and talked. . . .*

*(There must be, there has to be, no heart could beat if
this were not so,
That was an hour, a glittering hour, an important hour
in a tremendous year)*

*Where we talked for a while of life and love, of logic and
the senses, of you and of me, character and fate, pain,
revolution, victory and death*

*Is there tonight any shadow, at all,
Other than the shadows that stop for a moment and then
hurry past the windows blurred by the same warm,
slow still rain?*"

KENNETH FEARING, Memo

"*We were convinced that though we were living on the
edge of catastrophe, we had been uniquely blessed with
a knowledge of what was happening to us.*"

JAMES A. WECHSLER, The Age of
Suspicion

"*Suddenly she heard a little noise like that of a mouse in
the straw and, looking up, she saw a tiny man no higher
than her spinning wheel. Dressed all in brown, he had a
long beard.
"Why do you weep, miller's daughter?" he asked.
"I weep," she answered, "because for my very life I
cannot spin gold from straw.*"

Rumpelstiltskin

D R. J. B. MATTHEWS, who has at once gained and lost so much from his past, was talking one afternoon about the autobiographies of ex-radicals. A visitor wondered aloud why so many ex-Communists recount the events of their youth in terms repeating a common experience and then draw from it conclusions which seem so contradictory.

"Who," said J. B. Matthews, "can explain his own past?"

The time of being very young and madly hopeful comes to many men and deserts them all, and the lessons they take from its loss are very different. I was very young in the thirties; hard though it is to rouse that memory, I must have been madly hopeful. But the very young are spectators; the heart of youth, as Ellen Glasgow has said, is a hard heart. However intense the image, its feelings are detached from almost everything except itself. I have counted upon the devotion of my own children and lost it to a passing freight train too many times to believe again that it is possible to commit the very young.

And those of us who were young and fetched by the myth of the thirties were mostly spectators. Except for the very few who passed through the tragedy of the war in Spain, the fact of experience was not in us. And, hard as I try, I cannot muster up the reality of experience now out of the memory of our cardboard heads bobbing to an oath never to bear arms for the government of the United States or never to bend our cardboard knees to fascism or never to slow our paper-doll progress along the road to all power for the working class.

What the thirties used to describe as its youth movement was most of whatever part I knew of the thirties. I cannot think of it without thinking of myself. If I remember its characters as posturing in the main, it is because I remember myself as posturing. If I think of them as having conceived themselves as instruments of history without ever being a part of history, it is because I think of myself that way. In this excursion to a lost time, I have reached a lost self. The eye of the beholder has chanced upon its own skeleton in the graveyard. There is a warning in that observation which seems to me only fair to record: as J. B. Matthews has said, it is very hard for any of us to explain his own past.

The youth movement of the thirties began as it ended—in lamentation. Dr. Harold J. Laski opened the decade in August of 1931 by inquiring in *Harper's Magazine*: "Why Don't Your Young People Care?" It was a question that might be asked about the young in any moment of history, but Laski did not mean it that way. He had just finished a lecture tour of American colleges. In the second year of the depression, he had found only detachment from the social crisis and boredom about politics. It was plain, said Laski, that if the revolution comes to America, "there will be no Harvard or Columbia students on the barricades."

Over the next ten years, there would be many occasions when Laski could strike a happier key because, if he had a fault as an observer, it was in taking the word as the fact and accepting what people said as what they meant. The time came when even his question, "Why don't your young men care?" would seem cast in terms too individual and insufficiently impersonal, for it had begun to sound as though there were no "young men" singing solo, but only "youth" in chorale. The young in America seemed to have aroused themselves to crescendos of involvement. These reached their pitch by 1937, when an estimated 500,000 students took part in the student strike against war and were reported united in a pledge never to support any war declared by the United States government.

That was a statistic which no one could measure, since it was a compendium of the claims of the American Student Union, which sponsored the strike, and the estimates of college editors, who are suspect accountants because they tended more than the general to rouse themselves about the social question, perhaps because it made better copy than did press releases for college dances. In any case, the total included unaccountable hosts of the neutral and even the hostile. No one at the rear of the crowd could hear the oath, and no one on the platform could hear most of the testators because, even in those cases where partisans of the Reserve Officers Training Corps were not clustering at the fringe hurling eggs and engaging themselves to the detriment of communication, a failure of the public-address system seemed inevitably concurrent with the climax of the strike.

But there do exist statistics to indicate that, even at this presumed fever pitch, Harold Laski's question was not materially less valid than it had been in 1931. The American Student Union was the official mass expression of student revolt. At the height of its uproar, the ASU had only twelve thousand members and claimed another eight thousand who hadn't paid their dues but were otherwise totally committed. The Young Communist League had fewer than five thousand student members at any one time. As the thirties wore on, the Young People's Socialist League, the heroic and historic Yipsels, fell below one thousand members and the Young Trotskyites below five hundred.

Yet the few persons in those last three organizations made most of the history of student rebellion in the thirties. In 1937, as an instance, young Communists, young Socialists, and one young Trotskyite constituted eighteen of the thirty members of the National Executive Committee of the American Student Union; and all its national officers were either Socialists or Communists. There were close to four million high school and college students in the United States in 1937; the myth of their radical impulse was created, at the very most, by fifteen thousand persons. It has been said that these fifteen thousand set the tone for the American campus in the thirties, in which case they did it by default. A tone set by three-tenths of one per cent of a community can hardly, after all, be described as a tone.

What history there is asserts that in 1937 half a million American college students took an oath never to support this government in any war. The Selective Service Act came three and a half years later; fewer than one hundred men refused to register under it as a matter of principle. By 1943, just 1,400 young men of all sorts had gone to prison for ideological or ethical defiance of the draft law. And half of those were Jehovah's Witnesses, whose impulse hardly arose out of any movement of students.

It was that small and burned out that soon, leaving so few ashes behind. And even with its opening strains, its themes were set: the imitation of its elders, and the search ending in a revelation that quickly fled or twisted at its end to comedy.

The revolt of the students in the thirties appears to have begun with a group of sixty students, most of them from Columbia and the other New York colleges, who embarked in March of 1932 to investigate the conditions of coal miners in Kentucky's dark and bloody Harlan County. Most of them had been recruited by Donald Henderson, a Columbia economist. They were trailing four months behind Theodore Dreiser, John Dos Passos, and others of their elders, who had traveled to Harlan to study the left-wing National Miners Union strike there and had come home under the shadow of indictments for criminal syndicalism. Dreiser had charged that miners in Harlan were being paid as little as eighty cents a day, that eight of their children a week were dying of undernourishment, that twelve strikers had been killed by deputy sheriffs, and that the miners lived with terror, starvation, and official violence.

Dreiser had left Harlan County pursued by all its furies, but he at least had a chance to look around. Donald Henderson's flock was stopped at the Cumberland Gap by the high sheriff's party, driven to the Pineville, Kentucky, courthouse and there subjected to an inquisition by District Attorney Fred Smith before some two hundred deputies who mixed their representation of legal majesty with suggestions that the visitors be hanged without delay. The district attorney had apparently benefited from the research of some New York purveyor of dossiers on the Bolshevik conspiracy, and he subjected each tourist to extensive and detailed questioning on the subversive affiliations of self and parents.

It must have been a scene destructive of neutrality. Arnold Beichman, of the Columbia University *Spectator,* who had come with the expedition as a detached observer, turned to the man from the *New York Herald Tribune* and announced:

"I must take my stand."

And Beichman marched over to join the prisoners in their enclave and demanded that the district attorney question him too. Smith's memorandum from his premature J. B. Matthews was, of course, barren of reference to this interloper, but Smith manfully improvised the suggestion that Beichman's father was a member of the national committee of the Communist Party. "Oh, heavens," said Beichman, "my poor simple father."

The politics of commitment has its rewards at first. Beichman returned to Columbia to find a letter from the district attorney's daughter describing Pineville as a cultural desert and requesting suggestions on ways to escape to New York.

Their brain-washing at an end, Henderson's chicks were thrust aboard their buses and driven back to Tennessee under the escort of deputies ostentatiously fumbling their dumdum bullets. The party fled to Nashville, where not one of them felt safe from the terror. In his new involvement, Beichman was sitting at the typewriter in his hotel room when Joseph P. Lash, a young Socialist who was captain of the retreat, put in his head to say:

"We're not out of this yet. Remember nobody sleeps alone tonight."

And so Beichman began his report to the *Spectator* on the day's horror with a stark entry along these lines:

"Knoxville, Tenn.—Joseph P. Lash has just come to my room and said 'Nobody sleeps alone tonight.'"

The *Spectator* printed his lead with the utmost relish, and Beichman returned to the campus to find that his scars had earned him nothing so lasting as the nickname: "Nobody-Sleeps-Alone-Beichman." Men still fought for the meaning of their lives in Harlan County. But the student movement had begun, as it would almost always live, to the murmur of mocking laughter from the side lines.

Beichman was a pioneer among college journalists who could not keep their seats in the press box. The whole history of the student movement of the thirties could have been covered in the pages of an undergraduate *Editor and Publisher,* because its moments of high drama regularly played themselves out with college editors hurling manifestoes at college administrators, in a free play on the last chance most of them had for full expression with someone else paying the printer.

Columbia, under Nicholas Murray Butler, was habitually treated by its undergraduate editors almost as an extension of the University of Heidelberg under the Third Reich. The university appears to have shown notable tolerance to the pricks of a succession of alienated *Spectator* editors, among them Beichman and James A. Wechsler. Beichman is now in the service of the new aristocracy as public relations director for several AFL unions; Wechsler is editor of the New York *Post*.

Both went unpunished for their crimes against the university; the only Columbia student permanently expelled for radical excesses was an athlete named Robert Burke, who was separated because of an inflammatory speech supposedly written for him by a *Spectator* staff writer. Burke became a bravo for a CIO union; the reputed author of his downfall is now a foreign correspondent of moderately conservative views. As a former college editor, I am of course flattered by any suggestion that as a group we were more conscious of social evil than our fellows; but there remains the fact that, if we did not build the barricades ourselves, they would not have been built at all, and there would be no clatter and thunder to write about.

So much of the tumult was manufactured then, as detached from commitment in its way as the laughter was. The stage itself held very few people and most of those are gone. The tumult is gone, too, and the laughter, because no one seems to exercise the detachment of laughter about such matters any longer. Most persons who are articulate about that lost time treat it as seriously as only a very few of us did when we thought it had reality so very long ago.

So many of us are gone now, gone without trace, this bright young legion of the elect who were supposed to be the leaders of their generation and the beacon for its future. The American Student Union was at its zenith in 1937. Its pronouncements were taken seriously by adults, even the sort of adults whose custom it is not to bear fools gladly. It was discussed as a serious menace by the Hearst papers; and it set the tone of antimilitarist, antifascist fervor which many of its friends and enemies alike universalized as the mood of the college undergraduate in the mid-thirties.

The ASU's leaders believed, and some of their elders agreed with them, that they would play a great part, perhaps even the greatest, in America's future history. In 1937, the American Student Union picked thirty-two members of what must have been its executive-committee-elect of the advancing future. Four of them are now professional Communists; two are hired hands for conservative unions quite unlike the vision which took them into the labor movement; one was killed in Spain; three are journalists; the rest are gone, not dead but simply obliterated; they are housewives or businessmen perhaps. It would take all the resources of all the Congressional committees working for six months to find them and bring them together for a reunion, and much more than that to put them at ease with one another when they got there.

To approach them is to dive into a well of oblivion. A friend of mine once said that no history of the youth movement of the thirties could be complete without mention of the girl to whom he had once suggested that she take more pains with her appearance. "Millions are dying in Spain and China," she rasped, "and you ask me to wear lipstick." He thought about her a while, but he could not even recall her face; she has been gone so long now, married and settled somewhere, and doubtless blaming her appearance on the children.

There was Agnes Reynolds of Vassar, who lasted longer than most of them, and was seen last in the spring of 1941, dressed in colonial costume and preparing to ride a white horse to Washington and warn the country against imperialist war. Miss Reynolds called herself a modern Paul Revere; but then the Nazis invaded the Soviet Union and she did not ride. And she has not been seen since either, *disparue* like so many Charlotte Cordays or Rosa Luxembourgs of our childhood.

And they went, it is possible to think in many cases, without even having heard the name of the Rosa Luxembourg, who was the great revolutionary figure of the German Social Democracy, and thus the precursor of those buried young ladies of our youth movement. For this was a dismally ignorant radical generation, especially its Communist segment. My wife came up not long ago with a sheaf of letters from her friends in the thirties. One of them from 1936 ended, "As a last resort, I think I'll become a follower of Gandi (if that is the way to spell it.)" Another, from the summer of 1940, ended: "I'd have loved to visit you, but I'm afraid it'll have to be put off another year. Maybe we'll get around to it in the dismal future when all our men will be dead in the war and we'll have to take to Lesbienism."

And those two documents, neither of them from young Communists, seem to me typical of the period because the writers were incapable of spelling the names either of one alternative to Marxism (Gandhi) or of one dread consequence of its failure to come to power (Lesbianism). Not long ago, an apostate Young Communist told the House Committee on Un-American Activities that once, when he was in trouble with the Party, a sympathetic girl comrade explained to him that the revolution is occasionally cruel to its children and that a problem like his had once confronted a revered leader whose name, if he recalled it correctly, was "Rosie Luckenburg."

But still we assumed that we knew the course of history; what is often more important, we thought we alone knew the precise dimensions of the catastrophe that would engulf us and our generation. *Death* was a word frequently upon our lips. But the word *oblivion* came very seldom. Yet oblivion was the youth movement's catastrophe, although oblivion could hardly have been the catastrophe we thought it then, since I recollect no suicides from this roster of obliterated student leaders; and most of them must be living happily in limbo. Not long ago, I had word of one former editor of the ASU *Student Advocate*. He was living in the Deep South and had a newspaper job and some local esteem as a jazz clarinetist. He was quite proud of having resisted the temptation to vote Republican in 1952.

Of course, survival of itself is no special merit, especially in days like these; but failure to survive does require a few words of explanation from the departed.

That explanation might be more important if I could say with assurance that here was something which had life and is now dead before its time. The ASU had a certain reality when people talked about it, when a newspaper editorial decried its menace or watched its progress with serious, adult interest, when the President of the United States sent his greetings, when it was attacked or defended or anywhere treated as important on the outside. But it had no inner life; you had only to sit through one of its meetings to hear the interior voice saying that this had no reality of itself. The ASU would always wonder why so many professed to love it and so few paid it dues.

The student movement's leaders and followers were together victims and propagators of a legend. We can see their illusion nowhere more clearly than in the requirement that the myth of a great student anti-fascist movement be sustained by the counter-myth of a serious student fascist conspiracy in opposition to it. The signal to arms requires an enemy; where none exists, he must be invented. The ASU *Student Advocate* was always choked with accounts of fascist hordes arising on various campuses. As one instance, its December, 1936, issue contained an extensive assault on a Johns Hopkins student named Gordon Grahame Duce, who had formed what he called the Hopkins Americanistic League against Communism, with Italian fascism as its model and anti-Semitism as one of its tenets. At the moment, the ASU's correspondent reported, the Hopkins was resisting; its students appeared "aggressively opposed to fascist-terrorism."

Coming on this now, I can only remember poor Duce from the Hopkins as the creator of a crude and certainly tasteless joke.

Perhaps the saddest moment in his short life was his discharge from the Army Reserves because of a bad heart, which killed him a few years ago. The author of this portrait of him as fascist terrorist is practicing medicine in Baltimore and shows no recognizable trace of the passions which stirred him then. It is pitiful and somehow terrible to think that Duce left so little behind him, except a card in the War Department's dead file and this account of him as commandant of a storm troop that never existed, a shadow invented by a shadow and not only dead but in death distorted.

Reading and remembering things like that, it is hard to believe that we here discuss the passing of anything very deep and serious. For there is in these papers, as in the recollection of the time when they were written, somehow a continuing assault on reality, as though everything seemed to be happening and so much less was. These are the memorabilia of the very young; and first love may be sweet or bitter but it is seldom consequential. Conrad wrote once that there is a shadow line in all our lives which divides the young from the mature. It is a division between those who are setting forth and those who are coming back and it is the line between the idea and the reality. We were very young then, and properly speaking, the young have no experiences; experience is the price of their youth.*

The student movement spoke as though for legions but it was important only to companies of us. And fewer still carried it across the shadow line. To think of those few is first of all to think of those who went to Spain to fight Franco and of what they must have discovered there about the difference between what men think they can do and what is required of them, and of how some were killed there and others came home, strangers to what they had left behind, and terribly changed by reality.

What documents are available indicate that 2,800 Americans fought in the Spanish Civil War and only 1,200 returned. They learned, if nothing else, the certain lesson of the infantry soldier that, if he stays at his trade long enough, he is more than likely to be killed, wounded, or captured.

Some lost their faith and deserted, and others became policemen and shot deserters; those are equal consequences of being a soldier. Some died facing the enemy; some surrendered and were shot by the enemy, because of the inconvenience of taking prisoners or from simple malignity. Some died because they were careless or did not know their trade; some died as heroes shouting for liberty and the republic, meeting a tank with a Molotov cocktail, which was only a bottle filled with gasoline and a pitiable implement for grown men in a modern war. Those who were enlisted men sometimes hated the officers they had once called comrades. Many of them must have looked upon the distinguished revolutionaries come to bring them greetings from home, at those fresh clothes and those tailor-made cigarettes, through eyes that were alien.

---

* Morris L. Ernst and David Loth, in their *Report on the American Communist,* estimate that there are 700,000 ex-Communists in the United States and that a majority of them joined and left the Party between the ages of eighteen and twenty-three. The Communist was the dominant radical type of the thirties, in the sense that the anarchist was the dominant radical of the nineties and the Socialist the dominant radical of the period before World War I. If Ernst and Loth are correct in their estimate that the average Communist joined and left the Party before he was twenty-three, my judgment that the youth movement of the thirties was in the main ephemeral and its experiences largely trivial carries the implication that the experience of the average ex-Communist was ephemeral and trivial. And I think it was.

To almost every one of them there came with defeat that moment of being the hunted pursued by the hunter. When they returned to the rear, they named the scene of one of their few victories not Browder Ridge but Dead Men's Point. For they had the experience as common to the soldier of freedom as it is to the soldier of oppression, which is the experience of humiliation and acceptance of death. Late in their war, the bulletins of their International Brigade left off the language of political exhortation and became more and more a compendium of obituaries for the fallen and the most elementary suggestions for the soldier's art, suggestions especially pathetic to the eyes of a monumentally equipped, firepower-rich soldier of World War II.

There was the recommendation that, in firing their bolt-action rifles, soldiers of the Brigade remember to hold the breath and maintain a slow trigger-squeeze and be careful to keep the piece on the shoulder and not let it slip down the arm. There was the warning that these rifles are badly zeroed and tend to shoot high and wide. There were suggested patterns for a cone of rifle fire against planes. There was discussion of the black-tipped *anti-tank* rifle bullet. Behind all these words lies the barely concealed fact that so many young men went into battle untrained and ill equipped, and that they died at the end because they were outgunned. No one had suggested back in the States that, however glorious his cause or grand his spirit, the outgunned, outnumbered soldier must expect more defeats than victories.

The helmets that were issued to them seldom fit and were so much worse than useless that most of them took to wearing caps even against artillery and aerial bombardment. Robert Raven, who was blinded early in the war and became a hero of so many Spanish Aid rallies back home, was not wounded by the enemy but because a Canadian comrade, out of mere ineptitude, pulled the pin on a grenade and handed it to him and it exploded before he could throw it at Franco's trenches. The last words he heard from a man he could see were *"No Pasarán."* That was the Spanish for "They Shall Not Pass," and the crowds in Madison Square Garden shouted it together when he arose eyeless to speak to them.

The journalists came and wrote about their lives as an epic

among the olive trees but it could not have been quite that. People far away said they were losing and dying because the democracies did not understand their cause. It would be a long time before the world learned that even the Soviets had given them nothing and sold them precious little for gold on the line, and that if Stalin had done as much for the Spanish Republic as Hitler and Mussolini did for Franco, their deaths might have been more useful. But that is what governments have done to soldiers through all history. We did it to our troops on Bataan and the British to theirs in Norway. It is the history of wars that aggressors fight with iron and their victims with bare flesh.

It was a canon of the myth of the thirties that these were all heroes who died with their faces to the enemy. It is becoming a canon of the myth of the fifties that most of them fought, and most came to know they fought, only for a cause betrayed by the Soviets; before long we may be told that more were killed by Communist police squads than by Franco's troops. No safe evidence exists to support either canon.

We do not even know how so many of these men died. It seems enough to say that he who was at home when a soldier died degrades himself when he speaks of that death in terms of blame, rumor, or gossip or with anything but that certainty which is denied us here. If a soldier dies badly on the field because of a failure of nerve, or humiliated behind the lines because he had been betrayed, we cannot judge him or even his executioners entirely. The father of John Cookson, a young scientist killed in Spain, wrote him just before he died that "a man might better die young for a purpose than live a whole life without one." If Cookson died still sure of his purpose, we cannot say that his death was useless. The object of any purpose is always uncertain, and he who has pledged his soul to one may be lucky to die young.

It must have been so unlike what they thought it would be, but for those who bore the difference that lay across the shadow line, it was certainly no less glorious. And those Americans who joined the International Brigade and deserted and were shot as a consequence cannot be exactly described either as traitors or as men given a sudden vision of betrayal. It seems much more to the point to say that they had crossed the shadow line between the idea and the reality and that they could not bear the reality. We may someday be forced for our own protection to shoot those who became not deserters but the sort of policemen who shoot deserters. But they too in their way had crossed the shadow line, and how are we to judge them?

There was, as an instance, the student leader who had been the inspiration of all his comrades in the Young Communist League at his university, who went to Spain as their surrogate, and was wounded there. He wrote them later from the hospital that he had been offered a place as an undercover agent inside the "Trotskyite Fifth Column" in Barcelona. He could choose between that and the fighting and he chose Barcelona. He had gone forth to defend freedom; now he would go to a rear area as an instrument of repression. He too had crossed the shadow line; and the boys back home, even such of them as were capable of detecting the difference, had no real right to judge him.

It has been estimated that two-thirds of the Americans who fought in Spain were Communists. The other third included Socialists and the sort of adventurers who follow wars. The proportion of Communists hardly reflects the response of young Americans of all political descriptions to the Spanish War. Certainly ten times as many as ever got there wrote the Spanish Embassy asking to enlist; nothing was done to encourage them; the road to Spain was difficult and illegal and a long trip from the inclination. The Communists got through in disproportionate numbers largely because their Party had an efficient apparatus for smuggling them along.

Most of those who went to Spain were young, although some were as old as forty-five or fifty. Some were sent by the Communist Party because they were tested leaders and political-commissar material; and some were just young men who had gotten into trouble with the Party and were dispatched to Spain for reasons of atonement and expendability. But both these groups were a handful of the whole.

The great majority appear to have gone by their own choice and out of somewhat the same lonely impulse that had made them Communists or radicals in the first place, which was a combination of alienation and the search for adventure. That impulse may have told some that to be a Communist was not merely to be one who conquered but one who suffered and that the great end of life is to die for something greater than life. So many of them were seamen, those ceaseless wanderers, and so many others were the young who had never found themselves in what they called the movement.

David Cook, a Columbia graduate, wrote from Madrid just before his first battle:

"If I'm to be among those who don't get back, I'll have concentrated so much into the last short space that it will be as good as having lasted a normal span. I have no military experience, of course, and this would have kept me home if I had found a place in the movement back there. But I never managed to get functioning properly, partly through having no steady job."

Philip Detro, a Texan, went to sea and tried to settle down in New York and be a writer, but it did not work and he fell in with the Communists. First he felt the need to learn so much and then he began to feel the emptiness of what he had learned. When Spain came, he rushed to volunteer; he had to wait a long time and was bursting with the impatience of the long nights in Greenwich Village. At last he was accepted on one day's notice and he did not sleep before the boat left. In Spain he became a captain.

There was Sam, a runner for an infantry command post, whom Alvah Bessie asked why he came to Spain.

"Hell," said Sam, "I wanted to. I didn't like the way things were going back home. My folks didn't approve of me."

"Didn't approve of you, why?"

"Well I was only making ten a week in the curtain factory, an' I was taking up a lot of time organizing the workers."

They came, these three men now buried in time, looking for a home. Part of what took them may have been an impulse for glory, which is certainly no worse in a man than the impulse to refuse to accept experience. The youth movement they had left behind had its full quota of those who sought fulfillment in the domination of others, which is a sort of definition of glory for civilians; it could be said indeed that the impulse which led some of us to play at revolution carried an image of each of us with a marshal's baton in his knapsack.

Spain had that concept too; a 1938 decree of its Ministry of Defense declared: "It is necessary and just that each soldier of the new army should carry in his knapsack the baton of a Field Marshal." But that image is somewhat different from what ours was. Its *beau idéal* was Napoleon's Marshal Ney, who fought his last battle waving a saber in the front lines and crying "Come, see how a Marshal of France dies."

The difference must be that a soldier's dream of a marshal's baton is tied, not merely to the dream of dominating others, but to the acceptance of his own death somewhere at the end. That is the difference between the few who died in Spain and the many more back home who thought they were identifying themselves with Spain. It is the difference between those who sacrifice and those who only talk of sacrifice, between the soldier or the soldier's wife and the untouched civilian.

And yet it seems easier to think about those who fought in Spain at the moment of death, because so many came home terribly flawed and different from those they had left behind. A good many left the Communists and drifted away. Some have become simply soaks; I remember one who became a labor spy; another is a union leader of very flexible principles. I can think of very few who survive as they were and are not somehow aliens in their own country. Most of those who function politically, and they are a minority, are professional Communists, which in these days is an expression of alienation. They are Party functionaries more often than followers. Theirs is not a comfortable life, certainly, and some of them have gone to prison for it. But it is the life of policemen and not of prophets; it is hard to believe that the realists among them must not know that if they come to glory, it will be, not as leaders of any American revolution, but as proconsuls of a Soviet army.

The time when they were touched with fire has left so little trace upon their faces that it can be summoned up, as with so many soldiers, only by remembering those who died before they had time to grow old and wither.

Sam Levinger, who was only twenty when he died, can stand

for the best of them. His family was not poor; his life as a child was a comfortable one. But he seems to have been unable to resist the temptation to run away or throw himself away. He was eight years old the first time he tried to run away; after his family had moved from Wilmington, Delaware, to the Middle West, he tried to sail down the Mississippi on a raft as Huck Finn did and it sank three yards off shore. I confess that I would like to think of the men in Spain as having been carried there by Huck Finn and not by Lenin and as having mainly gone innocent to their graves.

Sam Levinger always went to school with a huge lunch and always gave it away and kept nothing for himself. His family took him to Europe in 1931, when he was fourteen. He went to visit Hitler's Brown House wearing a Boy Scout uniform. He followed the British troops fighting a native rebellion in Port Said. He came home, still a high school boy, to go down to Cambridge, Ohio, with some Ohio State students to watch a coal strike. He was the only one of them to be put in jail, because he was the only one who talked back to the sheriff.

He had become a Young Socialist by then, and he spent his first year at Ohio State almost as often as not away from the campus on some picket line. The strikers he helped used to call him "the kid who sings." He seems to have enjoyed life very much, and he did not posture about going to Spain. He died there after nine months of combat as a machine gunner in Belchite in Aragon.

He left behind him a poem; so many of them wanted to be poets:

Comrades, the battle is bloody and the war is long;
Still let us climb the gray hill and charge the guns,
Pressing with lean bayonets towards the slope beyond.
Soon those who are still living will see green grass,
A free bright country shining with a star;
And those who charge the guns will be remembered,
And from red blood white pinnacles will tower.

It is not a poem to be judged separate from the man who wrote it; and, after all, it is not entirely accurate, because the men who charge the guns are seldom remembered. But it is a very tired poem with no more hope of a marshal's baton in it. Sam Levinger had come to know what it is to be simply a target, and his was very different from the sort of poem which anyone who stayed home would have written about the Spanish War.

Spain was the passion of that small segment of my generation which felt a personal commitment to the revolution. For most of its members the greater war whose prelude Spain was came almost as anticlimax. Much of their attitude toward experience was conditioned by their attitude toward personal involvement in the Spanish War. If they had avoided that one, it was no wrench, so far as it was possible, to avoid World War II; and, if they entered it, a majority appear to have felt no compulsion to suffer by their entry.

I can find only one former student radical who won the Distinguished Service Cross in World War II; he was Robert Thompson, a veteran of the war in Spain. Thompson went to Spain from California, became a captain, and was invalided home with a wound and malaria. After he returned to the States, Thompson did Young Communist League work until the war; he does not appear to have been especially apt at it, and he went in the army as soon as he could. His 32nd Division was in New Guinea before anyone else; Thompson went in with them at Buna; after he had wiped out four Japanese pillboxes all alone, he was promoted to sergeant and given the DSC for "utter disregard of his personal safety."

A United Press correspondent who met him at Buna asked Thompson what his peacetime job was and reported that he answered, "Maybe you won't believe me, but I'm a Young Communist League organizer for Ohio."

Robert Thompson returned as a hero to the Communists and, mainly as a piece of adornment, was established as their New York State chairman and member of their National Board. For this distinction, he was sentenced to three years in prison in 1950 as one of eleven Communist leaders convicted of conspiring to overthrow the government of the United States. The court gave him three years instead of five for what he had done at Buna. He jumped bail and it took the government three years to find him. He was held in New York's West Street jail after he was caught; one evening in the chow line, a Yugoslav held for deportation struck him with a hammer and wounded him seriously. The Yugoslav did not know Thompson; he seems to have thought of this as the sort of affirmative anti-Communist gesture which might stay his deportation.

Today Robert Thompson is an enemy alien in his own country. But no one can say that he has not taken the chances of his time or that he ever turned his back on its fires or refused the full force of their flames. Somehow words of pity, contempt, or admiration have no meaning for Thompson's life, as though, when a man cannot act without being wounded by his act, he passes to a place beyond judgment by the rest of us.

For Thompson never lived in a world of words—whether in the great lights of Madison Square Garden or in the narrow warrens of his Party's headquarters on Thirteenth Street in New York. The words seem only empty spaces between those moments when he pulled the pin on a grenade and crawled alone up to somebody else's rampart and the moment when he was struck on a chow line.

These are, to be sure, extreme experiences in a man's life. They are given to or taken by very few of us in any degree as intense as Thompson's. But there are in almost every life moments of a special kind which are its moments of reality. Spain was a reality; no one who went there and was shot at could ever be the same again. But the student strike against war was a show, almost indeed a carnival. The young could take its Oxford Oath never to support a war and be just the same thereafter. A man was alone in Spain and in the company of hundreds at the student strike; but the first was real and the second was verbal. The fates have a way of demanding of a man that he suffer his greatest moments all by himself; being alone seems as often attendant upon reality as being in company is attendant upon the flight from reality.

Here at the end, I cannot think of those of us whose vision was bound by what we called the youth movement in the thirties as having been good or evil or of having damaged our time very much or having elevated it to any special degree. I can only think of most of us as having shared a malnutrition of reality.

The Young Communists set the tone for most of us after a

while, even when we turned against them, for we tended to live our dream lives in response to or reaction against the Soviet Union. The Soviet Union was not, of course, a major factor in our real lives, so that we reacted not so much to this distant drum as to its human embodiment in the form of a Young Communist League organizer.

I remember the first YCL organizer I ever met. He had been speaking at a meeting of a few students, into which I had drifted; when it was over, a friend introduced me to him. We had no conversation; I can recall now only his first name, which was Mike, and a mouth which was slack at the center and taut and determined only at the edges. My friend said afterward, "God, isn't Mike strong?" Looking back, I think this was as characteristic as anything one of my comrades ever said to me while I was a comrade. For most of them were weakness leaning upon fancied strength. An appalling number came into the movement and stayed in because they could be bullied by someone who could muster the illusion of decision, as Mike had mustered it to my friend's satisfaction if not to history's. Most of the people who testify against the Communists before the committees and in the courts have faces very like Mike's; and I am very sure that I saw his picture in the papers above an account of some such service a year or so ago.

Even our masters seem to have recognized this weakness in so many of their followers, and that recognition must have been the basis for the concern with heretical infection which I remember most from the Young Communist League meetings I attended. Our section organizer seldom let an occasion pass without reminding us that some fallen brother, in defiance of all incantations, was still alive and healthy and that any contact with him would bring inevitable corruption and hell fire. And there was some basis for these warnings; a single heretic accomplished the downfall of almost my entire YCL chapter, because so many of us evaded the admonitions of our leaders and continued to associate with him on the sly and were consequently corrupted. Most ex-Communists can remember similar Party efforts to establish the social untouchability of deviationists; most of them think it enough to assert that *they* as individuals never stooped to any such thing. Their pride on this score has always seemed to me odd, since they must have sat at meetings and listened without protest to speeches by persons who, if they could not realistically be described as lynching the innocent, plainly wished they could. All I know is that I listened to such speeches and did not at once arise and express my revulsion, a show of weakness hardly to be effaced by those occasions when I sneaked off to adopt the posture of common decency to the victim. We tend, I am afraid, to be by custom too harsh toward those who have done that which they ought not to have done, and too lenient with those who have left undone that which they ought to have done.

The element of mush in these young Bolsheviks was not universal, I am sure, but it seems to me insufficiently regarded in most discussions of them. I can remember one particularly dedicated Communist girl who held off joining the YCL until after the 1936 election because she was convinced that Alfred M. Landon was a fascist and would throw all Communists in jail if he won. There was a measure of cowardice in the student movement, as there is in any movement which suggests that victory is both imminent and a guarantee of absolute peace and security. The leaders of the student strike against war understood that theirs was a bold challenge against the odds. But their literature was such a succession of images of approaching mutilation and death that there had to be converts to whom it was most potent as an appeal to self-pity. My least pleasant recollection of the Communist experience was that so many people whimpered so often. And ex-Communists remind me most often of those days, not when they are wicked, which they are no more than most, but when they are abject.

The Communists set the tone for the student movement of the thirties—what there was of it—because they had the advantage of numbers, because they offered the weak the impression of strength, and because they had a church which no one else could match. They offered in short an available escape from reality. Most students, of course, managed to bear reality quite well enough to be apathetic about any avenues for escaping it. The Communists were a tiny fragment of the whole, but they were a majority of the committed. To reject them meant to surrender even the illusion of strength and condemn yourself anew to that alienation which had moved you to commitment in the first place. The Young Socialists and the Young Trotskyites, who were the competitors of the Communists, became thus more and more a minority of the minority and were a little warped by that process.

Of even the few students who struck against war or talked into the night about the why of it all or went home and told their parents that they were dedicated revolutionaries, only a fraction accepted even the minimal commitment of joining the Young Communists, the Young Socialists, or the Trotskyites. They were the special persons who felt that words were not quite enough and who had chosen, or thought they had chosen, an involvement more than verbal. But only a minority, even of them, carried that decision over the shadow line to maturity and lived any part of their lives still committed to that tender of their first youth. They were the few who may be said to have grown up as revolutionaries.

Most of them, as I have said, became Communists. But a few were members of the Young People's Socialist League and were thus the children of Norman Thomas. They began almost with the sense that history had passed them by. They had an outraged conviction that Franklin D. Roosevelt had stolen Thomas' clothes after 1932 and was still masquerading in them after 1936. And so they thought of Roosevelt as something of a confidence man, of themselves as the only true faithful, and of all who had abandoned the Socialist doctrine as fallen angels.

By 1938, too, the Young Communists, under the impulse of the Popular Front tactic, were talking more and more like New Dealers. And, perhaps because the reality of their lives was a quarrel with the Communists, the Young Socialists reacted more and more in the language of revolutionary activism.

If one was young in the middle thirties and felt compelled to dream revolution, there was no temple for it long except with the Yipsels, as the Young Socialists were called, or with the Young Trotskyites. The idea of force and violence may have stuck in the back of the heads of the Young Communists (very occasionally they read Lenin); but in practice they were so busy dressing themselves up as George Washington that any concept of irreconcilable class differences to be decided only upon the barricades was hardly a common subject for their fantasies. Their fantasies, as I remember them, had an even more romantic cast. They enjoyed the sense of being in the stream of great events, and some of them toyed with unfounded theories that Mrs. Roosevelt or Harold Ickes must be "one of us." This tendency of younger Communists to imagine and older ones not to deny that personages of substance were secret Communists was part of my own experience, although I cannot guess how general it may have been. There remains the grisly chance, of course, that extravagances of this type, borne by backsliders, have found their way into the files of the Federal Bureau of Investigation.

Association with the great and the triumphant was, I think, a staple of Communist day dreams. The Young Socialists tied themselves to the pure and the defeated—to the Karl Marx Hof in Vienna, the Spartacists of Rosa Luxembourg, and the revolutionary Jews of Poland, heroes whose moments of glory ended in the grave. True romance can be all the truer for ending in the defeat of everything but its purity. But a revolutionary's chance to die on the barricades is fairly limited in America; and these Young Socialists tended to die, at least as dreamers, sitting at meetings or framing resolutions that moved with iron logic through a world of fantasies.

Those in the grip of this species of unreality tended more than the Communists to recognize the peril of taint by the outside world. Revolutionary purity was no special problem for the Communists; they always assumed that, if they relaxed their day-to-day function as Bolsheviks for Hollywood, Washington, or the conservative labor movement, they could still go to Party meetings and pay dues and be part of their fantasy. But the Young Socialists understood that their dedication was not safe in lush grasses and that the eventual consequence of adjustment to capitalist society was abandonment of their party. They could not permit themselves to put the main purpose of their lives into a special compartment; but to bring it into contact with reality was to destroy it. Many Communists did not become renegades until the day they offered themselves to the FBI. But every Socialist was a renegade of sorts if he worked for a union, and, for practical considerations, endorsed a Democrat for public office. The process of defection was almost continual; the Yipsels formed people and then watched them drift off to the service of their enemies. But, in most cases, theirs was a farewell of sorrow more than anger, for they had a fellow feeling stronger than the Communists would ever know. They understood, if only by instinct, that they were losing their own flesh.

Looking back upon them, it is possible to say that unreality is not a bad thing, so long as there is no malice in it. I suppose more old Yipsels remain from the youth movement of the thirties, functioning in a fashion doing least violence to their image of themselves in those days, than survive from any other political group. The labor movement is full of them: not merely the Reuther boys, but a host of local union presidents, educational directors, and organizers. By contrast, I can think of none who could be described as making a personal profit out of red-baiting. Their numbers are too small and their achievements too modest to be offered as a compelling argument for the things we said in the thirties; but they are at least not better off forgotten.

They were, as I have said, Norman Thomas' children. He gave them much more than he took. In a sense, Thomas may have killed his own political party by visiting the fantasies of youth upon a movement which to live had to appeal to grownups. William Gomberg, of the International Ladies' Garment Workers Union, said once that, when he was eighteen and a Yipsel, he was flattered to have Thomas take his advice so seriously, but that, when he was twenty-one, he was simply appalled. And yet Thomas was a rare man for the thirties.

I remember once as a young Communist being taken to meet Earl Browder at Party headquarters in Baltimore. It was the most particular of occasions; each of Browder's callers was chosen for what passed for special promise and granted a fifteen-minute audience. I can recall now only a bare loft and a sodden man sitting lumpily in a chair at its center with his overcoat buttoned to his chin. I cannot remember anything he said; what words there were between us fell like lead. It is impossible to recreate exhilaration or disillusion or any other defined reaction; this was a moment absolutely without content, forgotten until by chance I rescued it from some dustbin of the memory. I have come to know Browder slightly since his fall; he has turned out to be an unexpectedly engaging man who dearly loves his wife and children and possesses unusual depths of passion and strength. And it may be that, while I struggled to communicate with him that afternoon, poor Browder was only alone and cold and longing for home and unable, because of his presumed place in history, to express so human a sentiment.

But what Thomas conveyed was no sense of critical place in history (when I knew him any such hope was fading) but rather a feeling that there is something glorious about being forever engaged. He seemed always just back from the side of the share-croppers or from being egged by the friends of Frank Hague. In that guise, he represented the only available piece of that buried tradition of the American radical about which John Dos Passos wrote. The old libertarian dream of spending one's life in lonely combat against every form of enslavement, to the extent that it was not a Communist confusion, appeared to us to have no vessel but Norman Thomas. There were times when he seemed to become shrill and bitter, just as there were times when he took the wrong road out of an inner need to take *some* road rather than not to be involved.

But I can remember him at his best sitting in the press room at the 1952 Democratic convention reading the platform of this party which had all but destroyed him as a politician. It was a platform fitted with planks from the Socialist program of twenty years earlier, full of promises of more social security, unemployment insurance, and special safeguards for labor and the farmer. Thomas said that night that he could feel a certain pride of authorship now: these things, now taken for granted, had seemed so wild when he began. America was, he decided, an extraordinary country, if it could change like this and remain so much the same. He seemed then to understand that his life had not been a failure.

The hardest experience for the doctrinaire radical is to have someone else create the things which he demands and to have history write its credit lines across someone else's tombstone. The resolution of that agony was Norman Thomas' triumph.

And the hardest thing to do with your youth is not to justify or apologize for it but simply to accept it. The thirties in their way were the youth of almost every protagonist in these studies; some grew up in them and others thought they were reborn in them. They are my youth too, and I think I share with most of these persons the memory of a common illusion, from which some are freed, by which some were destroyed, and which others still clutch to their disaster.

We were, most of us, fleeing the reality that man is alone upon this earth. We ran from a fact of solitude to a myth of community. That myth failed us because the moments of test come most often when we are alone and far from home and even the illusion of community is not there to sustain us. Elizabeth Bentley was alone when she went into the Communist Party; and she was alone when Jacob Golos died, and twice she stood her life on its head because she was alone. It is a notion of these studies that not politics nor religion was the mainspring of Elizabeth Bentley's life, but the fact of being alone. It is also their notion that in the relationship of Whittaker Chambers and Alger Hiss a political bond was less crucial than the fact that Whittaker Chambers was trying to get into the middle class and Alger Hiss to get out of it, and that each saw in the other his model of character. And it is their notion that Whittaker Chambers cried out that he had left the winning side for the losing one, not as an expression of historical prophecy, but because he believed, in his Communist phase, that he was part of a great company; and he knew, in his apostasy, that he was all alone.

Some of the men who died in Spain went to their graves recognizing that they were alone at the moment of death; many others did not. I would not argue that the fortunate are those who die young; but when a man tenders all of himself for a myth of community, his choice is very often between early death and later disillusion.

Part of our flight from reality was at the simplest level. It does not seem an accident that the calendar of events which shook the persons in this book to what they thought were their depths was so different from the calendar of events which shook most Americans. In forming the committed, for good or ill, the Sacco-Vanzetti case seems, as I have said, more important than the great depression; a hunger march on Washington more memorable than a four-billion-dollar public relief program; and John L. Lewis' endorsement of Wendell Willkie in 1940 more profound than the election itself.

For most of the real history of the thirties went on outside while the committed were legislating an historical myth. The thirties met their problems, or at least beat them back a little while and held the door open. Hitler, unemployment, the crisis of capitalism—all the things the revolutionaries said could only be solved on their terms—the America of the thirties met and dealt with, to a degree at least, and with very little help from most of us.

The failure of the ideas which obsessed so many of the radicals of the thirties did not lie in that part of them which was against the stream of our national history, for there is a not-inglorious record of an American radicalism which swam against the stream. The part that failed was the part which rode with a stream that was outside America. Most of our subjects were not rebels; they were rather persons desperate to conform or to enforce conformity.

The concept of a revolutionary dictatorship is old in many histories, but it remains an alien idea in America. The best instance of that from the thirties is not communism but fascism, which was the dominant revolutionary impulse in their world. The American fascist movement might as well not have existed so far as its effect on history is concerned. The totalitarianism which threatened America in the thirties was never internal despite all efforts to make it appear so; it was embodied in the armies of Germany, Italy, and Japan. In the same way, the threat to us today is the Soviet Union's possession of nuclear weapons. It is a measure of the domestic peril of Communist ideas that, if Julius Rosenberg was responsible for the Soviets having the atom bomb, this man, apparently unequipped to organize the shabbiest Marxist study group, did more to advance the cause of revolution in America than the whole Communist National Board.

For the life of the American revolutionary who was not engaged in espionage was lived without even ultimate effect on the consciousness of the people around him. It was dedicated to the degree that it was alienated. And, at those moments when it touched real events, it was changed beyond recognition.

The history of European communism is a history of death, terror, suffering, and hard courage. These people, say what you will of them, are in history. When Ignazio Silone predicts that the final conflict will be between Communists and ex-Communists, he speaks from a nation which feels the Communist problem as a piece of its very soul. But to say that in America, in peacetime, the ultimate struggle will be between Communists and ex-Communists is to make yourself ridiculous.

Yet the imagery of the European experience clutters the recollection of those ex-Communists who are presented to us as the great teachers on the struggle of our time. For these are men who used up their lives in the dream of Europe's barricades and in the reality of isolation. That isolation is the hardest memory of all for them to bear; they must say that it was terribly serious and apocalyptic; they must describe the little indignities which drove them out as horrors on the grand scale; and they must cling to the European image of the Bolshevik as a piece of iron, as immune to mercy as to torture, incorruptible, implacable, and infinitely superior to the soft and careless ordinary citizen. Their model remains the Communist in *Man's Fate,* who knew that to lose was to die and carried his cyanide pill with him for that end.

But where are the American Bolsheviks? Even Whittaker Chambers is reported to have said once that he and Alger Hiss were the only true Bolsheviks he ever met in the United States. Robert Thompson is the only instance of the pure breed I can think of who had been at large in the United States, and he appears to have been lost here. If we are to believe her story—and J. Edgar Hoover appears to believe it implicitly—Elizabeth Bentley must have been one of the most effective Communists in the Party's history; and Miss Bentley, by her own account, was a silly little woman with as much relation to the iron Bolshevik as tea to wood alcohol.

Even so, the European image distracted those who thought of

themselves as revolutionaries in the thirties. It distracts a good many persons still. I remember one former Communist who had gone on to success in Hollywood and, long after he had left the Party, was summoned in the fifties before the House Committee on Un-American Activities. He had no fresh information; he was being ordered to a ritual of absolution. He had no wish to lie or seek the Fifth Amendment, both being courses which he recognized as being degrading and impractical. His first impulse was to defy the committee and accept the chance of disgrace. Then he had a long talk with a famous refugee, an ex-Communist still carrying the dust of a dozen fascist prisons, where he had been tortured and had occasionally cracked under torture. This ghost of the Old World explained that there are degrees of pain which even the most principled man cannot be expected to stand. His conscience thus cleared, the beleaguered went before the Un-American Activities Committee and told what little he knew. It seemed to him irrelevant that the racks of Europe were miles away from the gentle, weary inquisitions of Committee Counsel Frank Tavenner and Europe's perils much more ultimate than the ouster from a confiscatory tax bracket which is so often the most extreme sacrifice required of the radical brought before the bar of counterrevolution. He was free of the fringes of the myth of the thirties; he remained locked in its center.

I cannot escape a certain sympathy for Whittaker Chambers, because he seems so plainly to have believed and suffered. But, when Chambers suffered, he suffered *in vacuo;* that dark night of the soul of which he speaks was a personal and not a political affliction; he hardly escaped it by leaving the Communists. The strongest feature in the careers of Elizabeth Bentley and Chambers, who lived as Communists more intensely than most in the thirties, is that their experiences were so empty. These are the dullest spy stories in history, and spying is a dull business: Elizabeth Bentley on a park bench in dragging conversation with Bill Remington; Chambers sitting all day in the Hiss apartment without so much as a respectable book to read, or riding the day coach to New York to be chivvied by a Russian. I have heard it argued that the Bentley story is so terrible because she is such a drab. But that is an argument using exterior reality to cover the absence of inner passion, because Elizabeth Bentley was only passionate when she was a woman wailing for her demon lover or holding back her tears at Yasha's chill funeral; she is just an office wife when she discusses the housekeeping details of Yasha's business, which happened to be espionage.

There were Communists who bore the loneliness of their life in America by reminding themselves of the early Christians, although Chambers is the only person in this book who appears to have seriously connected himself with that image. And yet their kinship with the early Christians was most often a kinship with the Augustine who prayed unto the Lord to make him pure but not yet, or with Spintho, the backslider of *Androcles and the Lion,* who said at the supreme test of his faith:

"I'll repent afterwards. I fully mean to die in the arena: I'll die a martyr and go to heaven; but not this time, not now, not until my nerves are better. Besides I'm too young; I want to have just one more good time."

Very few of them understood that safety and security are themselves sinful. It is strange how many of the Communists, those dominant radicals of the thirties, had characters shaped by the conditions under which the daily lives of most were a matter of deferring their test and concealing their aims. There were cases when this concealment suited the Party's convenience; but there were far more cases where it suited the individual's convenience. There were, as an instance, many more covert than open Communists in the student movement, where being an open Communist could hardly have been fatal. My first public act as a member of the Young Communist League was to resign and proclaim my allegiance to the Young Socialists. There have never been many places in America where it was more pleasant to be an open Communist than an open anti-Communist. And yet I think we would have helped ourselves as human beings if we had been public Communists; concealment is not good for a man, especially when it is concealment for his own advantage. The guilt of disguising ourselves was the worst guilt most Communists acquired in the thirties; for whenever they deceived anyone about

their true allegiance, they had told a lie and were adding that
much more to the burden of solitude which had made so many
of them Communists in the first place.

In most cases where a Communist was asked to function in the
real world, the adoption of disguise and the need to function as
something he was not did the most terrible violence to his nature.
If Hollywood was a reality, the life of the Communists there can
be taken as the pattern of the life of Communists everywhere
they joined the service of the enemy: they subverted the enemy's
castle far less than the comforts of the enemy's castle subverted
them. The Hollywood Communists, whatever their conscious in-
tent, were unable to corrupt the movies with their ideas; the
movies corrupted them and they got rich fabricating empty banalities to fit Hollywood's idea of life in America. It has been
argued that their heavy financial contributions to the Communist
movement were a menace to our safety. But a Leninist would
answer that movies of the sort they wrote corrupted the working
class to an extent which inhibited the successful propagation of
revolutionary ideas far more than their tithes advanced it. Some
of them, now that Hollywood is barred, have turned to the manufacture of open Communist propaganda; it is a measure of communism's hold on the American soul that none of them would
write as revolutionaries if they could make a living at anything
else.

There were, of course, two groups in these studies who were
open Communists. Most of the Communist sailors who built the
National Maritime Union were quite frank about their affiliation;
they inhabited one of the few areas in America whose inmates
were alienated by the fact of their condition and not by interior
quarrel, and where it was possible to proclaim yourself a Communist. They joined the Party out of a hunger close to physical,
the oldest of them at least; when that hunger was appeased
and they were no longer alienated, they departed without a backward glance.

The writers of the proletarian novels were, more often than not,
open Communists too. Theirs was an interior quarrel; alienation
is the brood mare of writers. And they were drawn from their
own inner struggle to seek the company of men like themselves

and the flame of exterior inspiration from a revolutionary working class. They must have had the sense that if an exterior inspiration would make them better writers, it was worth the price of political neutrality. For they at least understood that, to test the idea that to be a Communist meant to be a better writer, it was necessary to write as a Communist. After a while most of them learned, as every writer has to learn, that they were alone and that there were no crutches. When they made that discovery, their fires were out; they were hammering the cold iron and they had lost their chance.

The sailors pursued reality and the writers pursued fantasy; and, if one group survived and the other went under, it was perhaps because one group pursued its function and the other sought to escape it. But most of the other Communists in these studies pursued their function in disguise. Their inner and their outer selves were alike a mask. Lee Pressman could not have functioned as an open Communist; he was forced to a disguise which oppressed him so much that he all but threw it away at moments of private discourse. He was unhappy concealing his aims; when he had to choose between his own beliefs and those of his employer, he made the choice voluntarily. And yet, when he had made it, the habit of fiction was hardest for him to surrender; harsh, solitary existence with the Communists in America was an unbearable reality; he found himself alone, and departed.

This lie—this double level of existence—was the only crime committed by most Communists in the thirties, but it was not a small crime. The Communists are the only political party in our history with a great body of members consistently embarrassed to admit their allegiance. They tried at once to possess their dream and live outside it. When men follow that course for twenty years and are finally brought to crisis under it, they tend to act badly; and I do not think anyone could argue that the Communists of the thirties have acted well in the fifties. And, when the young adopt such a course, it does not long sustain itself in the face of maturity, which is the primary reason, I think, why so many of the young Communists of the thirties have simply gone away.

The guilt of those enchained by the myth of the thirties was not

the Moscow trials or a slave labor camp in Kamchatka or an assault upon Finland, because none of those things was a reality
in their lives. It was not even the pursuit of fantasy, because
fantasy is not serious so long as it is not malignant. Their guilt
was lying to and about themselves, and all the mean, uncounted
little tricks which so many of the repentant now blame on a
doctrine but which they were quite capable of thinking up and
executing all by themselves. I do not think it entirely my jaundice
which has left these studies so barren of remembered acts of
mercy or kindness or fraternity; I think that void exists because
there was less kindness, justice, and brotherhood in the radicals
of the thirties than in any other group of radicals in our history.

For Lee Pressman, telling Gardner Jackson that he is too old
and of no future use, was not a man who required instructions
from Josef Stalin. Anne Moos Remington, arguing in the last
ditch that, if she testified against her husband, he would have to
go to prison and she to work, had nothing to learn from the wives
of Lenin and Karl Marx. And Joseph Curran, not even a Communist, turning a face of stone to men with whom he had worked
for so many years, was no product of Bolshevik education. As
George Orwell has said, it is a waste of time to be angry, but the
stupid malignity of this kind of thing does try one's patience. But
it is the malignity of individuals; it is a malignity common to us
all, and I certainly, and you perhaps, cannot escape it by blaming
it upon a political doctrine.

I tend, coming back from them, to think of the thirties as a
time when we represented an island of guilt surrounded by a
sea of innocence. America went on about us, largely unconscious
of us. And that was in some ways the best of times. It was a time
when men in factories raised their heads and fought for a conception of their freedom and took a great part of it. It was a time
when the Negro began to fight for all his rights as a citizen. It was
a time when this nation decided that man has a duty to the lowest
of his brothers. Whether I am proud of myself in that period has
nothing to do with the fact that I am proud of my country,
prouder than I am now. For America then was not afraid of the
persons in these studies because it was not afraid of itself. It knew
then that the very many were too healthy to worry about infec-

tion from the very few. We were only a part of our time; it was our illusion that we were the most important part, but most Americans knew that we were not, and they were right. There remain some today who would tell us that we were the most important part of our time. If a nation of the healthy chooses to believe that its history was made by a little group of the sick, then it is in peril of the mistake only a few made in the thirties, trading the real for the malignant unreal.

We have not been here studying persons who were so very good or so very evil. I do not believe that the worst enemy of Lee Pressman or Alger Hiss or J. B. Matthews or Whittaker Chambers could really think that any crime any of them committed is matched by the totality of his destruction. If ever four men have gone to hell on earth, it is these four—one in disgrace, one in prison, and two in the world's eyes quite successful. They were very different men; they appear to have been together at one point in the thirties and now they are all alone.

And the fall of each was a fall of singularity, for each had a weakness from which no creed or call could summon him. Alger Hiss could not be a Communist organizer; he gave his car to one as surrogate for him. Lee Pressman could bring himself to leave comfort and safety for the lonely affirmation of what he thought he believed; but he had to temper the wind with the largest fee he could get on the way out. J. B. Matthews cried out for every strike except the one against himself. Whittaker Chambers was the great hope of revolutionary letters; and he left them at his own request to be an underground man. And the last thing any of them expected was to be defeated and alone.

But there has been a radical in America whose tradition was defeat and whose end was community. His was a voice almost stilled among the radicals of the thirties; and now, at a time when the radicals of the thirties have been driven to cover or recantation or dreadful isolation, we listen for his voice again. He was the radical who dared to stand alone, to whom no man called out in vain, to whom the lie was dishonorable and the crawl degrading. He would, I think, have found it in himself to pity Matthews, Chambers, Pressman, and Hiss alike because there would have been a part of each of them in him. I think of him as perhaps like

Sam Levinger, who is dead in a grave which is either unmarked or desecrated in Franco's Spain and who wrote before he died:

> Comrades, the battle is bloody and the war is long,
> Still let us climb the gray hills and charge the guns.

Those are tired words, and they have absorbed all the agony which is the truth of life. They are resigned, but they are undefeated. They do not suggest that somebody else charge the guns. They know the worst, but they will make the charge themselves. I miss them very much and I wish we had them back.

Afterword
to the 1967 Edition

THIS BOOK is twelve years old and its author twelve years older; and the mixed impulse of gratitude and apology with which he sees it issue forth again is defined in what Melbourne said about Macaulay, which was that he wished he were as sure of anything as that young man was of everything.

What was at that time a flat certainty about judging how people lived their lives is now unsettled by recognizing so many slights to some individuals and kindnesses to others, alike unmerited. There seems no way to clean off these blemishes without attacking the whole. And so they will have to stand; even so, their source ought to be examined if only as a lesson.

A great share of the whole fault is owing, of course, to particular personal pretensions. It is a bad practice to judge any man's life as finished while it yet has a term to run. No one could imagine from these pages that Lee Pressman, dismissed as a ghost, still functions usefully as a labor lawyer, or that Joseph Curran, celebrated as the triumph of useful service in the real world, has become the self-indulgent sultan of a protectorate of the teamsters union, or that the Reuther brothers, while remaining as responsible and as devoted as ever to the principles by which they were raised, are rather less consequential than they were expected to be.

The faults noted here were not so disabling nor the virtues celebrated so certain of reward as I had thought them then. For it is no trick at all to see through the conventional wisdom of a generation gone; the truly difficult is to escape the half-conscious acceptance of the wisdom of this one and, to avoid floating downstream, while assured that one struggles against the current.

This book was composed in 1954, when all but a very few persons believed that America had solved all its problems and that the radical criticism had nothing more to say to us. So now our government is in a war from which public men know of no way to extricate themselves and from which private men can conceive no method of extricating their government; and we are a society into which every day children are born for whose lives the economy has no productive use. These conditions were present, if perhaps not so obvious, in the fifties and ought to have proclaimed what is only faintly suggested at the end of this work: that the spirit of the thirties had as much reproach to lay upon the fifties as the fifties had upon them.

Our special mistake in the fifties was in undervaluing the system of Karl Marx, not as a device to anticipate the future but as a way to describe the present. We thus discarded that always useful part of Marx which was the historical pessimist along with the decorative element which was the Utopian.

By now we may be entitled to assume that the Utopian will always be irrelevant; Marx's Utopia was, after all, founded on the promise of the abolition of private property or, more particularly, of the distinction between the few who dispose of the means of production and the many who are thereby disposed of.

But the transfer of ownership from some private landlord to some Council of Soviets hardly altered that distinction in the Soviet Union. And so, to the extent that we dare anticipate the future we may expect that there, as here, the society will be divided between those who control property and those who work for a living and that what we shall always read will not be the history of socialism but only the history of Russia or China or Cuba, there being no history of socialism ever but just the continual history of social struggles.

Feeling that, we can begin to understand that all but a very few persons in these studies were Utopians, not merely those who are condemned for the assumption that the Soviet Union was, if not already perfect, moving that way, but also those who entertained, as I did twelve years ago, the same illusion about the United States.

What is surprising about that discovery, to me at least, is that it should be surprising at all: the puzzle about most men is not why they resist but why they conform, not why they occasionally insist they live in the worst of times but why they are so anxious to believe that they live in the best, not why they are alienated but why they want so much to fit in.

It now becomes possible, thinking about these people, to conceive of ordinary man's most intensely felt problem as being simply whom to follow. Stalin's only charm was that he so completely disposed of the problem. And yet, even after accepting him, the Communists in these studies still struggled through crises in their lives choosing between men of narrower but not much shallower pretensions. Those who were sailors chose between William X. Foster and Joseph Curran; those who were screenwriters had no more realistic choice than is usually provided to employees; but, even within that limitation, the Communist cadre in Hollywood seems to have been divided between those satisfied that socialist realism was completely served by the leadership of the brothers Warner and those who thought it would better be advanced under the leadership of Jerry Wald.

Yet, easy as it was in the fifties to wonder at persons who did not recognize that the movies were an article of commerce and they themselves only commodities in the transaction, it is as easy in the sixties to see the trade union, which is no more than an agency for employees, as unlikely to be more than the most limited instrument for decision in the disposal of commodities, at the very most an argument for children against their parents.

Such an argument is seldom effective unless defiant. Defiance was the great advantage of the thirties and it was too easily given up. The depression was a time when government had failed and when great numbers of persons felt themselves in revolt. In that spirit, there was something like the attack on the society from outside and below which the fifties were surprised to see beginning in the Negro protest movements and with much the same promise for national improvement.

But the real mistake of the thirties seems now to have been not in how much they demanded but in how little it took them to be satisfied. The Communists were most typical because they were happiest when they thought of President Roosevelt as their ally rather than their enemy; we are most American when we had rather be with our government than against it.

In this key, most of the instruments of social welfare which are the great monument of the thirties were cheerfully and almost automatically ceded to government by private men. Ordinary men would certainly be worse off if they did not exist at all; and yet every day we can observe the special penalty of the abandonment of private initiative in social adventure to the control of government.

One has only to enter those unemployment insurance offices whose appointed ceremony is to insult the unemployed while paying them to see how far the ordinary worker remains from owning what the society says is his. The true failure of the thirties then is not in its ruins but in its monuments; we have to begin all over again. Those who said in 1933 that government was an enemy made their worst mistake, not in saying that, but in too much changing their minds.

Because their author did not see this until too late, there flows too often through these pages the happy notion that he who is acceptable to a transient hour of his time is right and that he who is rejected is wrong. The idea that the survivor, merely by surviving, has proved himself an instrument either of Divine Providence or historical progress is a very ancient enemy of the understanding; and it has won too many battles here.

The most instructive failure in the whole work is that it was conducted through continual apostrophes to History as an abstraction with too little consideration for history simply as a job of work.

There are, in its grander monuments, two ways of writing history. One is Gibbon's, which is that of the detached observer with millenia separating himself from the subject. Its tone, for me at least, charms most when it moves in irony and with the delicate balance of antitheses. But, for Gibbon, this was not merely a grace but a necessity; his business was to work with documents, many in conflict with other documents almost as ancient and nearly all suspect. How does one know what to choose, what to keep and what to throw away in Procopius, to take a case, when the *Secret History* flatly contradicts the *Wars?* One cannot know and one can only try by balancing and sifting and calling other witnesses, all dead too, and by sitting through the night. One is the appellate court of history, dependent, as appellate courts are, on documents rather than flesh. So Gibbon writes as judges would in our ideal, because he could not have functioned if he had not made it his business to serve as judge between contending parties, *long ago dead.*

Ironic detachment was a style that very much tempted myself and a number of other young men in the fifties; those of us who enjoyed reading history would, I think, have agreed that we would rather have written in Gibbon's tone than in any other. I would not yet apologize for that judgment; detachment, moderated, seems to me still a virtue by itself; the danger was in our trying to put on the style as a judge's robe when the cases whose appeal one was dismissing had not even been heard out.

The other way of writing history is as a participant, self-imagined as Motley was or actual as the Earl of Clarendon was. This seems to me, for all its risks, the only fair way to struggle with events which took place in one's own lifetime.

Now, Clarendon, who began his *History of the Rebellion* as its victim and therefore as one condemned by the court of Divine Providence or historical progress, set down surprisingly hard rules for the historian who lived through the history:

"And as I may not be thought altogether an incompetent person for this communication, having been present as a member of parliament in those councils before and till the outbreaking of the rebellion, so I shall perform with all faithfulness and ingenuity; with an equal observation of the faults and infirmities of both sides, with their defects and oversights in pursuing their own ends; and shall no otherwise mention small and light occurences, than as they have been introductions to matters of the greatest moment; nor speak of persons otherwise, than as the mention of their virtues and vices is essential to the work in hand: in which as I shall have the fate to be suspected rather for malice to many than for flattery to any, so I shall preserve myself from the least sharpness, that may proceed from a private indignation, in the whole observing the rules that a man should, who deserves to be believed."

And so the thing can be done if one knows the perils and then tries to swim upstream.

It is one fault of this book that its author never quite knew whether he was participant or observer, having the excuse that,

in his own life, he was at most half the one and at least half the
other. But here he seems to be now observer and then participant,
according, one thinks, less to any real understanding of his own
involvement than to whatever literary convention seemed most
convenient for telling a particular story. At times, I judge as
though I were a participant in these events who had conducted
himself better than the person I am judging; at other times I judge
as though I were an observer entirely detached from the pains
and confusions of the person I am judging. In no case do I neglect
to choose for myself whatever happens for the occasion to be the
position of advantage; and so, on the one hand I can sound engaged and on the other I am responsible for the actions of no
one in the company with which I travel. And it would be a real
pity, for me at least, if this book seemed to have life in it only for
persons of the sort who are nostalgic for high moral positions they
would not themselves have taken at the time.

Still, what is left, after all these faults are discounted may be
"not unuseful to the curiosity if not the conscience" of those who
read it. The pictures of the actors, while colder than they should
be, do not seem to me crueler; they are at least formally just if
not quite fair; the stories seem to me generally accurate and not
unlively; the broad judgments, aside from that terrible complac-
ency about the triumph of God in America, are probably sound
enough, although there will certainly be young persons who will
wonder just what sort of time it must have been when things so
self-evident could be written and published as though everyone
didn't know them already.

But that is one of the deficiencies of existence; here, for example, is a book about persons who did not know certain things that
should have been obvious even in the thirties, written by someone
who did not know other things that should have been obvious
even in the fifties, and offered for the curiosity of persons who
can look forward to discovering just what particular piece of the
obvious they lived through the sixties without knowing.

TITLES IN SERIES